Transforming
Healthcare
Analytics

Wiley and SAS Business Series

The Wiley and SAS Business Series presents books that help senior-level managers with their critical management decisions.

Titles in the Wiley and SAS Business Series include:

Demand-Driven Forecasting: A Structured Approach to Forecasting (Second Edition) by Charles Chase

Demand-Driven Inventory Optimization and Replenishment: Creating a More Efficient Supply Chain by Robert A. Davis

Developing Human Capital: Using Analytics to Plan and Optimize your Learning and Development Investments by Gene Pease, Barbara Beresford, and Lew Walker

The Executive's Guide to Enterprise Social Media Strategy: How Social Networks Are Radically Transforming Your Business by David Thomas and Mike Barlow

Economic and Business Forecasting: Analyzing and Interpreting Econometric Results by John Silvia, Azhar Iqbal, Kaylyn Swankoski, Sarah Watt, and Sam Bullard

Economic Modeling in the Post Great Recession Era: Incomplete Data, Imperfect Markets by John Silvia, Azhar Iqbal, and Sarah Watt House

Enhance Oil & Gas Exploration with Data-Driven Geophysical and Petrophysical Models by Keith Holdaway and Duncan Irving

Foreign Currency Financial Reporting from Euros to Yen to Yuan: A Guide to Fundamental Concepts and Practical Applications by Robert Rowan

Harness Oil and Gas Big Data with Analytics: Optimize Exploration and Production with Data Driven Models by Keith Holdaway

Health Analytics: Gaining the Insights to Transform Health Care by Jason Burke

Heuristics in Analytics: A Practical Perspective of What Influences Our Analytical World by Carlos Andre Reis Pinheiro and Fiona McNeill

Human Capital Analytics: How to Harness the Potential of Your Organization's Greatest Asset by Gene Pease, Boyce Byerly, and Jac Fitz-enz

Implement, Improve and Expand Your Statewide Longitudinal Data System: Creating a Culture of Data in Education by Jamie McQuiggan and Armistead Sapp

Intelligent Credit Scoring: Building and Implementing Better Credit Risk Scorecards (Second Edition) by Naeem Siddiqi

JMP Connections: The Art of Utilizing Connections in Your Data by John Wubbel

Killer Analytics: Top 20 Metrics Missing from Your Balance Sheet by Mark Brown

Machine Learning for Marketers: Hold the Math by Jim Sterne

On-Camera Coach: Tools and Techniques for Business Professionals in a Video-Driven World by Karin Reed

Predictive Analytics for Human Resources by Jac Fitz-enz and John Mattox II

Predictive Business Analytics: Forward-Looking Capabilities to Improve Business Performance by Lawrence Maisel and Gary Cokins

Profit-Driven Business Analytics: A Practitioner's Guide to Transforming Big Data into Added Value by Wouter Verbeke, Cristian Bravo, and Bart Baesens

Profit from Your Forecasting Software: A Best Practice Guide for Sales Forecasters by Paul Goodwin

Project Finance for Business Development by John E. Triantis

Retail Analytics: The Secret Weapon by Emmett Cox

Social Network Analysis in Telecommunications by Carlos Andre Reis Pinheiro

Statistical Thinking: Improving Business Performance (Second Edition) by Roger W. Hoerl and Ronald D. Snee

Strategies in Biomedical Data Science: Driving Force for Innovation by Jay Etchings

Style & Statistic: The Art of Retail Analytics by Brittany Bullard

Taming the Big Data Tidal Wave: Finding Opportunities in Huge Data Streams with Advanced Analytics by Bill Franks

Too Big to Ignore: The Business Case for Big Data by Phil Simon

The Value of Business Analytics: Identifying the Path to Profitability by Evan Stubbs

The Visual Organization: Data Visualization, Big Data, and the Quest for Better Decisions by Phil Simon

Using Big Data Analytics: Turning Big Data into Big Money by Jared Dean

Win with Advanced Business Analytics: Creating Business Value from Your Data by Jean Paul Isson and Jesse Harriott

For more information on any of the above titles, please visit www.wiley.com.

Transforming Healthcare Analytics

The Quest for Healthy Intelligence

Michael N. Lewis

Tho H. Nguyen

WILEY

For general information on our other products and services or for technical support, please contact our Customer Care Department within the United States at (800) 762–2974, outside the United States at (317) 572–3993, or fax (317) 572–4002.

Wiley publishes in a variety of print and electronic formats and by print-on-demand. Some material included with standard print versions of this book may not be included in e-books or in print-on-demand. If this book refers to media such as a CD or DVD that is not included in the version you purchased, you may download this material at http://booksupport.wiley.com. For more information about Wiley products, visit www.wiley.com.

Library of Congress Cataloging-in-Publication Data:

Names: Lewis, Michael N., author. | Nguyen, Tho H., 1972- author.
Title: Transforming Healthcare Analytics: the quest for healthy
 intelligence / Michael N. Lewis, Tho H. Nguyen.
Description: Hoboken, New Jersey : Wiley, [2020] | Series: Wiley & SAS
  business series | Includes index.
Identifiers: LCCN 2019053586 (print) | LCCN 2019053587 (ebook) | ISBN
  9781119613541 (hardback) | ISBN 9781119613572 (adobe pdf) | ISBN
  9781119613589 (epub)
Subjects: LCSH: Medical informatics—Technological innovation. |
  Medicine—Data processing.
Classification: LCC R858 .L493 2020 (print) | LCC R858 (ebook) | DDC
  610.285—dc23
LC record available at https://lccn.loc.gov/2019053586
LC ebook record available at https://lccn.loc.gov/2019053587

COVER DESIGN: WILEY
COVER IMAGE: © MIRAGEC / GETTY IMAGES

Printed in the United States of America

V10017495_021220

This book is dedicated to my wife, Shelia, whose love, support and inspiration gave me the courage and strength to just write the damn book already! To my kids, Nicholas, Nevin, Natalie, Emily, Charlie, and Annie, who taught me that, through perseverance and determination, anything can be accomplished, you only have to try. To my dad, who taught me the important traits of being a successful leader and provided me invaluable career advice no matter how insignificant it seemed at the time. And finally, to my mom, who recently passed away from cancer. She was always there to lend a supportive ear and encouraged me to be the best person I could.

– Michael Lewis

This book is dedicated to my wife and kids who provided their unconditional love and unrelenting support with all the late nights, frantic weekends, and even working vacations to write this book. My family has been my greatest inspiration, giving me the flexibility and focus needed to complete this book in a timely manner. To all refugees around the world, hard work and persistence will open many opportunities.

– Tho H. Nguyen

Contents

Contents

About the Authors

Michael Lewis is Senior Director of Enterprise Analytic at Cleveland Clinic. Michael graduated from Cleveland State University in 1987 with a Bachelor of Business Administration with a concentration in Quantitative Business Analysis. He went on to receive his Master of Business Administration from Baldwin-Wallace College in 1991. He also earned the Health Insurance Associate Designation from America's Health Insurance Plans.

Michael was also a professor with Tiffin University where he taught graduate and undergraduate-level classes in Analytical Mathematics, Management Analysis and Research, Management Information Systems, and Information and Decision Support Systems.

He has spent his entire career of 30+ years in healthcare developing world-class analytics programs that promote a culture of fact-based decision-making and measurable continuous improvement. He has held the role of Senior Director of Enterprise Analytics since December 2015. He leads an industry-leading, cross-functional team to promote the design, implementation, and monitoring of innovative advanced analytical disciplines and solutions through the coordinated and systematic use of clinical and encounter-based data, related business insights, and multidisciplinary skill set for planning, management, measurement, and learning. Previously, he joined Cleveland Clinic in June 2012 as the Director of Contract Economics. He developed and implemented strategic reimbursement models, self-help analytics, and discovery dashboards to meet Enterprise metrics on US$8.0 billion+ of revenue.

Before joining Cleveland Clinic, Mike started his career in healthcare in 1988 working for Medical Mutual of Ohio (MMO) (formerly known as Blue Cross Blue Shield of Ohio). During his 24+ years at MMO, he held a variety of positions. As an Actuarial Analyst and Senior Financial Analyst in Provider Reimbursement and Data Analysis, he developed and implemented analytical models that enhanced the company margins by 3 percent. As a Regional Network Manager, he architected the building of proprietary hospital networks in Indiana and Northeast Georgia.

He built analytical models that help identify reimbursement unit costs opportunities that were contractually implemented network-wide.

In his spare time, Mike is an avid sports fan and options investor. He enjoys spending time with his wife, traveling, reading, and listening to podcasts. He is a foodie and craft beer enthusiast. Mike enjoys exploring exotic foods with Tho any time they are together.

Tho H. Nguyen came to the United States in 1980 as a refugee from Vietnam with his parents, five sisters, and one brother. As the youngest in the family, Tho has tremendous admiration for his parents, who sacrificed everything to come to America. Sponsored by the St. Francis Episcopal Church in Greensboro, North Carolina, Tho had enormous guidance and support from his American family who taught him English and acclimated him and his family to an opportunistic and promising life in America.

Tho holds a Bachelor of Science in Computer Engineering from North Carolina State University and an MBA degree in International Business from the University of Bristol, England. During his MBA studies, He attended L'École Nationale des Ponts et Chaussées (ENPC) in Paris, France – University of Hong Kong, Hong Kong – and Berkeley University, California. Tho proudly represented the Rotary Club as an Ambassadorial Scholar, which provided him a global perspective and a deep appreciation for the world of kindness.

With more than 20 years of experience, Tho has various leadership roles in data management and analytics. Integrating his technical and business background, Tho has extensive experience in alliance management, global marketing, and business/strategy management. Tho is an author, an active presenter/keynote speaker at various conferences, and a technology enthusiast.

In his spare time, He does volunteer work for various non-profit organizations and has held leadership positions for the Vietnamese-American Association of Raleigh, NC and Asian Focus NC. He has donated all of his proceeds from his first book to charities locally and globally, and gave two scholarships to pay it forward. Tho enjoys spending time with his family, traveling, running, and playing tennis. He is a foodie who is very adventurous, tasting different and exotic foods around the world.

You can connect with him via LinkedIn https://www.linkedin .com/in/thohnguyen/.

Acknowledgments

First, I would like to recognize my co-author, Tho H. Nguyen, for his understanding, guidance, and support during this new chapter in my life. Tho is a leading expert in how technology can play a role in your analytics strategy. Tho's first book, *Leaders and Innovators*, is a must read and inspired me to share my experiences. Second, I would like to recognize you, the reader of this book. By showing interest in learning how to bring to life an analytics strategy, your quest for health intelligence will be a positive disruptor for the healthcare industry.

There are many people at Cleveland Clinic, who started this journey before I arrived, who believed in me and allowed me to help shape the analytics strategy of the future. First is Chris Donovan, whose leadership, mentorship, and relentless pursuit of perfection gives me the drive to put forth world-class analytics for a world-class organization. Second is Andrew Proctor and Eric Hixson. As business partners in Enterprise Analytics, it is their clinic and operational knowledge and expertise that allows the converging work to be more meaningful to the organization. An extra thanks to Eric for always taking the time to debate the merits of any and all methods and models considered. To my analytics team, especially, Don McLellan, Cathy Merriman, Joe Dorocak, Michael Bromley, John Urwin, Colleen Houlahan, Dan Rymer, and James Allen, and those not named, for your tireless attention to details and putting up with my crazy ideas. I know we are making a difference and it starts with your dedication to our patients and organization.

I cannot thank everyone enough who tirelessly spent long nights reviewing and providing input, chapter by chapter, especially Lauree Shepard, Tho Nguyen, and Michael Bromley. Trying to bring to life real-world learnings, following my logic, opinions, and trying to understand how you put an analytics strategy into words can be maddening, but you did it with kindness, compassion, and thoughtfulness. I owe you gratitude beyond expression for your tremendous dedication to making sure the message is easily consumable and usable to the readers.

A special salute to all healthcare professionals whom I have interacted personally with and those I have not. Your dedication to caring for the sick and trying to cure life-changing medical events continues to ignite my passion to solve healthcare challenges as they arise. Finally, to my wife and children, thank you for brightening my life every day and allowing me to share yours.

– *Michael N. Lewis*

First, I would like to recognize my co-author, Michael N. Lewis, for his passion and patience writing this book with me. Mike brings the deep knowledge and insightful experience to make this book relatable. Second, I would like to recognize you, the reader of this book. Thank you for your interest to learn and be the agent of change in the healthcare industry. I am contributing the book proceeds to worthy charities that focus on technology and science to improve the world, from fighting hunger to advocating education to innovating social change.

There are many people who deserve heartfelt credit for assisting me in writing this book. This book would have not happened without the ultimate support and guidance from my esteemed colleagues and devoted customers. A sincere appreciation to my colleagues who encouraged me to share my personal experience and helped me to stay focused on what's relevant.

I owe a huge amount of gratitude to the people who reviewed and provided input word by word, chapter by chapter, specifically Lauree Shepard, Clark Bradley, Paul Segal, and Michael Lewis. Reading pages of healthcare jargon, trying to follow my thoughts, and translating my words in draft form can be an overwhelming challenge but you did it with swiftness and smiles. Thank you for the fantastic input that helped me to fine-tune the content for the readers.

A sincere appreciation goes to James Taylor, all healthcare professionals, IT specialists, and business professionals whom I have interacted with over the years. You have welcomed me, helped me to learn, allowed me to contribute, and provided real intelligence for this book. Finally, to all my family (the Nguyen and Dang crew), the St. Francis Episcopalian sponsors, the Rotary Club (the Jones Family, the Veale Family) – all of whom have contributed to my success – I would not be where I am today without them. To my wife and children, thank you for being the love of my life and bringing light and purpose to my day.

— Tho H. Nguyen

DISCLAIMER

The views expressed in this book are those of the individual authors representing their own personal views and not necessarily the position of either of their employers.

Foreword

by James Taylor[1]

I have been working with advanced analytics for nearly 20 years. The market has matured dramatically to the point where analytics, machine learning, and AI are now common topics of conversation in every industry. Once, analytic models were handcrafted for a few high-value scenarios. Now, companies are automating the creation of advanced analytics and using them to solve a wide range of problems. The time to develop and deploy advanced analytics has gone from months to seconds, even as the amount of data being analyzed has exploded. Every industry is focused on being more data-driven and healthcare is no exception.

Tho and I met many years ago through our work as faculty members of the International Institute for Analytics. We have a shared interest in the technologies and approaches of analytics and in how organizations can truly take advantage of their data.

Healthcare is an industry that impacts everyone throughout their life. New drugs, new treatments, and new understanding drives continual and rapid innovation. Yet even as healthcare technology and treatments get more effective, populations in many countries are struggling with older populations and an epidemic of obesity. Drug resistance is an increasing problem and costs continue to rise. The healthcare industry needs to find ways to use data to tackle these and many other challenges.

[1] James is CEO and Principal Consultant, Decision Management Solutions and a faculty member of the International Institute for Analytics. He is the author of *Digital Decisioning: Using Decision Management to Deliver Business Impact from Artificial Intelligence* (MK Press, 2019) and *Real-World Decision Modeling with DMN* with Jan Purchase (MK Press, 2017). He also wrote *Decision Management Systems: A Practical Guide to Using Business Rules and Predictive Analytics* (IBM Press, 2012) and *Smart (Enough) Systems* (Prentice Hall, 2007) with Neil Raden. James is an active consultant, educator, speaker, and writer working with companies all over the world. He is based in Palo Alto, CA and can be reached at james@decisionmanagementsolutions.com.

Healthcare organizations have a particular challenge when it comes to analytics. Healthcare data is uniquely complex and uniquely sensitive. It must capture the state of a complex, living person. It is only imperfectly digitized and much of it is image related, time series related, or both – hard classes of data to manage and analyze. It is also intensely personal, so its use is regulated and controlled to protect people's privacy and prevent health-related discrimination. Taking advantage of this data to reduce costs and improve outcomes is both essential and complex.

Over the years I have worked with hundreds of organizations that are using analytics to improve their decision-making. Like Tho and Mike, I have come to see that people and process are as essential as technology – perhaps even more so. Building cross-functional teams, engaging a broad set of skills, and having a process that focuses on decision-making are all necessary if analytic technology is to be applied effectively.

Take one healthcare provider I was working with recently. A technical team had developed some potentially useful analytic models. But working alone they could get no traction. We engaged clinical and operations staff in a discussion of the current decision-making. We applied design thinking and decision modeling to see how that decision might be improved with the analytic. With this shared understanding the technical team could see what a minimum viable product would require and could execute a series of Agile sprints to deliver it. People, process, and (analytic) technology.

With this book, Tho and Mike hope to show healthcare professionals how to transform their industry with data and analytics. Right from the start, they emphasize the importance of people, process, *and* technology – not just the coolest, newest technology. Real-world stories of healthcare problems addressed by insight-driven decisions show healthcare professionals what's possible and what technology exists. The stories help bring to life how analytics might create a more effective future state in healthcare.

The core chapters on People, Process, and Technology are full of great advice. There is a discussion of the skills needed, especially in analysis and business understanding. The need to invest in a wide range of roles (not just hire unicorns) and the importance of changes in sponsorship culture are emphasized. Three critical elements of process are discussed next. Design Thinking – something we find very effective in defining how analytics can improve decision-making – Lean and Agile. Our experience is that the hardest problem is defining the business problem so analytics can be applied effectively. As the authors point out, success therefore requires process change and the creation of a repeatable, sustainable playbook. The technology chapter gives a succinct but complete overview of available technology. All of this is pulled together into a framework for integrating people, process, and technology to drive culture change and move up the analytic maturity curve. The authors talk about the importance of focusing on data as an asset, bringing together cross-functional teams, providing clear leadership, and investing in growing analytic talent. All of this is illustrated with real-world case examples. A final chapter lays out what's coming and how will it change healthcare, especially the growth in sensors and devices connected through the Internet of Things, the growth of the cloud, and the adoption of artificial intelligence.

If you are a healthcare professional concerned about applying data and analytics to improve your organization, this book will give you valuable insights. The advice and framework will help you organize, recruit, train, and develop the data analytics capability you need.

Healthcare needs to become more data-driven, more analytic. This book will show you how.

CHAPTER 1

Introduction

"Without data, you're just another person with an opinion."
— W. Edwards Deming

PURPOSE OF THIS BOOK

While there have been many improvements and changes in healthcare, Mike and I strongly believe there is still a lot to do and we want to share with you our journey to make healthcare better one patient at a time. Our motivation for this book is to share with our valued readers real-world, personal experiences and to show how technology coupled with people and process is paving the way toward the adoption of the digital transformation in healthcare. Digital transformation also makes a strong case for how healthcare organizations can do so much better because of the innovative analytical practices that we have readily available today but they are not implemented or being considered in many instances.

Whether you realize it or not, healthcare affects everyone – young and old. When you, Mike, or I were kids, healthcare was not a topic of concern. Most of us had parents or guardians to oversee our healthcare. Personally, as I have gotten older and more mature mentally and physically, healthcare has become a necessity with more regular visits to the doctor or hospital. When we become guardians and parents ourselves, we have others to think about, whether it is looking after our own kids, taking care of an elderly family member or our own parents, or even fostering children. As a new parent, healthcare is definitely a priority for my wife and kids, not only having access to healthcare but also the quality of care that we seek when needed. Healthcare affects all of us one way or another throughout our life cycle, from birth, toddler, adolescent, adult to end of life.

Healthcare affected me very personally about a year ago when my wife was misdiagnosed or missed diagnosed due to lack of data and empathy in the plan of care. It was a brisk winter morning in February when it all started when my wife complained about some back pains and stomach discomfort. My wife and I had our daily routines where I was working in my home office and she was getting our daughter ready for school. That afternoon, my wife's agonizing back pains and stomach discomfort escalated to a level beyond tolerable.

Having had these symptoms in the past, she had been taking over-the-counter medications to see if they would go away. Unfortunately, they didn't and this time the pain became so much worse. Since our family doctor's office was closed due to it being after business hours, urgent care was our best option. It was late afternoon on Valentine's day and it was a day that we will never forget. Once we arrived at the urgent care, we filled out forms about my wife and symptoms that she was experiencing. The nurse asked her repetitive questions and took notes at the same time. We provided our insurance coverage details and were asked to wait. Because it was Valentine's day, the urgent care waiting room was nearly empty and the doctor was able to see us pretty quickly. The urgent care doctor asked my wife the same questions that the nurse had asked, then examined my wife but could not pinpoint the cause and a cure for the pain. The urgent care office suggested that we go directly to a nearby hospital emergency room (ER) to get a better diagnosis of my wife's condition. The urgent care nurse said that all of my wife's visit and information would be transferred to the ER and they would know what was done at the urgent care since it is affiliated with the ER hospital. Upon arrival at the ER and at check-in, there were no records and no one was aware of our arrival, situation, and condition. Thus, the traumatic drama escalated and continued on Valentine's evening.

Because all the data that was collected at the urgent care office was not in the system at the ER hospital, my wife and I had to relate all the same information again. In the midst of severe pain, I responded to most of the questions on behalf of my wife. The most obvious data such as name, address, birth date, Social Security number, insurance numbers, and gender were needed and entered on a form again before we could be checked into the ER. At this point, I could see my wife's pain had worsened and asked why there were no records and information from the urgent care office which is affiliated with the ER hospital. I questioned the repetitive process and why we had to enter the same data on the forms when my wife is a patient at the hospital and had history at the facility for over five years. The response was "We needed the data and forms to admit your wife" and we had no choice but to abide at that moment in time. After a few hours of waiting, we finally saw a nurse who asked the same, repetitive questions from the forms that we had filled out and then documented my wife's symp-toms. A few more hours of waiting and we finally saw an ER doctor. The ER doctor asked the same questions as the nurse did and we felt like a broken record repeating the same information for the fourth time. Finally, the ER doctor ordered blood tests, x-rays, and a mag-netic resonance image (MRI). Each procedure was executed by a dif-ferent personnel and department, so we had to wait even more in the hospital room in between each test. As you can imagine, hours passed waiting for results from each test and the pain continued.

Being helpless had to be the worst feeling – unable to do any-thing except sit and wait with my very young daughter, whom we had brought along, thinking that we would be home within a few hours. Having a two-year-old toddler in an ER at the peak of winter when colds and flus were highly contagious was nerve-racking and worri-some. The doctor finally visited our room to give us the diagnosis. Based on the results, the diagnosis was an infection and the doctor gave my wife some prescription medication to help with the pain and antibiotics for what was diagnosed to be a urinary tract infection (UTI). I vividly remember it was 4 a.m. the next day that my wife was released from the ER and we got to go home. We would never forget how we spent that year's Valentine's Day and were happy to head home. It was a blessing that there was a path to alleviating the pain for my wife.

A few weeks later, once the antibiotics were completely con-sumed, my wife was feeling better and we thought she was cured with no pain in the stomach and back. Regrettably, that was not the case as the back pain and stomach discomfort returned with a vengeance. Over a six-month time span, from February when the pain started to August when it was correctly diagnosed and my wife had an opera-tion, we had multiple visits to our family doctor, specialists, and the ER. Each time we visited a clinician and the ER, my wife had a differ-ent diagnosis which the doctors were unsure how to treat and what to do about it. Each visit required more bloodwork, x-rays, and MRIs – all of which were captured in fragmented, siloed systems from each office and there was no clear path to a cure in sight. Each ER stay was one week long and I had to communicate the history and recent visits to each nurse, doctor, and specialist at each hospital. During this time, my wife had multiple procedures and operations at various hospitals within one healthcare system but much of the data and details were not related or communicated among nurses and doctors. In the middle of summer, we had our final procedure and it was to remove an infected gallbladder, an insertion and removal of two stents to isolate the gallstone and an extremely stubborn, oversized gallstone. What should have been a simple diagnosis to detect the gallstone and removal of the gallbladder dragged on for six months with extreme pain and agony. In addition, we had multiple hospital stays that were costly and stressful.

What I learned from this experience is that:

- Healthcare has become shallow with longer wait times and shorter face-to-face time with the doctors and clinicians with redundant processes for each touchpoint.
- Clinicians have become data clerks and their notes are not well captured and not well communicated among themselves and within the healthcare ecosystem.
- Healthcare data is so overwhelming due to its volume and lack of data in the same ecosystem that clinicians are unable to review and correctly diagnose the ailment and provide a cure in a timely manner.
- The cost of each visit was astronomical and accumulated with every point of contact – the hospital check-in staff, nurse assistant, nurse, physician assistant, physician, and specialist. When we received the bill for each line item, we were very thankful to have health insurance; otherwise, we would have been in great debt. I can't imagine not having insurance.
- Illnesses cause stressful times for families, especially the kids. Being sick and not knowing or having a care plan in sight for a cure was very traumatic for me and my daughter (who missed her mother terribly during overnight stays). My wife is a strong and patient woman who endured so much pain and agony.

The above scenario spawned the idea for this book. Mike and I have been in the data and analytics profession for over 45 years collectively and we want to educate you on concepts that can lead your organization to sustained changes and to improve clinical, operational, and financial outcomes. Over the years, data and analytics have changed considerably and have become more convoluted – particularly in the healthcare sector. Health data volumes have skyrocketed, legacy data archives are on the rise, and unstructured data will be more prevalent in the healthcare sector than in any other sector. Healthcare is the only industry that keeps all types of records from birth to end of life and that volume puts a tremendous amount of burden on healthcare organizations to maintain and manage. But it is definitely an exhilarating time that generates many challenges and great opportunities for healthcare organizations to investigate and implement new and innovative technologies to accommodate data management and analytical needs. Thus, Mike and I invite you to join us on our journey to improve healthcare outcomes with insights and to integrate data and analytics in a harmonious environment.

When Mike and I met over five years ago, we both had attended a number of conferences and presented to both business and technical audiences about solutions that help healthcare organizations to be more effective managing the exponential growth in healthcare data and more efficient by streamlining the analytical processes that provide insight-driven decisions. As we shared our experiences, we received in return an overwhelming insight into healthcare organizations' challenges and issues. The biggest and most common questions were around people, process, and technology:

- What skill sets do I look for when hiring people, business analysts, or data scientists?
- What can I do to challenge my staff to do things differently and more efficiently?
- What are some ways to improve processing time since there is more data than ever to analyze?
- How can I deliver results to my leadership team with information that is real-time and improves decision-making?
- What technologies should I consider to support a digital transformation?
- Is cloud the right strategy for my healthcare organization?
- Is open source being implemented in other healthcare organizations?

- Where does artificial intelligence and augmented intelligence fit in?
- Are healthcare organizations keeping pace with other industries?
- What services should I consider training my organization in to be self-reliant?

As Mike and I attended a conference in sunny San Diego, California, we had a *eureka* moment over a meeting. What if we wrote a book that combines real-world problems focused on data and analytics in healthcare and share with our readers the challenges and successes? Mike would bring the business perception while I would bring my technology background to provide a complete perspective. We realize there are many books about healthcare, but this book is unique in ways that connect people, process, and technology to prepare for the digital transformation in healthcare from our direct experiences and backgrounds. We approached an editor who is also a mutual colleague with this idea and concept, and she was very enthusiastic about our book proposal. After several months of negotiations and developing the outline and timeframe, the publisher accepted our pitch. Our goals for this book are to:

- Share real-world healthcare problems and use cases focusing on connecting and integrating people, process, and technology to deliver insight-driven decisions.
- Educate healthcare professionals in what innovative technologies are available to manage data and apply analytics with some best practices to transform your organization.
- Provide a unique perspective of the future of healthcare and what to expect with the rise of digital transformation, machine learning, and artificial intelligence.

Whether you have a business or technical background, we truly believe you will appreciate the real-world use cases presented here. Before we dive into the details, we believe it is very appropriate to set the tone with what is health data and some challenges in the healthcare sector that demand the connection and integration of people, process, and technology. It is needed to maintain and sustain leadership in a very complex and growing healthcare industry.

HEALTH DATA DEFINED

Many years ago when I was a child, I could recall sitting in my doctor's office as my parents filled out forms about me and my health that contained fields such as name, date of birth, address, Social Security number, medications that I was taking, what is the purpose of this visit, and history of family members for each visit to each type of clinician. All of these forms have been kept in a folder that can stack up as high as the ceiling and stored in file cabinets (see Figure 1.1). When you visit the doctor and hospital, they retrieve those records, sift through all of that historical data, and review them to assess your condition. As the nurse called my name to go back to see the doctor, they would measure my weight, my blood pressure, and body temperature – all of these data points were also captured and entered in my file. Once the doctor was ready to see me, he would ask me some simple questions based on the information provided on the forms. At the same time, the doctor also evaluated and observed my physical and emotional attributes to see if any of these intangible factors provided any insights to my wellbeing, both physically and emotionally. From my pediatrician to my current doctor, all of my records have been maintained in some manner.

This photo by an unknown author is licensed under CC-BY-2.0.

Figure 1.1 Storage of Your Medical Records
Source: S.J. Howard, 2010. https://sjhoward.co.uk/in-support-of-a-national-nhs-computer-system/. Licensed under CC-BY-2.0.

With technology advancements, these forms can now be scanned, notes from paper can be entered into computers, and observations get captured in a dialogue – all of which can now be archived in electronic health systems. As I have gotten older, I had to fill out the same forms myself with the identical data points and the repetitive information continued to get captured. If you are a healthy person, you would visit your doctor once a year for a wellness checkup; otherwise, you may have additional visits when you get a cold, cough, or an injury. Unfortunately, if you encounter a serious illness such as injury, cancer, stroke, or a heart attack, x-rays and magnetic resonance imaging (MRI) are needed and these images are combined with your other data points to diagnose a problem and plan a treatment. All of these health data are kept from year to year, from birth to end of life, and become very voluminous and complex.

Thus, health data is defined as any data that relates to your health and comes from many sources such as behavioral observations, environmental factors, and socioeconomic data. Health data can be structured or unstructured. For example, your name, date of birth, blood type, or gender is considered as structured data and can be standardized in columns and rows. Most structured data can be stored in a data warehouse. Unlike structured data, unstructured data such as your doctor's notes, x-rays, MRIs, audio recordings, or emails are not standardized and have become more prevalent. Unstructured data are typically not stored in a data warehouse and require a different data storage mechanism. All structured and unstructured health data are collected over time to help understand the past, assess the present, and foresee the future of your health.

Besides our own personal health data, other health data sources can come from clinicians, pharmacies, labs, hospitals, health agencies, and devices (mobile) as described below and shown in Figure 1.2:

- *Clinicians* – an encounter with your family physician, specialist doctor, physician assistant, or nurse that examines your condition and recommends a cure for a diagnosis.
- *Pharmacies* – medications that are prescribed by your doctor to maintain your health or cure an illness and distributed at your local or online pharmacy. It can be generic as antibiotics to destroy bacteria or specific as lowering your blood pressure. These prescriptions are captured and regulated to avoid possible abuse.

■ *Labs* – this can be as simple as blood work to determine your blood type, cholesterol level, vitamin deficiency, or as complex as tests to determine if you are a sickle cell anemia carrier. Each lab work is carefully analyzed and the results are reported to your doctor for diagnosis.

■ *Hospitals* – visits to the hospital that normally require a doctor's attention for more serious procedures such as heart surgery, removal of a tumor, or giving birth.

■ *Health agencies* – agencies such as Centers for Disease Control (CDC) or National Institute of Health (NIH) provide medical research using our health data to control the spread of diseases or find cures of deadly diseases so that we can live longer and healthier.

■ *Devices (mobile)* – these can be both apparatus that gets installed in your body or wearables on your wrist to collect vital data such as heartbeat, blood pressure, number of steps, etc.

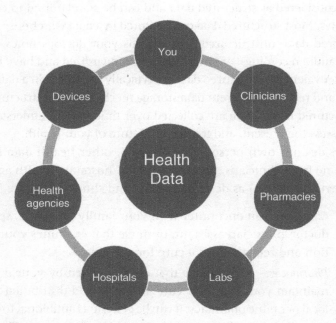

Figure 1.2 Sources of Health Data: From Paper to Digital
Source: Author.

HEALTHCARE CHALLENGES AND FOCUS AREAS

Now that the definitions have been established, let's examine some high-level challenges and how they translate into focusing on people, process, and technology to move forward into the twenty-first century and beyond. Many organizations, not just healthcare, are sharing with us similar challenges they encounter in the ever-changing world of economics and competition.

The first challenge is shortage of resources. Providing quality healthcare starts with people. Nurses, physician assistants, doctors, lab technicians, specialists, and therapists, etc. are always in high demand. According to Mercer's US Healthcare External Labor Market Analysis, the United States will need 2.3 million new healthcare workers by 2025 in order to take care of its aging and growing population adequately. These professions interact with patients on a daily basis, collect your data for analysis, and document the diagnosis and treatment to help you become healthy and on your way to wellness. Currently, there is a shortage and a challenge to keep talented professionals in healthcare while other sectors such as retail and manufacturing are displacing workers. Some healthcare organizations are welcoming these displaced workers and train them to fill some jobs such as lab technician, data entry, and medical assistants. There are many reasons as to why there is a shortage, but healthcare organizations are exploring strategies and offering incentives to avoid high turnover. Some of the strategies will be explored in a later chapter that revolves around people. In a nutshell, treating people as an asset becomes a competitive advantage to fulfilling the needs in healthcare.

The second challenge is using data effectively. As Figure 1.2 illustrates, the multifaceted sources of health data each person produces, managing the data is the biggest challenge healthcare organizations are facing today. Much of the data are in multiple places and systems. There is no industry standard or governance to allow patients to see their own data and there is no one system to host all of the patient data for easy access that clinicians and hospitals need to provide high-quality care for their patients. In the healthcare sector, we have plenty of data but lack the comprehensive knowledge because organizations are unable to access the many dimensions of data and analyze all the data they have about a patient. To borrow a quote from W. Edwards Deming, "Without data, you're just another person with an opinion." Opinions in healthcare can become a liability and have high risks of being incorrect. Clinicians need to have data-driven insights to make informed decisions so that mistakes can be avoided. In addition, the ability to analyze the data has become more complex with a variety of data types (structured and unstructured) and healthcare organizations may not have the right infrastructure and/or tools to mitigate the complexity. As data become more voluminous, it is imperative to have a solid foundation of technology and a well-defined process for managing data, analytics, and decisions.

The third challenge is innovating toward a digital transformation. All industries are challenged to innovate and prepare for the digital transformation. Digital transformation requires organizations to re-think their overall business processes. It is about using digital technologies and leveraging all your data to put the customer at the heart of the business. Other industries such as retail, travel and transportation, and telecommunications have embraced and started the path toward a digital transformation, placing emphasis on enhancing the customer experience. We believe the healthcare sector is lagging behind and has not yet developed a comprehensive strategy to overcome a highly siloed, fragmented ecosystem that many healthcare providers are dealing with toward obtaining a holistic view of the patient. In order to succeed in digital transformation, healthcare organizations must start evaluating a strategy and determine ways to become more effective and efficient in connecting and applying the data, deploying technology to improve communication to better engage with the patient, and enhance the patient experience. We believe healthcare companies are in catchup mode and the digital transformation initiative must be in the forefront to elevate the healthcare industry.

The above challenges that we hear from colleagues, vendors, and customers translate into three areas of focus for the rest of this book:

- *People* – many industry articles, thought leaders, and trends tend to indicate that data is the most important asset. Mike and I disagree and strongly believe that people are the most important asset, regardless of the industry or organization. You and I are the ones who are the creators and consumers of data. You and I are the ones who have to provide the intelligence into systems to transform data into action. Thus, investing in people, especially in healthcare, is a priority to become more patient aware and more friendly in communication as an industry.

- *Process* – as described earlier, everyone accumulates data and stacks of paperwork are collected over the years. The one constant struggle and the biggest challenge in healthcare is the push to move away from paper. Pushing healthcare professionals in that paperless direction is an uphill battle and a change that is greatly needed to have better communication within the healthcare ecosystem. In addition, the ability to streamline the process from data to intelligence to action becomes an exercise that will drive efficiency and effectiveness between the patient and the clinician.

- *Technology* – it is not about automation of processes to eliminate jobs; it is about exploring, considering, and adopting existing or new technology to augment the human interactions in the healthcare ecosystem. Because health data can grow exponentially and with the pace of change intensifying faster than ever, healthcare organizations are investigating and beginning to implement the latest innovation in technologies to prepare and support the digital transformation era. It is also an enabler to move away from a paper-led industry to a paperless culture that allows healthcare organizations to move forward and on par with other industries.

We truly believe the new and innovative technologies such as in-database analytics, in-memory analytics, open source, artificial intelligence, cloud, and virtual reality (to name a few) will help tame the challenges of managing health data, uncover new opportunities with analytics, and deliver a higher value care by augmenting data management with embedded analytics.

AUDIENCE FOR THIS BOOK

The intended audience is business and IT healthcare professionals who want to learn about new and innovative technologies, process improvement, and managing people to be successful in their line of work. The content in this book is for the business analysts who want to be smarter delivering information to different parts of the organization. It is for the data scientists who want to explore new approaches to apply analytics. It is for managers, directors, and executives who want to innovate and leverage data and analytics to make insight-driven decisions affecting the healthcare sector.

You should read this book if your profession is in one of these groups:

- Executive managers, including chief executive officers, chief operating officers, chief strategy officers, chief information officers, chief marketing officers, or any other company leader who wants to integrate people, process, and technology for efficiency.
- Line of business managers that oversee technologies and want to adopt innovative technologies providing quality healthcare.
- Business professions such as data scientists, business analysts, and quantitative analysts who analyze data and deliver data-driven insights to the leadership team for decision-making.
- IT professionals such as data engineers, database administrators who manage the healthcare data, ensuring its readiness, easy accessibility, and quality for analytics and reporting.

This book is ideal for healthcare professionals who want to embrace the digital transformation. It provides insight to improve the data management and analytical processes, explore new technologies applying analytics to complex data, and learn new skill sets to become pioneers in their healthcare organization.

HOW TO READ THIS BOOK

This book can be read in a linear approach, chapter by chapter. However, if you are a reader who wants to focus on a specific aspect such as people, process, or technology, you can simply jump to that specific chapter. If you are not up to date with the healthcare industry, we highly suggest starting here with Chapter 1, as it highlights the demand for and the state of healthcare. You can proceed to Chapters 2–4 to see how healthcare organizations are leveraging people, process, and technology. Chapter 5 brings all of the elements together and shows how you can unify and connect people, process, and technology to better manage health data and apply advanced analytics to derive intelligence for strategic actions. Chapter 6 is a must-read since it talks about the future of healthcare and how to anticipate the digital transformation with innovative technologies. Chapter 7 provides final thoughts from me (a data and analytics leader) and Mike (a business executive) and what actions you can take to advance in healthcare. Nonetheless, each chapter can stand on its own with minimal context from other chapters. The table below provides a description and takeaways for each chapter.

Chapter	Chapter purpose	Takeaways
1. Introduction	Highlights the demand and state of the healthcare industry. Shows how the industry has changed and how much demand there is for healthcare with evolving regulations.	• What has changed? • How can data and analytics have provided better information for healthcare? • What are some things organizations can do to improve healthcare? • What are innovative healthcare companies doing?
2. People	Demonstrates that humans are the most important assets in an organization and investing in people can prepare the healthcare sector for a more promising future.	• What kind of human investment is needed? • What skills are needed? • What roles are in high demand? • How do you build a resource library?
3. Process	Examines how to improve current processes from data collection to analysis to reporting.	• What is the current process? • How can it be improved? • Why do you need to develop a consistent process? • What sponsorships are needed?
4. Technology	Evaluates the technology landscape and what is available today. Considers what you can do to integrate data and analytics.	• What is available today for immediate implementation? • Should you consider open source technology? • What are some pros and cons using each type of technology? • What are the costs and benefits of each technology?

Chapter	Chapter purpose	Takeaways
5. Unifying People, Process, and Technology	Connects and summarizes how to unify people, process, and technology in a cohesive approach.	• How do you influence culture change? • How do you get your organization to move up in the analytical stages? • What are some considerations using analytics in healthcare? • Share some examples and use cases.
6. Future in Healthcare	Examines new technologies and emerging technologies that can improve healthcare.	• What does the future hold for healthcare? • What are some focus areas being considered? • How does human intelligence play a key role? • What should you consider as a professional in healthcare?
7. Final Thoughts	Concludes the book with the power of you delivering insight-driven decisions and intelligence. Final thoughts about the future of the healthcare sector.	• What are some actions you can take today to impact the future in healthcare? • Recommendations. • Final thoughts.

Let's Get Started

The healthcare sector is one of the most data-intensive industries. All healthcare organizations have data and much of that data is in a siloed, fragmented ecosystem that is collected in multiple channels from a multitude of sources that stream in from every direction. Mike and I want to share with you a real-world use case of a healthcare company focusing on integrating and connecting people, process, and technology. We want to provide details on how to transform the healthcare industry with a unique perspective from a finance executive and a technologist to give you a holistic view of IT and business. By integrating people, process, and technology, it will give your organization a strong foundation for the inevitable digital transformation in healthcare. Let's get started.

STATE OF HEALTHCARE

The topic of health comes up in many conversations and it happens every day in many of our salutations. When you see or meet other

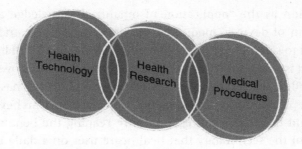

Figure 1.3 Major Advancements in Healthcare
Source: Author.

people such as family, friends, and perhaps someone you have just met, it is very common and customary for us to start a conversation with an expression "How are you?" Most of time, we receive a response "I'm good," or "We're okay," or "I'm fine." Other times, and more likely with family and close friends, we get intimate details such as "I am not feeling too good," or "My wife and I have been sick with a cold," or "My daughter was recently in the hospital for a sports-related knee injury." These conversations normally lead to further and more detailed discussions about us and our wellbeing. Conversations and discussions around health can be attributed to its natural presence and ominous impact on all of us.

The state of healthcare is ever-evolving, highly dynamic, and thought-provoking. Over the past few decades, the world of healthcare has changed dramatically and presents many opportunities for healthcare organizations to embark on an exciting journey. Many things have improved, new discoveries have been made, and change is constant. Over the course of the authors' careers, there are three major areas shaping the state of healthcare (See Figure 1.3). They are health technology, medical research, and medical procedures. Let's with health technology.

HEALTH TECHNOLOGY

In every direction you turn, technology has played an important role and it has an enormous impact on how healthcare has evolved over the last decades. Health technology is defined by the World Health

Organization as the "application of organized knowledge and skills in the form of devices, medicines, vaccines, procedures and systems developed to solve a health problem and improve quality of lives." The simple fact is that, as technology advances, many new innovations are created and developed every day. We believe technology has changed healthcare dramatically and patients, clinicians, researchers, practitioners, and healthcare professionals are reaping the benefits. Think about all of the technology that healthcare uses on a daily basis. For example, computerized tomography (CT) scan machines take x-rays of our bodies from multiple angles and clinicians can examine the x-rays in near real-time to diagnose our symptoms. These images can be stored and shared simultaneously to other doctors as needed. You can even carry x-rays with you if you desire to have them read by another doctor or practice. This is something that we take for granted now but it is such an important piece of technology that is used every day by clinicians.

Other advancements, such as surgical technology, breathing apparatuses, and technologies that deliver and administer medicine have improved and are helping to save people's lives. It's not just the equipment that has changed. Take, for example, the administration of anesthesia. Decades ago, when patients needed to numb pain, they either had no anesthesia or had to be put under completely. Today, clinicians can administer anesthesia locally or to a certain area and patients are more comfortable because they will not feel the pain when having a minor operation.

The biggest change that technology is able to deliver is the way healthcare professionals communicate. Long gone are the days where doctors can only be reached via a beeper. When a doctor was beeped, that clinician would need to find a phone to call that number. Now, however, hospital staff can communicate with one another more effectively and update each other in near real time. We have personally witnessed the use of speech to text when nurses or doctors are documenting their patients. In addition, speech commands can be used to call a specialist or doctor without having to pick up a mobile phone. It is similar to using a cloud-based voice service like Alexa, Siri, or Cortana. Nurses and doctors can simply use speech commands such as "Call Dr. Smith" or "Is Nurse Jo available to come to room 311?"

In addition to calling and connecting clinicians, the advancement of technology also allows medical records to be stored electronically. Compared to a few decades ago, when most medical records were still stored physically in cabinets with thousands of notes spilling out, these electronic records can all be aggregated in a safer and more secure environment for future use. There is less of a chance that information can be misplaced or lost since medical records are now stored electronically. Other ways technology has played a role include hospital booking systems, helping the staff to be better organized and better manage the workload of staffing. A more structured and organized environment leads to better healthcare from hospitals and clinicians know what they have to do with minimal disruptions.

Technology changes how we all live and work but we believe it has improved and benefited the healthcare industry the most. Compared to a few decades ago, we are seeing more tablets, mobile devices, and digital monitoring systems being used to improve lives. Lives are being saved every day because of the progress made in technology for healthcare.

HEALTH RESEARCH

Advances in research have accelerated in the past 10 years. Think of all the discoveries for managing diseases such as diabetes, new drugs and treatments for managing HIV thanks to clinical pharmacology, and procedures for minimizing recovery time for heart condition victims. However, the biggest advancement in health research has been combating cancer and increasing the survival rate. Cancer is one of the most debilitating and deadliest diseases and claims many lives annually. Historically, if you were diagnosed with cancer, you were guaranteed not to survive and may have had only days or weeks to live. Today, more and more people are surviving each and every day. While some people can see cancer going into remission, others live long and fruitful lives with the aid of medications. The key to this advancement is medical research. It has allowed clinicians to detect early signs of cancer and prepare a regimen plan before it can spread or become deadly. If cancer is detected early, the chances of survival are higher, thanks to advanced research in medicine, chemotherapy, and radiotherapy.

It is not just cancer research: other health areas have progressed by leaps and bounds. Recent research unveiled discoveries in the development of more prescription drugs available in the market to aid with pain and treat infections faster than before. Procedures such as gall balder removal or stent insertion that used to take hours to execute are now done in minutes. Some diseases that were considered untreatable decades ago such as HIV are now more manageable. Thanks to medical research, new developments have progressed that allow clinicians to treat or cure the symptoms faster and safer.

Healthcare professionals and executives continue to push the envelope and invest in health research, which has continued to accelerate in the past decades. Although it is impossible to discover everything or have a breakthrough all at once, there will always be new discoveries and ways to augment healthcare through research. There are technicians in labs across the world pouring over research data to advance medical research and find innovative discoveries made every day and that is a terrific thing for healthcare in the medical research field.

MEDICAL PROCEDURES

Many medical procedures have also advanced to be more effective and efficient. Take, for instance, cataract surgery, which can now be an outpatient procedure where patients can be admitted and released on the same day. Knee surgery patients can go home within a day compared to the past, where patients would have to stay for days in the hospital to recover. Inserting stents for heart patients can be done in hours and patients can also go home within a day to rest and recover in the comfort of their own homes. But no one wants to be in pain during any of these procedures. Anesthesia has been an area undergoing continued improvements. Decades ago, either you had no anesthesia or had to be completely under. Looking back a few decades, patients were worried about the harmful effects of anesthesia. Clinicians used gas that would knock the patient out completely and that would leave them feeling dazed and groggy for hours or even days. Obviously, no patient wants to feel any pain when having surgery. Thankfully, medical procedures such as local anesthetics for simple procedures are more prevalent today and administering anesthetics is also safer. Today, there are options. Anesthesia can be administered locally, meaning only the operating area is numbed. Doctors use injections to numb an area and the patient can be more at ease with the ability to feel other parts of their body. Other times, anesthesia is given to patients who need to be completely asleep.

Thanks to medical research and innovation, heart surgery and stroke victims have shorter operating times with smaller incisions and sharpened techniques. The progress in this medical field has saved many lives, as well as allowed patients to get back on their feet much faster compared to a decade ago. As this book is being written, a friend had just experienced a minor stroke that progressed to a massive stroke within hours after being admitted to the ER. Stroke happens when a blood vessel feeding the brain gets clotted or bursts. He felt numbness on the right side of his body and had collapsed at home while trying to get back into bed. In the ER, the doctors operated on him with two small incisions to unblock the blood flow to his brain. Within hours he was awake and was able to go home within a day. After two days he was on his feet and back to work. It is truly a testament to how far medical procedures have progressed. Researchers are still investigating ways to make things better and more efficient in this field since stroke is the third leading cause of death in the United States.

Of all the ways healthcare has evolved over the years, health technology, medical research, and medical procedures have made the biggest impact. Patients, medical professionals, and healthcare organizations all benefit from these advancements. In addition, these three areas will change and advance even more and make healthcare better for all.

The topic of healthcare has gained a lot of attention in the United States and around the world. Discussions in healthcare can be highly controversial, debatable, and personal. On the other hand, these healthy conversations can be very engaging, uplifting, and impactful. Consumers and healthcare organizations are taking notice of this matter and have begun to acknowledge how healthcare affects everyone on a global scale. The healthcare industry is fascinating for its growth, demand, and influences. In examining the healthcare industry more closely, let's start with its market size and consistent growth.

GROWTH IN HEALTHCARE

The healthcare sector is a multi-trillion-dollar industry that contin-ues to grow exponentially. Research studies and reports consistently show that the healthcare industry is not slowing down anytime soon. A recent 2018 study published by Deloitte, a consulting company, in collaboration with *The Economist* Intelligence Unit, reported double-digit growth from 2015 to 2020. In 2015, the global healthcare mar-ket was US$7.077 trillion and is expected to grow to US$8.734 trillion by 2020.[1] Another study and report recently revealed that the global healthcare industry will swell to US$11.801 trillion by 2021.[2] Health-care is currently ranked the number-one industry driving the United States economy above technology, construction, and retail, based on data and industry perspectives from the Bureau of Labor Statistics.[3]

There are many reasons for the enormous growth in the health-care sector. The primary reason is an aging population that requires diagnosis, treatment, and prevention of diseases or illnesses. The healthcare industry offers products and services to treat patients like us (you and me) with preventive, curative, and rehabilitative care for physical and mental impairments. These products and services are in high demand from the aging population, which uses healthcare the most. According to the United States Centers for Disease Control, citizens over the age of 65 experience three times more hospital days than the general population. From the same source, folks who are over 75 years of age have four times more hospital days compared to other population groups. As we age, healthcare becomes more essen-tial in our daily lives.

[1] DreamIt (24 August 2018). "Just How Big Is the Healthcare Industry? Here's What You Need to Know." Retrieved from https://www.dreamit.com/journal/2018/4/24/size-healthcare-industry.

[2] https://www.marketwatch.com/press-release/healthcare-global-market-report-2018-2018-09-17.

[3] https://www.investopedia.com/articles/investing/042915/5-industries-driving-us-economy.asp.

Another reason for the growth in healthcare is the rise of chronic illnesses such as diabetes, heart disease, and cancer. According to Centers for Disease Control, six in ten adults have a chronic disease and four in ten have more than two chronic diseases in the United States. Diabetes is considered one of the top three diseases and diagnoses continue to increase. The International Diabetes Federation predicts that the number of people around the world who have diabetes will expand from 425 million in 2017 to 625 million by 2045, which is a staggering 47% increase in less than 20 years. Much of the chronic illnesses are attributed to poor nutrition, lack of exercise, and excessive alcohol and tobacco use.

Similarly, heart disease is also on the rise. The American Heart Association expects the number of people who have heart disease in the United States to escalate from 6.5 million between 2011 and 2014 to 8 million by 2030, making it another chronic disease that has double-digit growth of 23% in less than 15 years. The cost of caring for these types of conditions will lead to drastic growth in healthcare spending, higher expenses for patients and families, and added costs for providers.

Another rise in healthcare diagnoses and growing concern is mental diseases, which affect millions globally. While diabetes and heart disease have some type of treatment and/or cure, mental diseases such as dementia or Alzheimer's are often untreatable. This chronic disease has personally affected me. Several of my sponsors who brought me to America have been diagnosed with dementia. As many of you know, once a person close to you or a loved one is diagnosed with this chronic disease, it is heartbreaking to see how quickly that person's wellbeing and memory deteriorate. One minute they can recognize you and be very sound in their communication, then the next minute you are a stranger and there is no recollection of short-term memory. It is very hard to carry on a conversation and a struggle for the patient to find the words to converse with you. Mental illness is debilitating and drains the physical and emotional aspects of the patient, their family, and loved ones who are providing care.

Having witnessed this awful disease and cared for a loved one, it is extremely depressing that there is no cure in sight for dementia that is affecting millions of senior citizens. In 2017, Alzheimer's Disease

International did a study and reported that there were about 50 million people living with dementia. In the same report from the same organization, it is projected that more than 125 million people will have dementia by 2050. This chronic condition will contribute to the rapid increase of healthcare expenses. It was reported in the same study that one trillion dollars was spent on treating and caring for dementia patients in 2017.

As the healthcare industry continues to grow and the demand remains high for services, there are many factors to consider. These factors all begin with data from you and me, who are the end users in a complex healthcare system. Let's examine what healthcare providers such as Cleveland Clinic are doing to improve healthcare with data and analytics.

HEALTHCARE DATA

Data exists in every organization, whether it is in finance, manufacturing, retail, or government and it is no different in healthcare. Data is even more critical in healthcare since data is turned into information that clinicians rely on to make informed decisions that can mean life or death. Because we are collecting many more data (from telehealth, images, mobile devices, sensors, etc.) than ever before and the speed at which we collect the data has significantly increased, data volumes have grown exponentially. In particular, healthcare providers have at least doubled their data volumes in less than 24 months, which is beyond what Moore's law (that the rate of change doubles in 24 months) had predicted over 50 years ago. With the pace of change accelerating faster than ever, healthcare providers are looking for the latest, proven innovation in technologies to better manage all of the data and apply analytics to help transform every challenge into opportunities to impact positively the patient's experience.

The data explosion in healthcare exacerbates the challenges that healthcare organizations are facing. IDC, a research firm, conducted a study in April 2014 and reported that healthcare data grows to 2,314 exabytes or 2.314 zettabytes (which has 21 zeros) in 2020. To give you a sense of how much data this is, the report illustrated an analogy to where all of the patient data stored in tablet computers would stack up to 82,000 miles high. This is equivalent to a third of the way to the moon. Data in healthcare is expected to continue to increase by 48% annually and much of the data will be in an unstructured format where it cannot be stored in columns and rows. Traditionally, clinicians have documented clinical findings and facts on paper, and even now tend to capture data in whatever method is most convenient for them, often with little regard for how this data is eventually captured, integrated, and analyzed. Electronic medical record (EMR) systems have attempted to standardize the data capture process and documentation of the patient data but it has not been able to accommodate the cumbersome data capture process.

The healthcare sector and its data are unique compared to other industries. Compared to other industries, data in healthcare is more difficult to deal with (see Figure 1.4) because it is:

- Multifaceted and resides in many systems (silos)
- Often unstructured
- Under strict regulations

The next sections will go into more depth on each of these issues.

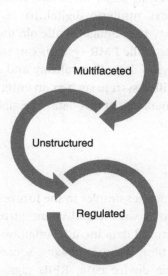

Figure 1.4 Uniqueness of Healthcare Data
Source: Author.

MULTIFACETED AND SILOED DATA

Healthcare data comes from many sources and various systems. It is multifaceted and not linear. One data point does not necessarily follow or precede another since our health or diagnosis does not follow any regimen. As data points can come from handwritten notes, electronic systems, or piles of folders, data quality may be an issue in many organizations. Healthcare data involve many variables that make it challenging to centralize and analyze. Like our human body that consists of many parts to make it work together, healthcare data is very similar. Healthcare data is a combination of individual systems or silos that are very complex and unable to work together. Collecting and managing the healthcare data from each of those systems is often done with disparate applications, which makes it impossible to share and leverage that data across an ecosystem of fragmented applications.

Healthcare data comes from various departments across the organization. Data source systems such as electronic medical records (EMR) and electronic health records (EHR) software store certain data while different departments like radiology or intensive care units also have their own silos of data. In many instances, these types of data are in different formats – text, numeric, digital, paper, pictures, videos, etc. For example, radiology uses images while old medical records exist in note or paper formats while EMR systems can store hundreds of rows of textual and numerical data. Centralizing and aggregating all of this data into a single, unified system such as an enterprise data warehouse is a logical choice to make all of this data accessible and apply analytics for actionable decisions.

UNSTRUCTURED DATA

Healthcare data will not get simpler in the future and will only become more complex due to its variety and volume from unstructured data. Examples of unstructured data include email, social media data, XML data, videos, audio files, photos, images, sensor data, spreadsheets, web log data, mobile device data, RFID tags, and pdf documents. In the report referenced above from IDC, about 80% of the world's healthcare data is unstructured and needs to be treated differently than structured data that are normally in row-and-column format.

Approximately 1.2 billion unstructured clinical and medical documents are created every year. Critical medical information is often kept in these documents since it is so difficult to extract and analyze to obtain insights from them. One important way to improve healthcare, enhance patient care, and accelerate clinical research is by gathering, understanding, and analyzing the insights and relationships that are confined and contained in unstructured data. Such free-form medical text, hospital admission notes, and a patient's medical history are pertinent and relevant data points to help uncover opportunities.

As we embark on the digital transformation, healthcare organizations collect and leverage even more unstructured data from patient-generated tracking devices such as blood pressure sensors, heartbeat monitoring, and location identification. These mobile devices are constantly collecting your data that can be every minute or hour. Over days, months, and years, these data points can become massive in volume and they can be useful for clinicians to have more insight to prescribe to their patient a regimen toward preventive care.

STRICT REGULATIONS

Each time you and I visit a clinician, there are many forms to sign prior to seeing the clinician. One of them is the HIPAA (Health Insurance Portability and Accountability Act) form. This act was developed in 1996 to protect the patient's privacy as much as possible. Under HIPAA, the Department of Health and Human Services (HHS) establishes boundaries on the use and releases of our personal health records. HIPAA also outlines precautions to protect our information and establishes civil and criminal penalties for any violations. The law applies not just to hospitals and medical practices but also to chiropractors, dentists, nursing homes, pharmacies, and psychologists, as well as to business associates such as third-party administrators, pharmacy, benefit managers for health plans, billing and transcription companies, and professionals performing legal, accounting, or administrative work. Misuse of sensitive information about the patient can lead to serious liabilities.

For each clinician, we must sign this form to allow healthcare providers, hospitals, and small practices to collect, store, access, and manage patient data to be HIPAA-compliant. Once the form is signed, your medical records and history are made available for healthcare professionals to access, analyze, and diagnose. HIPAA addresses the use and disclosure of our Protected Health Information (PHI). PHI refers to any information that can be used to identify a patient, including telephone or fax numbers, websites or photos, names of relatives, any number or code that may lead to identifying a patient's identity, and much more. As we transition to the digital world, HIPAA compliance will be enforced to access our personal health records and share what is needed to get quality healthcare.

Healthcare organizations across the country are faced with several data challenges. Managing a tremendous amount of data that includes medical and patient along with an increased demand for on-time access to medical records is an opportunity for improvement. In addition, healthcare organizations want to streamline their application portfolios to protect our health data in a secured environment that is accessible for compliance, reporting, and sharing. Now that we have discussed the data in detail, let's examine the value of analytics and the analytic applications that healthcare organizations use.

VALUE OF ANALYTICS

There are many definitions for analytics and the emphasis and focus on analytics has been in the forefront of many organizations. Analytic applications have surged in the marketplace because many companies globally have recognized the value of analytics, in particular, healthcare analytics which analyze the past, understand the present, and predict the future from all the healthcare data that organizations collect. Analytics can be very broad and has become the generic term for a variety of different business initiatives. According to Gartner, analytics is used to describe statistical and mathematical data analysis that clusters, segments, scores, and predicts what scenarios have happened, are happening, or are most likely to happen. Analytics have become the link between IT and business to exploit the tsunami of data. Based on our interactions with customers, we define analytics as a process of analyzing all of the data to gain knowledge about your business and deliver insight-driven decisions within an organization. Let's examine some common use cases and the value analytics provide in healthcare.

Risk Score on Chronic Disease – With the right data, analytics can help to derive a risk score and predict the likelihood of a person getting the disease and prevent it before it becomes fatal. With analytics, healthcare organizations will be able to identify patients with high risk of developing chronic diseases quite early and provide them with better treatment so they don't have to encounter long-term health issues. This information minimizes long-term care, which could mean nominal costly treatments to alleviate complications that might arise.

Quality Patient Care – Stellar patient care is extremely important. Doctors need to evaluate the symptoms and quickly provide a course of action to pull in other doctors and/or nurses to execute. Analytics can positively impact quality care by analyzing all of the data points of the symptoms and prescribe actions to be carried out based on the diagnosis. Analytics answers the question of what to do, providing decision option(s) based on current and historical data points.

Proactive Patient Analysis – Clinicians often advise patients that there is a chance of infection when there is a procedure or operation conducted on the patient. Patients encounter a number of potential threats to their recovery or wellbeing while still in the hospital. These threats include the development of sepsis, hard-to-treat infection, or an unexpected downturn due to their existing medical condition. Data such as vitals from the patient can be analyzed and analytics can provide clinicians insight to changes in a patient's vitals and allow them proactively to identify relapse before severe symptoms manifest themselves that the naked eye cannot detect.

Operations Management – Analytics help with managing staffing needs and operations such as emergency care or intensive care departments. Having the right staffing in areas of quick response time can save lives. With improved technological infrastructure and proper analytics, it is possible for healthcare providers to make key operational decisions. They have begun to adopt a proactive instead of a reactive approach to manage patient flow, alleviate operational bottlenecks, and reduce clinical workload stress. Operational decision-makers are able to make informed decisions.

Appointment Management – Any unexpected gap in the daily calendar can have an adverse financial effect for the healthcare provider while throwing off a clinician's or an office's entire workflow. Healthcare organizations are using analytics to analyze and identify patients' patterns such as the likelihood of skipping an appointment without advance notice. By doing so, it can reduce revenue losses, offer open slots to other patients in need, and minimize the workflow disruption. Duke University conducted a study[4] and discovered that by using predictive analytics, there is a higher accuracy than looking at patient patterns to detect a no-show. Providers can leverage this insight to send reminders to patients at risk of failing to show up, offer other services such as transportation to make their appointments, or suggest alternative dates and times that are more suitable.

Financial Risk Management – Similar to other industries, using analytics to analyze risk is highly useful and strategic. Risk management is a burden because it can help and hurt a healthcare organization to determine a patient financial risk of payment and decide on what kind of payment may be appropriate in case a patient does not have coverage. Analytics can help to uncover unpaid bills, identify the cash flow to the hospitals by determining the accounts that demand payment, and also determine which payments are likely to be paid or remain unpaid in the future.

Fraud and Abuse – Fraud and abuse is a big problem and an ongoing issue in healthcare. Leveraging data and analytics can help in detecting and preventing fraud and abuse. There are several types of fraudulent occurrences in healthcare, and they range from honest mistakes such as erroneous billings, to dishonest mistakes such as double charging, wasteful diagnostic tests, false claims leading to improper payments, and so on. Leveraging data and analytics helps in identifying the patterns that lead to potential patterns of preventing fraud and abide in healthcare insurance as well.

Managing Supply Chain – Healthcare providers, hospitals, and clinicians have very tight budgets. The supply chain is one of a provider's largest cost centers and is an area that constantly needs improvement

---

[4] https://healthitanalytics.com/news/predictive-analytics-ehr-data-identify-appointment-no-shows.

to trim unnecessary spending and improve efficiency. Hospital and healthcare executives are honed into reducing variation and obtaining more actionable insights into ordering patterns and supply utilization. In a survey conducted by Navigant,[5] using analytics to monitor the supply chain and make proactive, data-driven decisions about spending could save hospitals almost US$10 million per year. Furthermore, leveraging analytics provides insights to negotiate better pricing, reduce the variation in supplies, and streamline the ordering process.

New Therapies and Precision Medicine – Research and development are constantly evolving and new ideas and innovation are on the cusp of every healthcare practitioner. As precision medicine and genomics gain popularity, researchers and providers are using analytics to augment traditional clinical trials and drug discovery techniques. Analytic and clinical decision support tools play key roles in translating new medicine into precision therapies for the patients. Analytics support the use of modeling and simulation to predict outcomes and design clinical trials, for dose optimization, and to predict product safety and potential adverse effects. In addition, analytics enable researchers to better understand the relationships between genetic variants and how certain therapies can affect the patient.

Healthcare Transformation – There is a shift in healthcare to focus on patient-centered care. Healthcare executives have started to reevaluate how they engage and interact with patients in their care as consumer expectations increasingly demand more personalized and less fragmented healthcare experiences. Consumers have more expectations and know that they have more choices. Not all providers cost the same and even the quality of care is not the same. With analytics, healthcare organizations are able to drive healthcare improvement and transformation, and this will in turn drive impressive levels of change to focus on the patient. Analytics can deliver insight to influence enhancements and changes in the present hospital-centric delivery model from volume and activity to value and outcomes.

Of course, there are many use cases for analytics in healthcare. This chapter only scratches the surface to illustrate the value of collecting the data, making it available so that analytics can be applied and deliver analyses so that clinicians can make insight-driven decisions. In the next few chapters, we will examine closely how people, process, and technology are crucial to further improve the healthcare industry.

CHAPTER **2**

People

"Pleasure in the job puts perfection in the work."

— Aristotle

Peter Drucker said, "The most valuable asset of a 21st-century institution, whether business or non-business, will be its knowledge workers and their productivity."[1] When you think of the healthcare industry, there are thousands of different job titles. Many of these are jobs that exist across every industry. When you think of professions, from accounting to human resources to information technology, many of the roles are present in most typical organizational structures.

Accounting

- Accounts receivable analyst
- Bookkeeper
- Budget analyst
- Chief financial officer
- Controller
- Treasurer

Human Resources

- Benefits officer
- Compensation analyst
- Employee relations specialist
- HR coordinator
- HR specialist
- Retirement plan counselor

Information Technology

- Business systems analyst
- Database administrator
- Information architect
- Mobile developer

[1] https://www.educba.com/employee-most-valuable-intangible-assets/.

- Software engineer
- Systems administrator

The healthcare industry is usually defined by several different economic sectors. If you consider the International Standard Industrial Classification nomenclature, you can group organizations into the following high-level categories: hospital activities, medical and dental activities, "other human health" activities, healthcare equipment and services, and pharmaceuticals, biotechnology, and other related life sciences. Some job titles specific to the healthcare industry are:

Administrative Healthcare/Medical Job Titles

- Accountant
- Administrator
- Billing Specialist
- Business Analyst
- Case Manager
- Chief Financial Officer
- Customer Service Representative
- Financial Analyst
- Hospital Administrator
- Information Technology Specialist
- Medical Billing Specialist
- Medical Coder
- Operations Manager
- Patient Services Representative

Clinical Healthcare/Medical Roles

- Ambulatory Nurse
- Anesthesiologist
- Hospice Counselor
- Intensive Care Nurse
- Paramedic

- Pharmacist
- Physician
- Registered Nurse (RN)
- Registered Nurse (RN) Case Manager
- Surgeon

You have probably heard the following in some form or another: "People are the most important asset of an organization." How can you not agree with that statement? Without people what would an organization produce? However, when you think about the way typical organizations account for people, they are not an asset.

Think about an organization's balance sheet. Table 2.1 shows the asset side of accounts.

Nowhere do you see people as an asset. Why? Because they are listed on the liability or expense side. Counterintuitive to think an organization's most important asset is really a "liability" from an accounting perspective in a typical company.

As the economy of humankind continues to evolve, the importance of people and the differing types of skills they will require, from quantitative techniques to analytic interpretation to data management to storytelling, continues to get more complex. The following excerpt from Mayor Michael Bloomberg's Commencement speech at University of Michigan in 2016:

> For the first time in human history, the majority of people
> in the developed world are being asked to make a living
> with their minds, rather than their muscles. . . .

Table 2.1 Assets Within an Organization

Cash	Long-Term Investments
Short-Term Investments	Land
Accounts Receivable	Buildings
Accrued Revenues/Receivables	Equipment
Prepaid Expenses	Vehicles
Inventory	Furniture and Fixtures
Supplies	

Source: Author.

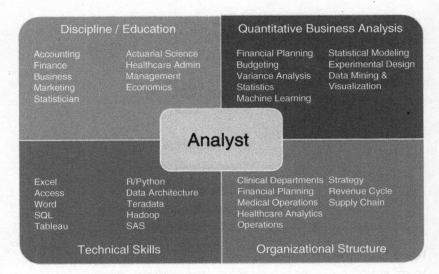

Figure 2.1 What Is an Analyst?

Source: Author.

> Now, we have an economy based on information: acquire the knowledge, apply the analytics, use your creativity. Hard to do, hard to learn, and even once you've mastered it, you'll have to start learning all over again, pretty much every day.[2]

As he describes the nature of our changing economy over the past 3000+ years, people are at the center. The concluding years of the twentieth century into the twenty-first century are known by many names – the information age, the computer age, the digital age, the digital transformation, etc. As he points out, it is the ability of our workforce to use data and turn that into information that is actionable that is the key job skill. It is a skill that requires continuous learning.

When you think about your current organization's job roles, it is just as varied. Even though this chapter is labeled "People," we are narrowing the focus to analytically focused people. Many organizational job titles include the word "analyst." When you review the employees who populate those job titles, something like the list in Figure 2.1 comes to mind.

[2] https://www.mikebloomberg.com/news/mike-bloomberg-delivers-commencement-at-university-of-michigan/.

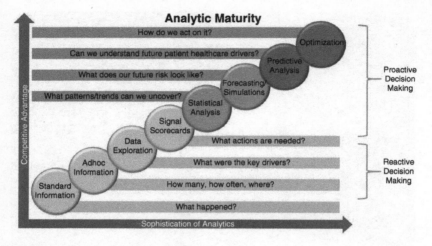

Figure 2.2   The Analytics Maturity Curve

Source: Adapted from Analytics Maturity Goal: From Reactive to Predictive, SAS Institute Inc.

Analysts come in all of the proverbial shapes and sizes, only this time we can distinguish them across your organization. They have a wide range of academic training that correlates to certain types of quantitative skills. They have a wide range of technical skills. They reside in virtually every department. Some people may only have one skill; others will have multiple skills.

In this new age, every organization in one way or another will require analytical talent to be successful. It has been noted by Thomas Davenport in his book[3] that your organization's competitive advantage increases with more sophisticated analysis. Logically, that makes sense. When you think about what sophisticated analytics means, it is the use of prescriptive and predictive analytics and the use of machine learning to drive insights and actions that were not once apparent.

Figure 2.2 illustrates what Thomas Davenport was driving at.

People will drive your movement in Figure 2.2 from lower left to upper right. The increased sophistication and competitive advantage

[3] Thomas H. Davenport and Jeanne G. Harris, *Competing on Analytics: The New Science of Winning* (Boston, Mass.: Harvard Business Review Press, 2007).

can create challenges to your workforce. Why? People. Those who have analytical backgrounds will continue to use advanced analytical techniques to produce outcomes. People that need to use the output of those techniques need to keep pace with analytical sophistication. This will require all members of your organization to keep up with the ability to interpret and use these techniques in decision-making.

People will fall into one of these two fundamentally important abilities that you need to address:

1. The ability to produce results
2. The ability to consume results

The first ability is centered around what types of people do you have in place? How do you define what you need to produce results? The second ability is centered on how do you "upskill" your organization to use analytics daily? As you think about raising the analytic expectations across your organization, what opportunities can you provide? How do you increase the understanding of analytics?

As your organization matures in its journey, you will need to keep in mind the following:

1. How do each of these abilities change?
2. How do they change relative to each other?
3. What are the implications for managing these changes?

The objective of your people strategy is to achieve analytic maturity, which requires understanding of and investment in your workforce.

THE ABILITY TO PRODUCE RESULTS

As you think about "people," your strategy should have two main foundations. The first foundational component is identifying what skills or disciplines are needed for analytics. For the purpose of this book, I use the words *skills* and *disciplines* interchangeably. Once you define the skills required for analytics, you can determine the second foundational component – what types of job roles you will need to execute within your organization. Without doing this work, you will have roles and skills that are not clearly defined or understood and won't work in harmony.

What skills are required to be analytically competent? Type in the word *analytics* in Wikipedia, Google, etc. and you will be flooded with all types of skills that you can list. While this can be useful to gather a comprehensive list, there is no structure and it will not relate to your analytics strategy. Use the analytics maturity chart to help you define the types of skills you need.

In Figure 2.2, for each question going from the lower left to the upper right, take an inventory of the current work your organization completes. Make a list of the work you would like to complete. This will create your "starting" list of skills required. You can then take that list and understand those skills you have today and those that you will need to fill.

The skills required in the lower left of Figure 2.2 have been around for the past 30+ years. They are all about reactive decision-making skills. These are usually reports that show history, usually lagging from at least one day behind to maybe even a month behind, depending on the focus. There are all kinds of financial reports, key performance indicators, and metrics that you can report past trends on. These retrospective and descriptive analytics were the traditional jobs of business intelligence analytics and basic skills included data extraction using Structured Query Language (SQL) and visualization tools.

As you think about the skills in the upper right of the analytics maturity chart, these skills are more focused on predicting or prescribing and finding patterns and correlations within your data. They tend to focus on using statistics and mathematics.

The important thing is to gather the list of skills you want your organization to possess. After you list your skills, you can align them into different categories. When grouping into categories, you can get as detailed as you feel is necessary to create the appropriate job roles. There is no one magic or right answer. The important point here is about gaining consensus in your organization. It is about agreeing to the principles and not allowing them to change or deviate. Success is dictated by sticking to those principles. It is so easy to allow "principle creep" or the continuously tweaking or changing of what you agree upon to derail movement or bring to a screeching halt the execution of your strategy. You need to remind your organization constantly what was agreed upon.

As you think about the number of categories you want to group your skills into, a radar chart is one way to help understand the skill profile you are driving toward. Many thought leaders tend to have six to nine groups of capabilities (e.g. strategic thinking, data visualization, data exploration, data management, predictive analytics, etc.). Your analytics strategy should help guide you to your capability groupings.

The four capability pillars or supports that we believe to be the foundational structure around determining what roles your analytics strategy requires to be successful can be found in Figure 2.3. These capability pillars are a way to group your skills when thinking about assessing proficiency and knowledge and applying these in your daily work. Each pillar in Figure 2.3 is not a comprehensive list by any means. It highlights what we believe are some of the important people skills required. Let's examine what belongs in each of these pillars.

Every organization should strive to be an analytic innovator. These organizations strategically apply analytics, value data, and have a highly competent analytical workforce. Having people with highly competent skills in each of these pillars will enable your organization's journey to become an analytic innovator. The quantitative analysis pillar is understanding what types of skills your people will need to be considered analytic innovators.

Building Analytic Capability

Redefining Analyst Roles & Requirements

Quantitative Analysis	Leveraging Data	Communication & Visualization	Business Acumen
Machine Learning	Computer Science Fundamentals	Building Visualizations	Healthcare Proficiency
Statistical Modeling			Financial & Operational
Experimental Design	Data Blending	Storytelling/ Communication Skills	Enterprise Strategy
Data Discovery & Mining			Problem Solving
Optimization	Information Management Principles	Translate Insights into Decisions & Actions	Strategic, Proactive, Innovative, Collaborative

Figure 2.3 Four Capability Pillars to Support Your Analytics Strategy
Source: Author.

Everyone has probably heard the phrase, "Data is the new oil." Being able to leverage data is more critical now than ever. This pillar covers those technical skills and jobs that can deliver structured or unstructured data to end users. Data management roles apply their fundamental understanding of designing and configuring data warehouses and solutions architecture to make sure the most valuable asset, "data," is available to the organization.

The communication and visualization pillar describes people skills that allow the organization to consume the results of these new advanced methodologies. Being able to choose the right visualization to share a complex idea in a simple, easy to understand manner is challenging. The ability to drive actions through insights is easier said than accomplished.

The business acumen pillar centers not only around industry knowledge, but organizational knowledge, problem solving, and strategy. Healthcare proficiency can be argued to be the most important skill in the business acumen pillar. Every organization has "lifers" who are a wealth of not only industry knowledge but organizational knowledge too. The ability of an organization to pass along this knowledge is critical.

WHAT TYPES OF ROLES?

Over the past decade or so, many new job roles have emerged. In order to attract new talent, we continue to try and give these job roles "sexy" titles to attract talent. No matter what the job title, the following roles below are keys to building a strong analytics workforce. Each role can have a slightly different definition, have overlapping responsibilities, or may be combined into one job role. We are sensitive to job role titles and by no means are we insulting anyone by combining job roles together in the descriptions below. Many times when you are searching job boards, certain job roles are used to ensure "hits" when trying to attract talent.

Let's take a quick look at what each of these titles may do in your organization. When we think of these job roles, we think of the following responsibilities:

Business Analyst This person interacts with members of your team as well as the stakeholders in your company where a business problem has been identified. They will work with outside Subject Matter Experts (SMEs) or project team members in problem formulation, solution design, and project development. They use business analysis, problem solving and reporting techniques, and/or enterprise developed tools to provide guidance and insights into the daily operations of specified business units. The business units will depend on how your organization is structured. They oversee the identification and definition of the business rules, metrics, key performance indicators, and business intelligence reports required to support enterprise-wide functions and business partners. These are specialists in your organization who have subject matter expertise (understanding revenue generation, longitudinal costs analysts, etc.) and a deep understanding of your organization and how it operates. They will continuously examine data to uncover insights to keep the business moving in the right direction and provide recommendations for operational efficiencies and process improvement that assists in change initiatives.

Citizen Data Scientist   These are people who are not formally trained in data science. They use technology advancements to perform data science functions. As software continues to evolve, the Citizen Data Scientist will not be required to "know" how to program or code, but rather they will use drag-and-drop techniques on their data sets. They will leverage their business acumen and model interpretability to drive insights.

Data Analyst   This person performs analysis of data. This is a process of inspecting, cleaning, transforming, and modeling data. They also look to discover useful information, suggest conclusions, and support decision-making. Many times data analyst responsibilities lie within other job roles. However, this important niche is starting to be singled out.

Data Architect   This person is the brains behind the ability to access your data. They need to have the ability to take all of your data and transform it into "views" that can be easily used by your organization. They provide strategic guidance to technology solutions to maximize the value of information.

Data Engineer This is your data access "go-to" person and is a tactical position for your analytics team. They will be responsible for optimizing and fine tuning access to your data. They will have two primary tasks: (1) optimizing access to your data for normal daily work and (2) collaborating with your analytics team to understand requirements to create optimal data sets. In the course of supporting their primary tasks, their daily work will consist of cataloging data sources, supporting the end-to-end data processes to create your enterprise data warehouse. They design, specify, and configure the database environment, to ensure efficient functionality by performing activities related to day-to-day administration, monitoring, and maintenance of applications tier, middle-tier, and database-tier functions and database environments. They will administer, install, maintain, develop, and implement policies and procedures for ensuring the security, availability, and integrity of these environments.

Data Ethicist This is a newer, emerging role. This person will help answer the question, "What should we do with data?" They will help determine risks and opportunities. Are there any unintended consequences? Does the use of the data match the organization's value? They will be leading the ethical awareness of using data for good.

Data Hygienist This is the person who makes sure your data is "clean." They will be looking over the data to ensure the data is stored in a consistent manner. For example, it is not enough that your data field contains a date: the date should be stored the same way for all records, in such a way that the dates make sense. You want to deliver the "cleanest" data to your analyst as possible.

Data Scientist A data scientist is a person who has knowledge across the four capabilities. We liken this person to the "Unicorn" below. Normally, this person excels in utilizing data modeling techniques to address complex business problems and analyzing large, unstructured data sets. They will design, implement, and champion data modeling and advanced analytic methods. They will demonstrate a deep domain expertise in healthcare, statistical and machine learning techniques, high-performance data architectures and technologies, and academic curiosity. They will extract insights from structured and unstructured data. They will also be able to explain through visualizing and storytelling. This end-to-end knowledge across all four capabilities will foster a culture of fact-based decision-making. They will lead a cross-functional team to promote the design, implementation, and monitoring of innovative advanced analytical disciplines and solutions through the coordinated and systematic use of clinical and encounter-based data, related business insights, and multidisciplinary skills set for planning, management, measurement, and learning.

Data Wrangler/Data Warehouse Specialist This person delivers data acquisition, transformations, cleansing, conversion, compression, and loading of data into data and analytics models. They work in partnership with data scientists and analysts to understand use cases, data needs, and outcome objectives. They will perform data discoveries to understand data formats, source systems, file sizes, etc. to inform analytics teams. They are a jack of all trades in the collection of data delivered in various formats or from various systems (relational databases, FTP sites, file sharing sites (e.g. Box), external hard drives, etc.).

Software Engineer/Software Programmer/Application Developer This person is writing much of the code behind the scenes. They are using a variety of languages. They are writing, testing, debugging, and maintaining the code necessary to collect and process your data to keep your technology platform up and running for your analysts. They integrate internal systems with third-party tools.

Solutions Architect/Visualizer This person leads the overall development and implementation of a business solution. They understand the business requirements and expectations of the final product to be delivered to the end user. They provide the overall technical vision for the solution to the appropriate teams for build. They will use user-based design principles to create an optimal end-user experience in understanding how they make decisions. The focus on the end-user makes it clear that the solution will be optimized to support the decision-making process.

Statistician/Biostatistician This person will use their statistical expertise to develop complex predictive/prescriptive models, forecasting models, survival models, etc., to provide solutions to business problems and organization operations.

Visualizer This person will be responsible to understand how to tell the most compelling story visually. This includes choosing the right visual and highlighting the insight to be derived. They are creative thinkers. They will need to understand all data elements in your data warehouse, as well as how your analytical teams apply statistical methods and machine-learning methods to build the "right" story.

Unicorns Do they exist? Yes; however, we are not talking about the mythical animal that has a large, pointed, spiraling horn projecting from its forehead. We are talking about a person in the workforce who can do all of the job responsibilities in the list above and do them all at a high level. We would be incorrect to say that none exist. In our opinion, there are a very small number of people whom you can call unicorns, mostly due to two factors: (1) technology is continuously changing at a rapid pace; and (2) industry business acumen is undoubtedly that one factor that takes a decade or more to be considered a "know-it-all."

WHAT JOB ROLES DO YOU NEED?

Many of the roles described above will be part of your analytics team. Whether you create specific job responsibilities for each of the roles defined above or merge some roles together is an organizational decision. We think about four major job families. They are (1) Data Engineer, (2) Business Analyst, (3) Quantitative Analyst, and (4) Data Scientist.

This book is not going to recommend to you what you ultimately decide to call job roles within your organization. It is a guide to understanding the skills required to succeed in analytics and the different types of job roles required to support that success.

What Capabilities Do You Need?

The key to defining the roles required is to understand and map your analytic capability requirements. As you can see in Figure 2.3, we have listed different capabilities examples into the four foundational pillars to determine what your team makeup will consist of.

Quantitative Analytics

The first pillar is around quantitative analytics. This grouping contains the necessary skills to produce your quantitative analytics. It is around two key disciplines: (1) "doing the math;" and (2) using processes to find anomalies and patterns in data. "Doing the math" centers around individuals who have been trained in educational programs like statistics, actuarial science, econometrics, physics, biostatistics, applied mathematics, or engineering. They have a thorough understanding of how the math works. Computers of course will do the math, but these individuals have also "done the math."

How do you determine what types of skills your organization needs? Think about it this way: if someone were to ask you what types of reports or analytics you do, would you be able to produce a list of all of the work your team has accomplished over the past few years and what analytics were involved?

When you produce typical reports and analysis today, it most likely entails the "way you have done it in the past," with not much new thinking or analytical techniques. With the volume of work that is asked of us, we tend to stick with what has worked in the past and produce "the number" that is required to be placed in the presentation to your upper management. Occasionally, they may ask for some "supporting numbers," which can easily be produced without much fanfare.

The list of potential quantitative skills in Table 2.2 is a good place to start. It is by no means a comprehensive list; nor should the entire list be used. Again, brainstorming around a list of potential skills will help you understand how you would incorporate them to advance your analytics capabilities. The "new requirements" of quantitative skills are a combination of traditional business analytics techniques for

Table 2.2 Traditional Quantitative Business Analytics Techniques

- Statistics (Risk Analytics)
- Forecasting
- Simulation
- Game Theory
- Algebra (Business Math)
- Budgeting
- Reserve (IBNR) Analysis
- Markov Chains
- Data Collection / Sampling
- Probability
- Normal and Binomial Distributions
- Sampling Distributions / Central Limit Theorem
- Confidence Intervals
- Hypothesis Testing
- Analysis of Variance (ANOVA)
- Correlation
- Solving Systems of Linear Equations
- Gauss-Jordan Elimination
- Variable Selection
- Multicollinearity
- Residual Diagnostics
- Matrix Manipulation

understanding and use of algorithms and statistical models. Tables 2.2 and 2.3 give you a sampling of skills to consider when defining your quantitative analytics pillar.

Leveraging Data

The second capability pillar is around organizing the data, deploying and leveraging the data, data security protocols, and data engineering skills. The skills are technically based and usually are accompanied by a technology solution. These capabilities center around designing, building, and integrating data from various resources, internally and externally.

People use complex programs, queries, and/or data models to optimize performance. They need to be able to align technologies solutions to enable business capabilities. Always keep in the forefront – how do you build a data warehouse solution that integrates an advanced analytics solution? Do you need a data model as well as an analytics

Table 2.3 Machine Learning Algorithms[4]

1. Instance-based algorithm
   - K-nearest neighbors algorithm (KNN)
   - Learning vector quantization (LVQ)
   - Self-organizing map (SOM)
2. Regression analysis
   - Logistic regression
   - Ordinary least squares regression (OLSR)
   - Linear regression
   - Stepwise regression
   - Multivariate adaptive regression splines (MARS)
3. Regularization algorithm
   - Ridge regression
   - Least absolute shrinkage and selection operator (LASSO)
   - Elastic net
   - Least-angle regression (LARS)
4. Classifiers
   - Probabilistic classifier
     - Naive Bayes classifier
   - Binary classifier
   - Linear classifier
   - Hierarchical classifier
5. Dimensionality reduction
   - Canonical correlation analysis (CCA)
   - Factor analysis
   - Feature extraction
   - Feature selection
   - Independent component analysis (ICA)
   - Linear discriminant analysis (LDA)
   - Multidimensional scaling (MDS)
   - Non-negative matrix factorization (NMF)
   - Partial least squares regression (PLSR)
   - Principal component analysis (PCA)
   - Principal component regression (PCR)
   - Projection pursuit
   - Sammon mapping
   - t-distributed stochastic neighbor embedding (t-SNE)
6. Ensemble learning
   - AdaBoost
   - Boosting
   - Bootstrap aggregating (Bagging)
   - Ensemble averaging – process of creating multiple models and combining them to produce a desired output, as opposed to creating just one model. Frequently an ensemble of models performs better than any individual model, because the various errors of the models "average out."

(Continued)

[4] *Source:* Based on data from https://en.wikipedia.org/wiki/Outline_of_machine_learning.

(Continued)

- Gradient boosted decision tree (GBDT)
- Gradient boosting machine (GBM)
- Random forest
- Stacked generalization (blending)

7. Reinforcement learning
   - Q-learning
   - State–action–reward–state–action (SARSA)
   - Temporal difference learning (TD)
   - Learning automata

8. Supervised learning
   - AODE
   - Artificial neural network
   - Association rule learning algorithms
     - Apriori algorithm
     - Eclat algorithm
   - Case-based reasoning
   - Gaussian process regression
   - Gene expression programming
   - Group method of data handling (GMDH)
   - Inductive logic programming
   - Instance-based learning
   - Lazy learning
   - Learning automata
   - Learning vector quantization
   - Logistic model tree
   - Minimum message length (decision trees, decision graphs, etc.)
     - Nearest neighbor algorithm
     - Analogical modeling
   - Probably approximately correct (PAC) learning
   - Ripple down rules, a knowledge acquisition methodology
   - Symbolic machine learning algorithms
   - Support vector machines
   - Random forests
   - Ensembles of classifiers
     - Bootstrap aggregating (bagging)
     - Boosting (meta-algorithm)
   - Ordinal classification
   - Information fuzzy networks (IFN)
   - Conditional random field
   - ANOVA
   - Quadratic classifiers
   - k-nearest neighbor
   - Boosting
     - SPRINT
   - Bayesian networks
     - Naive Bayes
   - Hidden Markov models
     - Hierarchical hidden Markov model

9. Bayesian statistics
   - Bayesian knowledge base
   - Naive Bayes
   - Gaussian naive Bayes
   - Multinomial naive Bayes
   - Averaged one-dependence estimators (AODE)
   - Bayesian belief network (BBN)
   - Bayesian network (BN)
10. Decision tree algorithms
    - Decision tree
    - Classification and regression tree (CART)
    - Iterative dichotomiser 3 (ID3)
    - C4.5 algorithm
    - C5.0 algorithm
    - Chi-squared automatic interaction detection (CHAID)
    - Decision stump
    - Conditional decision tree
    - ID3 algorithm
    - Random forest
    - SLIQ
11. Linear classifier
    - Fisher's linear discriminant
    - Linear regression
    - Logistic regression
    - Multinomial logistic regression
    - Naive Bayes classifier
    - Perceptron
    - Support vector machine
12. Unsupervised learning
    - Expectation-maximization algorithm
    - Vector quantization
    - Generative topographic map
    - Information bottleneck method
13. Artificial neural network
    - Feedforward neural network
      - Extreme learning machine
      - Convolutional neural network
    - Recurrent neural network
    - Long short-term memory (LSTM)
    - Logic learning machine
    - Self-organizing map
14. Association rule learning
    - Apriori algorithm
    - Eclat algorithm
    - FP-growth algorithm

(Continued)

(*Continued*)

15. Hierarchical clustering
    - Single-linkage clustering
    - Conceptual clustering
16. Cluster analysis
    - BIRCH
    - DBSCAN
    - Expectation-maximization (EM)
    - Fuzzy clustering
    - Hierarchical clustering
    - K-means clustering
    - K-medians
    - Mean-shift
    - OPTICS algorithm
17. Anomaly detection
    - k-nearest neighbors classification (k-NN)
    - Local outlier factor
18. Semi-supervised learning
    - Active learning
    - Generative models
    - Low-density separation
    - Graph-based methods
    - Co-training
    - Transduction
19. Deep learning
    - Deep belief networks
    - Deep Boltzmann machines
    - Deep convolutional neural networks
    - Deep recurrent neural networks
    - Hierarchical temporal memory
    - Generative adversarial networks
    - Deep Boltzmann machine (DBM)
    - Stacked auto-encoders
20. Other machine learning methods and problems
    - Anomaly detection
    - Association rules
    - Bias-variance dilemma
    - Classification
    - Multi-label classification
    - Clustering
    - Data Pre-processing
    - Empirical risk minimization
    - Feature engineering
    - Feature learning
    - Learning to rank
    - Occam learning
    - Online machine learning

- PAC learning
- Regression
- Reinforcement learning
- Semi-supervised learning
- Statistical learning
- Structured prediction
  - Graphical models
    - Bayesian network
    - Conditional random field (CRF)
    - Hidden Markov model (HMM)
  - Unsupervised learning
  - VC theory

model? They need to be able to bring in best practices in data architecture to support the new analytics frontier.

You also need to consider conditions around security, backup, and recovery.

Here is a small sample of skills and technologies that fit into this capability pillar:

- Hadoop
- Spark
- MapReduce
- Hive
- Pig
- AWS
- EMR
- MySQL
- MongoDB
- Cassandra
- Data streaming
- NoSQL
- SQL
- R
- ETL
- Developing reports

- OLAP
- Cubes
- Web intelligence
- Business objects design
- Tableau
- Dashboard tools
- SAS
- SSIS

Visualization and Communication

The third capability pillar is around storytelling. The ability to tell a story about the data is an increasingly important skill. Many colleges and universities are starting to incorporate this skill into their curriculum. Normally, it is just a course in their educational process, but eventually degrees around storytelling with data could emerge. Collaborations between businesses and universities will continue to drive and develop this skill. Anyone attending any type of analytical conference will see storytelling as a prominent theme that is emerging. You see many presentations and panel discussions between business and educational professionals talking about developing this skill set.

But what do we really mean by storytelling? What are we trying to achieve? In the most basic sense, it is action that you want someone to take. It is not only the ability to create insights that will drive an action, whether it is an operational objective, a financial objective, or a planning objective. It is also the ability to understand what happens after the action is taken.

Telling a business story with data should still contain the five essential elements to a story: characters, setting, plot, conflict, and resolution. It is how you use these elements. Storytelling skills need to be able to effectively communicate data that culminates in a business choice.

Many organizations confuse storytelling with a technology solution that enables self-service analytics and many technology solutions incorporate data preparation, analytics, and visualization and sell this as a storytelling solution. Technology solutions help drive capabilities to the end user as an important part of your analytics strategy and should not be confused with a storytelling role that drives capability to drive insights, actions, and outcomes.

This capability covers a vast amount of business territory. Storytelling with data not only illustrates a compelling story, supports business arguments, and informs decisions, it also informs daily business operations and supports daily business decision-making. You need to think about the capabilities you need. Is it storytelling? Visualization techniques? Design-based thinking? What combinations of skills do you need? The right capability mix can provide a faster path to insight and/or action. No longer is the skill around building a dashboard that contains factual information. The skill is using storytelling skills and user-based design principles to develop tools that lead to actionable insights that support the way we make decisions. What is "newsworthy"? How do we know what is interesting from the end user's perspective? How do we draw them to that information?

Our knowledge is limited to the data we have. There are unpredictable events. There is information we lack. This environment creates friction between the three elements – planning, actions, and outcomes. A good storyteller can minimize this friction and continuously works to maximize the art of action. This friction can be translated into three types of gaps: knowledge, alignment, and effects. A good storyteller must be able to piece each of these gaps together like a puzzle. A missing piece, and the puzzle is incomplete. However, being able to provide the necessary pieces will complete the picture, thus telling the complete story.

What skills are required to bridge the knowledge gap? What are we trying to answer? Think of an investigative journalist. Their inquisitive mindset helps us understand what we know and what we would like to know. They do this through information gathering. It is the ability to navigate the organization and get to the right people. How do we ask effective questions? Can we develop the right rapport and trust? Can we effectively eliminate clutter that can cause confusion?

What skills are required for the alignment gap? The concepts around "agile" play a role here. We want to empower lower-level employees to make decisions that align with upper management. We want to create user stories to show alignment. By using agile techniques, you can quickly understand if you are "not on the same page." Knowing "scrum" skills can minimize organizational miscommunication and mistrust and can get you realigned.

What skills are required for the effects gap? It is being able to effectively show our actions before and after. It is about understanding the importance of context. To show what went right and what went wrong. How we visualize the good and the bad. To be able to choose the appropriate visualization.

These skills usually require an investment in individuals. Sometimes, that investment comes in the way of hiring someone with experience. Sometimes, it comes from identifying individuals in your organization who want to develop this capability. A natural place to look is in business intelligence roles. These roles already possess some of the skills since they continuously develop and maintain dashboards supporting operational key performance indicators (KPIs), financial performance, reports, data discovery, etc. These roles will continue to develop the necessary capabilities by investing in books, online courses or workshops, time, opportunities to learn, and practice, etc.

Table 2.4 is a small sample of skills in this typical visualization and communication pillar. While the table is only a small sample of the types of general skills that we feel are important, content organization, collaboration, and scrum skills stand out as key skills.

When you need to present your story to reveal insight and want to be ready to take action, content management is a skill that will prove

Table 2.4 Typical Storytelling Skills

• Public speaking
• Oral communication
• Written communication
• Content organization
• Critical thinking
• Business strategy
• SWOT analysis
• Interviewing skills
• Visual skills
• Collaboration
• Scrum skills

Source: Author.

most valuable. Content management is all about collecting, managing, and publishing. These visualization and communications roles need to be able to collect all of the information available. As they collect the information, they are categorizing it into the parts of your story. Managing content involves understanding what information is pertinent, adding value, and producing actions. Information that does not add to the outcome desired only generates chaos and introduces questions and concerns that may not be relevant.

Publishing is how you put the presentation together. In effect, you want the presentation to be simple and powerful. Yet, you want this person to exhibit creativity and create a compelling story. At the end, you want to elicit a desired response, from approval to making a decision to taking an action.

Collaboration is a skill that is easy to define and difficult to execute on. Basically, every dictionary will define collaboration as the ability to work jointly with others or together especially in an intellectual endeavor. While there are still projects that are siloed, many of today's business problems require collaborative solutions, especially in the healthcare industry. When you think about every project you are considering, each one will most likely have some footprint in financial, clinical, and operational terms. Having a person who keeps a team together on solving problems faces many challenges.

The list of challenges can be lengthy. A person who has the skill to navigate two key challenges successfully will provide much smoother sailing in your collaboration – resources, specifically time and people and scope. This person needs to understand if team members are "all-in." Collaborations seem to break down when the most important piece, people, creates trust issues. Trust issues can take many forms – lack of time, lack of commitment and participation, attitude: you get the idea.

Another piece that often derails collaboration is around scope. The ability for this person successfully to define the scope in a clear and concise manner will gain alignment, eliminate scope "creep," and create consistent expectations among the team.

The last skills we want to touch on are scrum skills. We will talk a little more about the agile process in the next chapter and how that might look to your organization, but scrum skills in this sense are about the people skills needed. The specific subset of scrum skills we are talking about here are advisor, coach, and facilitator. The successful orchestration of these skills often leads to alignment and achievement of the team's overall mission.

That subset of scrum skills when executed properly enables the team by gaining consensus on objectives, process, workflow, and deadlines, assisting in conflict resolution by understanding what divides the group and assisting in closing the gaps, and supporting constructive open and transparent dialogues between team members. These skills allow a person objectively to remain neutral, provide business meeting management skills (agenda, meeting notes, timekeeping) to make sure time is not wasted, and offer advice and guidance to empower the team to work effectively through self-organization and cross-functionality, getting all members of the team to respect one's business capabilities.

Business Acumen

The last capability is around business acumen. This skill set is more nebulous and many of the skills here are considered "soft" skills. When you think of the previous pillar and this pillar, some of the skills will overlap. It is how you think about using them.

Let's take critical thinking as an example. In the third pillar, how you use critical thinking skills is slightly different than under the business acumen pillar. When storytelling, you are using your critical thinking skills on making the five elements of the story flow and tell a complete and comprehensive story. In this fourth pillar, it is centered around your business and industry as a whole, not just a particular story, and how all fundamentals of your industry and business interact.

Some of the skills in this group are not conferred upon you by a university or college upon graduation. They are learned skills. When you look at Table 2.5 to help build your skills list, you will see there are some skills where universities or colleges offer a class to help with the basics. However, the growth of these skills requires effort on your part.

It is not only understanding the business of your industry, but also around learning problem solving skills, navigating your organization to leverage a collaborative solution, understanding what drives financial and operational KPIs. It is what you learn the day you start your job. It is how much effort you put into advancing this skill.

Some of the skills in this pillar are transferable from one job to another. However, the most important one, knowing your industry, can only come from the experience of working in the industry and your thirst for tapping every critical resource in your organization to understand the underpinnings of your business.

A sample of general business skills are listed in Table 2.5.

While Table 2.5 is only a small sample of the types of general skills that we feel are important, decision-making, critical thinking, problem solving, and relationship building stand out as key skills. How do we evaluate if a person has some of these skills? Our thoughts below can help drive questions during an interview process to gain a greater understanding of the person's abilities.

Decision-making is generally a combination of intuition or "gut feel" and logical thinking. Information plays a key role informing our decisions, but doesn't make our decision. Over the course of your career, you have probably made decisions based on your intuition. It just feels right. No matter what information you have, whether it supports your gut feel or contradicts your gut feel, you make a decision based on instinct. As you collect these "feel right" decisions and they correspond to successful outcomes, your brain seems to develop a process to enable you to make a decision when it feels right to your "gut." When you are indecisive, there is conflict between your intuition and logical thinking. Information as well as other potential influencers play critical behind-the-scenes roles as well. Questions start

Table 2.5 General Business Skills

Project Management	Leadership
Mentoring	Relationship Building
Decision-Making	Margin Analysis
Critical Thinking	Quality Audits
Problem Solving	Financial Accounting
Professionalism	Cost Accounting
Business Strategy	Income Statements

Source: Author.

to formulate that you need to investigate: Have you done enough information gathering? Have you left every stone unturned? Do you have personal bias? What alternatives do you have? When you have indecision, consistently exploring these types of questions can lead to dependably making better choices.

When evaluating a person's critical thinking skills, we look to see if the person has experience demonstrating certain behaviors. While there is no specific number of skills that define critical thinking, we will explore a few of the more important behaviors below from our experiences. We need to understand how a person performs an analysis. Can they only see big picture? How granular can they get? As they break an analysis down piece by piece, are they able to recognize when meaningful insights cannot be garnered? Let's look at an example. One of the most common knee injuries and very common among athletes is the torn anterior cruciate ligament (ACL). How do we eliminate healthcare costs for people who tear their ACL? What type of analysis needs to be done? Once you tear your ACL, it starts you down a clinical carepath that includes physician visits to evaluate operative or non-operative treatment. If you go down the operative path, you will have pre-surgical testing, the surgery itself, post-op recovery, and post-op physical therapy. Each of these parts of the clinical carepath has more levels of complexity. Ultimately, you could example each and every item that was part of this clinical carepath. Understanding how "deep" you need to go is important to delivering the appropriate insight.

Is the person with these critical thinking skills able to understand and apply standards? For the same torn ACL example, what is the expected outcome, clinically, financially, and operationally? There are benchmarks and standards that we can measure against. Being able to apply these standards suitably against the desired outcome and articulate your findings is not always easy.

Do they possess information curiosity? Do they always think there are more data, facts, evidence, or relevant sources of information they need to seek out? Are they only relying on internal data that is easily available? Are they looking for industry trends? Are these trends local, regional, national, or global? Are they searching for research articles in medical journals? Are they seeking out clinical leaders to tap into their expertise? Someone who is not inquisitive will normally fall short in providing the most comprehensive conclusion.

Depending on the type of data (financial, clinical, or operational) you are working with, they may not be able to assist in providing insights. Can they demonstrate the ability to transform data? Are there instances when applying a mathematical function to a data element to transform it makes sense? Are they able to produce reasonable, well-balanced, coherent, and sound conclusions? Simply put, are you able to follow their logic? Does it make sense? Is it rational? Can you poke holes in it?

Problem solving takes many forms. A person may not have this skill coming into your organization, and the Cleveland Clinic Improvement Model teaches their caregivers the way they expect their caregivers to build a culture of improvement. One of the tools they use is called A3. A3 has many variations of process flow and Cleveland Clinic uses the follow steps: (1) Background, Problem Statement, Business Case; (2) Current Condition; (3) Goal Statement; (4) Analysis; (5) Countermeasures; (6) Planning and Implementation; (7) Follow-up. The series of trainings instills an approach that all caregivers understand and follow. They are given specific tools throughout each step to ensure consistency. Figure 2.4 shows how the Cleveland Clinic approaches A3.

Relationship building is vital. Theodore Roosevelt said, "The most important single ingredient in the formula of success is knowing how to get along with people." We will touch on a few skills required to guarantee success. When you meet a person for the first time, we believe the most important transaction is knowing their name. Ask them how they prefer to be addressed. Often repeating their name in the course of conversation strengthens that initial bond. Our experiences suggest that you tend to connect more with people who use your first name and remember it. During the course of your conversations, people will reveal pieces of personal information, an event, family, hobby, book read, etc. You do not need to know everything, but often remembering one of these tidbits also enhances the bond.

It is difficult to listen effectively. You don't realize you are doing it, but when a person is talking to you, you are processing what you want to say next, and in some cases, interrupt before the person's

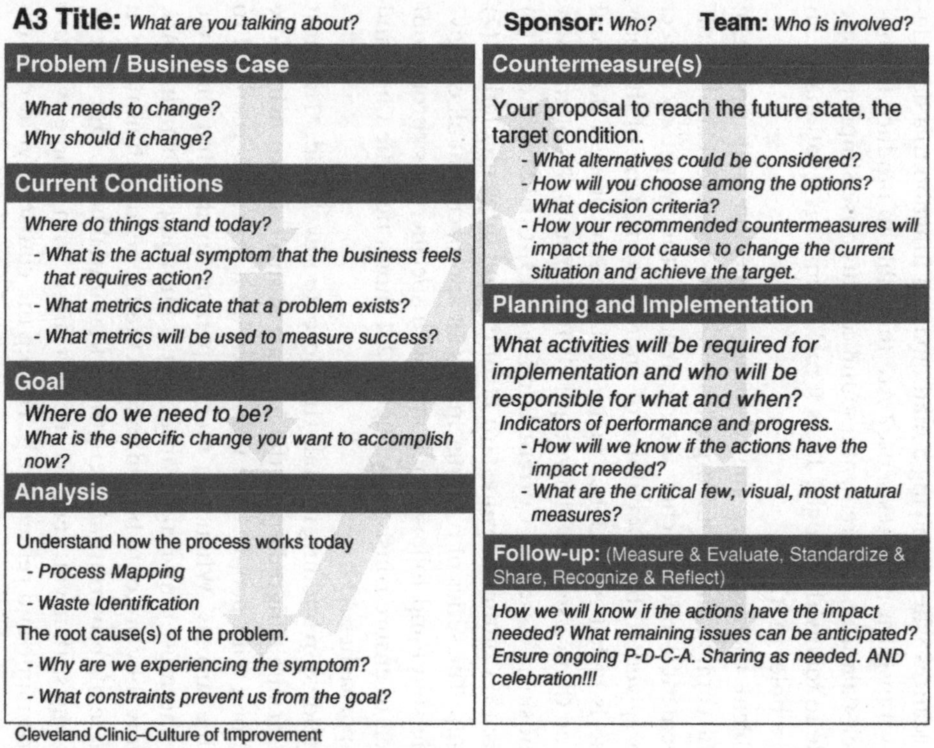

A3 Title: *What are you talking about?*　　　　**Sponsor:** *Who?*　　**Team:** *Who is involved?*

Problem / Business Case

What needs to change?
Why should it change?

Current Conditions

Where do things stand today?
- *What is the actual symptom that the business feels that requires action?*
- *What metrics indicate that a problem exists?*
- *What metrics will be used to measure success?*

Goal

Where do we need to be?
What is the specific change you want to accomplish now?

Analysis

Understand how the process works today
- *Process Mapping*
- *Waste Identification*
The root cause(s) of the problem.
- *Why are we experiencing the symptom?*
- *What constraints prevent us from the goal?*

Countermeasure(s)

Your proposal to reach the future state, the target condition.
- *What alternatives could be considered?*
- *How will you choose among the options? What decision criteria?*
- *How your recommended countermeasures will impact the root cause to change the current situation and achieve the target.*

Planning and Implementation

What activities will be required for implementation and who will be responsible for what and when?
Indicators of performance and progress.
- *How will we know if the actions have the impact needed?*
- *What are the critical few, visual, most natural measures?*

Follow-up: (Measure & Evaluate, Standardize & Share, Recognize & Reflect)

How we will know if the actions have the impact needed? What remaining issues can be anticipated? Ensure ongoing P-D-C-A. Sharing as needed. AND celebration!!!

Cleveland Clinic–Culture of Improvement

Figure 2.4　A3 Title: What Are You Talking About?
Source: Cleveland Clinic.

thought is complete. Instead of thinking what you want to say next, follow-up with clarifying questions. This often shows your desire to understand rather than moving on to what you think is important and keeps the person engaged.

When it comes to feedback, it should be a two-way street. Some people focus on the combination of criticism and feedback. Criticism is always connected to negative feelings. Focus on feedback. This is free information for both of you and delivering feedback in a constructive way can be mutually beneficial. Whether you ultimately do something with the feedback is your choice.

Ultimately, you are looking to build trust. Trust is earned and not given. Earning that trust can be supplemented through a couple of different techniques. First, try scheduling regular times to meet in-person or talk to them. These don't need to be hour-long check-ins. They should be short, 15-minute check-ins. This way, you are always making sure you understand what challenges they face and what objectives are important to them. The cadence of regular check-ins will depend on you. With all of the relationships you will build, you cannot possibly do weekly or monthly check-ins. Often, biannually will be effective.

When you think about the healthcare industry, it is important to think about questions that will help you understand what types of business acumen are important for the different roles. Depending on what type of organization you work for (hospital, physician practice, insurer, drug company, etc.) your list of questions will be more comprehensive and differ from the list in Table 2.6. Table 2.6 is a sample of questions that help shape your business acumen skill set from a provider of healthcare services' perspective.

As you think about how these four pillars translate into job roles, Figure 2.5 is an example of what they may look like on a radar chart.

When you think of all the potential skills that you can rate, you could get a radar chart with between 7 and 13 different skills to plot. How can you meaningfully compare that many skills? Could you really understand what a job role's profile would visually look like? That's why we took Figure 2.3 and turned it into a radar chart. Instead of scoring, we tried to use some simple terms like *familiar*, *capable*, and *expert* to help us shape what job profiles would look like. We believe this is an incredibly

Table 2.6 Sample of Healthcare Business Acumen Questions

What is a bundle? How is it defined?	What is population health? What tools do we need? What are Health Cost Guidelines? How do you use them?
What is an episode treatment group?	How does Payer Contracting impact you short-term and long term?
How do you define transplants?	What are risk scores? How do you use them?
What are the different reimbursement methodologies? (DRG, APC, ASC, per diem, fee schedules)	How do scheduled and unscheduled patients move through your facility? What are your capacity constraints?
How are healthcare services coded? (CPT , ICD-10, principle procedure)	How does scheduling work across the continuum of care? How does this impact planning, from staffing to operating room scheduling?
What are the following organizations? How do you interact with them? How do they impact your organization? (JACHO, AHRQ, CMS, NQF, NAHQ, etc.)	How do you track patients from registration and appointments to final payments of balance?

Source: Author.

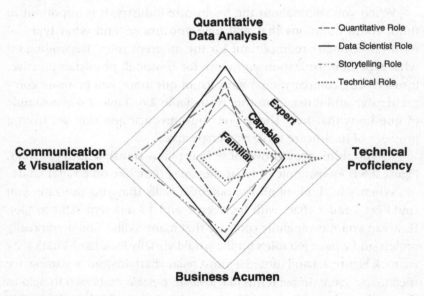

Figure 2.5 Skills Map
Source: Author.

important exercise. This can help you understand the types of job roles you will create in your organization and if some of them overlap.

ORGANIZATIONAL STRUCTURES FOR YOUR COMPANY

When thinking about staffing your analytics team, the analytics governance structure will play an important role. Normally, you will see between five and six common structures your organization can consider. Figure 2.6 shows five structural models to guide your discussion around organizing your analytical talent along with the appropriate analytics governance, where analysts would reside, and the coordination of analytical activity throughout the organization.

Each model can be described by governance, analyst location, and project management support:

Centralized Model

■ Governance – Stronger ownership and management of resource allocation and project prioritization within a central pool.

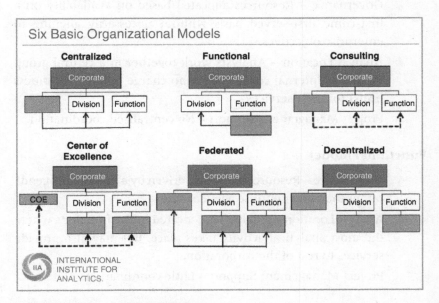

Figure 2.6 Basic Organizational Models

Source: International Institute for Analytics: Organizing Analytical Teams.

- Analyst Location – Analysts reside in central group, where they serve a variety of functions and business units and work on diverse projects.
- Project Management Support – Coordination by central analytic unit.

Centers of Excellence Model

- Governance – Better alignment of analytics initiatives and resource allocation to enterprise priorities without operational involvement.
- Analyst Location – Analysts are allocated to units throughout the organization and their activities are coordinated by a central entity.
- Project Management Support – Flexible model with right balance of centralized and distributed coordination.

Consulting Model

- Governance – Resources allocated based on availability on a first-come first-served basis without necessarily aligning to enterprise objectives.
- Analyst Location – Analysts work together in a central group but act as internal consultants who charge "clients" (business units) for their services.
- Project Management Support – No centralized coordination.

Functional Model

- Governance – Resource allocation driven by a functional agenda rather than an enterprise agenda.
- Analyst Location – Analysts are located in the functions where the most analytical activity takes place, but may also provide services to rest of the corporation.
- Project Management Support – Little coordination.

Decentralized Model

- Governance – Resources allocated only to projects within their silos with no view of analytics activities or priorities outside their function or business unit.
- Analyst Location – Analytics are scattered across the organization in different functions and business units.
- Project Management Support – Little to no coordination.

Model Source: Julio Hernandez, Robert Berkey, and Rahul Bhattacharya, "Building an Analytics-Driven Organization," *Accenture* No. 1 (March 2014), 1–2.

Cleveland Clinic uses a hybrid model using the Centralized and Centers of Excellence models. The organization has agreed to guiding principles for the data and analytics team as well as for itself. This allows us to stay focused on the mission of our analytics program. This is important because it is easy to stray and it reminds us of the principles we agreed upon.

It is a shared effort:

Responsibilities of the data and analytics team:

- Provision of trustworthy, available data.
- Deployment of modern, useable analytics tools.
- Development of enterprise scale vision, training, and support.
- Development of expertise and "consulting" around measurement, performance management, and "math."

Responsibilities of the enterprise:

- Become facile users of data-related insight.
- Broadly disseminate an analytically oriented culture.
- Commitment to developing required skills.

Your organization may gravitate toward one of these structures or may even use a hybrid of these structures. Ultimately, it is your organization's responsibility to choose the structure that fits your organizational business needs and how you want to deliver analytic capabilities. Again, your analytics strategy will guide your choice. There is no right or wrong choice, just an adoption of a structure to best implement your strategy.

ROLES TO EXECUTE YOUR DATA AND ANALYTICS STRATEGY

Once you have decided on an organizational model to implement, it is now about hiring the people who will execute your analytics vision. As we described above, there are capabilities pillars that will help identify the types of people.

It is truly about defining roles that you want people to play. Again, there is no playbook that says hire "x" data engineers, "y" quantitative analytics, "z" data scientists, etc. It is understanding the work: Where are the projects coming from? What types of analytics are required? What types of technical skills are required? How do we need to communicate the results or outcomes? How much business acumen is required?

By setting out the answers to these questions along with the work around the capabilities pillars, you will be able to understand the types of people you will need. Some will be new hires; some will come from within the organization. In the next chapter, we will discuss what the analytics process will look like. This will help you understand the potential velocity of projects at current staffing levels.

This book is a program and each chapter can help you appreciate each piece of the puzzle and its complexity. However, you need to put the entire puzzle together to get a complete understanding of how a successful well-oiled analytics program will operate. That's not to say it will operate smoothly from the start. There will be growing pains, and it is a journey that will take more than days or months to complete.

CHALLENGES TO GETTING THE RIGHT PEOPLE

It has been seven years since Davenport and Patil declared the role of Data Scientist as the sexiest job of the twenty-first century.[5] In 2015, data science and analytics job postings totaled more than nursing and truck drivers job postings combined, two of the largest hiring occupations in the United States.[6] A poll revealed that, by 2021, 69% of employers will require data science and analytics skills while only 23% of the college and university leaders say their graduates will have those skills.[7] By 2020, new job postings for data science and analytics skills are expected to reach 2.72 million.[8]

The healthcare industry in general has been slow to adopt these new analytically competent workers. We could argue many reasons why. What is the competitive advantage to be gained by this new job skill? Can we replace clinical decision-making by using algorithms? The healthcare reality is, we need these new skills as the industry tries to gain ground on reducing physician documentation burnout, gaining new insights to reducing organizational costs, creating ways to understand patient risk, and creating prescriptive and predictive algorithms to help inform the physician decision-making process to optimize the patient experience.

As healthcare organizations look to address the need for these new analytically skilled jobs, we can point to four key challenges: (1) lack of appropriate HR-related job descriptions; (2) total compensation; (3) lack of student engagement/involvement/understanding in colleges and universities; and (4) alignment to organizational mission, priorities, and/or values. (For the purposes of this book, we will use the

---

[5] Thomas H. Davenport and D.J. Patil, "Data Scientist: The Sexiest Job of the 21st Century," *Harvard Business Review* (October 2012), hbr.org/2012/10/data-scientist-the-sexiest-job-of-the-21st-century/ar/pr.

[6] http://www.bhef.com/sites/default/files/bhef_2017_investing_in_dsa.pdf.

[7] Ibid.

[8] Ibid.

word *universities* to include post–high school degree learning institutions.) In order to grab this new talent, each of these facets requires attention.

The first challenge can take the most time to solve properly. Writing the appropriate job descriptions that include career paths is laborious, carefully choosing the right words throughout the job description, clear understanding of the responsibilities, hiring game theory to test your descriptions, compensation market studies to understand base salary ranges, and understanding bonus programs.

The second challenge is around total compensation. Solving this challenge is not simply a local problem. Solving this problem means understanding globally and across industries how these types of professionals see compensation. Sure, salary is important, as well as bonus potentials, but let's not forget culture. Some people may not see culture as a component of total compensation, but when you are recruiting talent, both sides are interviewing each other and, if there is not a cultural fit, that will ultimately lead to both sides parting ways at some point. We consider culture benefits things like working from home, business casual dress code, good work/life balance, etc.

Consider an employer like Google. Benefits for their employees include perks like laundry and fitness facilities, generous paid parental leave, onsite childcare, free meals, etc. Google also pays above market for its employees. Healthcare cannot enjoy that type of luxury. Remember, every dollar spent on compensation is a dollar that cannot go toward taking care of a patient. One of the biggest complaints dogging the healthcare system is how expensive it is.

The third challenge is a failure to collaborate with universities. We've talked to many university students over the past few years in analytical programs across the country. When you mention careers in healthcare, many students think of occupations like physician, surgeon, nursing, radiologist, accounting, financial planning, and so forth, those jobs that normally take care of patients or are necessary for daily business operations. When we explain how analytics are being used today and will grow in the future, we normally hear the response, "I didn't know that," or "I wasn't aware of that."

You can solve the university dilemma by:

1. Identifying internship/co-op opportunities for their students.
2. Being actively engaged in your university partner's school calendar events.
3. Seeking opportunities to speak in a lecture series or classroom.
4. Providing projects for professors and students.

You probably already have a list of universities, local or neighboring (usually within a 4-hour driving radius), that have analytic programs. We have not found one university that is unwilling to invest time and energy in helping their students find quality internship/coop opportunities. The fact that you can do "day" visits to universities within a 4-hour driving radius is vital. There is no better substitute than face-to-face interaction with students.

Success in your internship programs relies heavily on having meaningful work that your students want to take back and "brag" about. When we have interviewed students, one of the first questions asked is, "What type of work will I be doing?" These students do not want to enter data into spreadsheets, "shadow" you around, or grab your coffee. They want the opportunity to show you they can produce. Our internship programs are centered around a team-based project approach. The interns are broken into teams and given a project that we expect to apply in the course of business. Also, we assign the interns "mentors," who also provide additional tasks. Some examples of projects were alert-based dashboards, helping developing dashboards to monitor predictive models, and helping programming of population health risk-based scoring.

You need to work with university faculty and administration to understand what school calendar events are important to participate in and add value to you and the students. Sometimes, attending the "all-day" career fairs may not be suitable to develop the right relationship with the students. Look into special "fairs" that only have students who have the skills you are looking for. These smaller occasions tend to allow more facetime with students and the ability to get your message across without having to do a "30-second infomercial." You will be surprised at the ways universities are willing to work with you to get you on campus. We have found sending frontline workers with a management person to be most effective. The students want to hear from the people "doing the work," not "managing the projects." When students and frontline workers have the chance to connect, you get a much better talent pool to choose from. Not only are they discussing the work, they are discussing other important non-tangible benefits, most importantly workplace culture.

We believe every university wants to supplement their curriculum with real-world case studies. Seek out opportunities to get students geeked about the work you do. When we present case studies at conferences or talk to students during "fairs" about case studies like forecasting corporate statistics with simulations to project key metrics, forecasting OR Utilization or volumes for key operating metrics, contract economics simulation modeling from fee-for-service to shared savings, pricing optimization models, using control charts on alert dashboards, primary care risk model, and rate realization model to enhance service line business decisions, their interest level peaks as they realize the opportunity for an exciting analytical career in healthcare. Why not capitalize on this opening to speak throughout the students' calendar year? From freshmen to seniors, the work you do will provide insight and excitement to the work they are being trained to do.

We believe your organization is just like everyone else's from the perspective of workload. There is always a backload of projects that seem never to make it high on the priority list and yet are important enough to hang around. What better way to engage students than with projects that can be professorially led?

While engaging students in healthcare projects can be difficult due to the Health Insurance Portability and Accountability Act, there are numerous ways to interact. Let's explore two different ways:

1. When you think about skills like storytelling, many universities have classes around this. Have them redesign your dashboards. You can always provide a dataset that has fictional names, and the other important data elements with random numbers. Their creativity is not brought about because the data you provided is real or fake; it is brought about because you

are providing guidance on how you do your work, make decisions, and are looking for them to help you logically use the dashboard for success.

2. Helping you with forecasting can be another good opportunity. How many times do you create your initial forecast models with the intent to add new variables to the mix? Most likely all the time. There is always a delicate balance between having a production-ready forecast model and "Oh, wait, what if we try adding this variable to the mix." There will always be new data that can be introduced and tested in your forecast models to see if you can improve the outcome. Whether it is forecasting emergency department visits to physician office visits to admissions, there will always be potential variables to explore. As we continue to collect and make available all kinds of data, internally or publicly available, there will always be chances for students to help explore these. What if you wanted to use public data like flu data from the CDC, or weather data (temperature, pollen counts, etc.)? This is the kind of classroom experience that does not have the answer in the back of the book.

Lastly, while mission, values, and culture are not normally a "challenge," we consider them here since finding individuals that match mission, values, and culture can be difficult. Many people will go to organizations' websites to understand their mission and values. We believe what differentiates healthcare in this respect is it is normally someone who has either (1) had a life changing healthcare event or (2) had a life changing healthcare event happen to a family member or friend.

At the beginning of the book, you read about Tho's experiences. Mike has also had some experience that has resonated with missions. Mike's triplets were born at a Cleveland Clinic facility at the gestation of 26.5 weeks. They were in the Neo-Natal Intensive Care unit for over 60 days before coming home. Mike's wife also had a frightening time when she was hospitalized with a pulmonary embolism. He recently lost his mother to cancer. These types of events are motivators and can help steer individuals to healthcare organizations. For me, they continue in my thoughts daily and help remind me of our mission.

Finding the right individuals will not be easy. Sometimes it is luck, sometimes it is fate, sometimes it might be a patient. One thing is for sure: it is a combination of each of the four facets above that will make your recruitment less demanding.

THE ABILITY TO CONSUME RESULTS

What good are all of these newly produced analytics if we cannot use them? This is a workforce transformation question. How do you "upskill" your organization? This will be a combination of educating, coaching, and training current employees on how to use these new analytics and hiring new employees that can use these new analytics. This is also not a one-and-done situation. As analytics and industry are constantly evolving, education and training need to be updated and current with the changing times. Do you develop internally or use external training? Or is it an amalgamated approach? There are many elements to consider: cost, size of workforce, how quickly you want your workforce to complete education and training, by way of example.

If you are developing internally, the typical continuous improvement cycle is in play. You need to design your curriculum, develop it, deliver it, evaluate its effectiveness, and improve. Not only do you need to understand the curriculum you need, but also for whom you are developing it. Curriculum objectives will be different for business analysts versus leadership. The curriculum should run parallel so leaders and business analysts are being educated and trained on the same topics.

You may not want leaders or business analysts to "know the math"; however, they do need to know what analytical methodology is appropriate and how to interpret and use the results. For example, let's assume you have data on a group of patients. Maybe you want to understand why certain patients require a great deal of medical care during the year. The goal of this transformation is to move from "Let's apply AI or ML to solve this problem" to "What if we apply some clustering techniques to find insights into like patients." Understanding the learning objectives will help set the tone for the curriculum.

When you are developing your curriculum, you need to consider the following characteristics of your workforce: current abilities, their availability for training, learning styles, complexity of the material that needs to be ingested, etc. Who is going to develop the curriculum? Who will peer review the curriculum? Will they be able to update the program continuously when needed?

Delivering your material can be accomplished in many ways, from online to video-based to webinars. Choosing a method will also have considerations, like how often you think the material will change, how many people will be learning at one time, etc. When you think about the effectiveness of the training, this is really centered around assessing a person's knowledge consumption by some type of skill demonstration or completion of a "knowledge test." Monitoring all of the steps involved in internal curriculum development will allow you to improve your training continuously to make sure you are meeting your number-one objective, "upskilling your workforce." As an example, let's consider you are looking to upskill leadership. Here might be an outline for the start of leadership curriculum:

Leadership Curriculum

Class: Analytic Lifecycle

Objectives:

- Business Problem Formulation
- Data Acquisition and Preparation
- Data Exploration
- Data Cleaning, Transformation, and Substitution
- Model Building
- Model Validation
- Production Deployment and Workflow Integration
- Results Monitoring

Class: Introduction to Analytics for Leaders

Objectives:

- Overview of Tools for Analytics
- Basic Statistics for Managers

■ Survey of Common Analytic Methods

- Supervised Methods

- Unsupervised Methods

- Clustering

- Forecasting

- Simulation

- Statistical Process Control

■ Managing Analytics Projects

Class: Introduction to Data Preparation

Objectives:

■ Data Acquisition

- Standards associated with acquiring data from the data vault

- Data governance

■ Data Merging

- How to use different tools to merge data

■ Data Preparation and Cleaning

- Preprocessing data

- Handling missing data

Class: Introduction to Analytics for Leaders

Objectives:

■ Basic Statistics for Managers

- Overview of sampling

- Overview of probability related to estimation and prediction

- Overview of probability related to inference (p-values)

◼ Overview/Use Cases of Common Analytics Tools

   - Regression

   - Logistic Regression

   - Cluster Analysis

   - Forecasting

   - Simulation

◼ Managing an Analytics Project

   - Process for Analytics Project Management

As your organization introduces new methodologies, education, coaching, and training will need to be developed. This is where the continuous lifecycle comes into play.

If you decide to consider external training, you need to weigh the costs of off-the-shelf training programs versus custom training for your organization. Again, due diligence will be necessary around how often this type of material will change, how different is your organization when it comes to a custom solution, and how much will these types of training cost. Is the training too general?

When your organization is changing a business system to a software vendor, you most likely have in place a request for proposal (RFP) process to select a vendor. This is no different. You will define your requirements and will find a short list of training specialists to evaluate. Following a structured process like an RFP will ensure that you are meeting your defined objectives and goals.

THE "REAL ANALYTICAL EMPLOYEE COST" TO AN ORGANIZATION

These new analytically focused jobs will allow us to create a deeper understanding of the health of the populations we manage, predictive algorithms that will surface opportunities for intervention and prevention, and forecasting models to support your operational efforts or long-range planning. This will require new skills, knowledge, and pipelines for our existing and future analysts and leaders.

Understanding the investment required to make the new skills, knowledge attainment, and potential new hires will tax the organization with costs at the expense of productivity. As you look to upskill your current employees to hiring new employees, your organization will incur costs, normally a larger upfront investment in the first few years (Phase I) and then a "maintenance" type of costs in the out years (Phase II). The timeline is yours to determine, but in organizations with over 50,000 employees, this is most likely a two- to four-year outlay of higher analytical costs before you get to this "maintenance" cost of continuous training.

Phase I will consist of four buckets of potential costs. The buckets are: (1) upskilling current employees using internal training; (2) upskilling current employees using external training; (3) hiring new employees (leaders and business analysts); and (4) hiring new employees (analytical roles). You may have costs in any combination of buckets. Phase II will consist of three buckets. They are: (1) continuously keeping employees current; (2) hiring new employees (leaders and business analysts); and (3) hiring new employees (analytical roles).

We will examine some examples of what costs you will need to consider for each of the buckets. Depending on your organization, some costs may not apply, and you may identify some costs that are not described below. Outlooking the spend will help you understand the overall cost and lost productivity to increase the analytical maturity of your organization; however, the implications are that you are driving improved decision-making, putting your organization in a position to outperform its competitors, and driving stronger organizational performance. The costs below can serve as guiderails as you try to quantify the effort.

Identified below are typical types of costs that you will need to estimate. Once we define each of the typical types of costs, we will put together a simple formula for Phase I and Phase II buckets. Here are those costs:

- *Salary* – This is the annual salary you are budgeting for the position you are hiring.
- *Benefits* – Most organizations provide you with a Total Compensation amount that includes your benefits. You can usually

call your compensation department and they should be able to provide you with a good estimate to use here. Expect a figure here to range around 25%–30% of salary.

- *Sign-on Bonus* – Will you need to make a one-time sign-on bonus?
- *New Employee Productivity Costs* – These are related to your new hire. Many estimate it takes one to two years for an employee to be fully productive. While this statistic can be jaw-dropping, we believe in healthcare this number is accurate; in some instances, it may be conservative with the complexity of healthcare. We believe the minimum amount should be at least one year of salary. In addition, you need to estimate the amount of costs associated with training your new employee. Estimate the number of hours you will spend training the new employee (make sure you include time with management, not just frontline to frontline). You will need to use a salary estimate. We like to use the midpoint of the salary range for this job. Convert the annual salary into an hourly rate based on your organization's standard and multiply by the number of hours you logged.
- *Human Resources* – You will need to estimate the number of hours they will spend on filling your position. Tasks that they will be performing include posting your job, internally and externally, reviewing resumes, performing initial screen interviews, and job offer letters. You will need to use a salary estimate. We like to use the midpoint of the salary range for this job. Convert the annual salary into an hourly rate based on your organization's standard and multiply by the number of hours you logged.
- *Advertising* – Job board listings (indeed.com, careerbuilder.com, monster.com, zipRecruiter.com, etc.).
- *Third-Party Recruiter* – Is this person salaried or do they work on commission? If salaried, you can use the human resource costs above as a start. If they are commission, understand whether it is fixed or a percentage of salary or some other metric.
- *Employee Referral Bonus* – Do you have a program like this? If so, add it.

▨ *Employee Relocation* – Do you pay for relocation costs? Do you pay a fixed sum? Some percentage of the salary? Make sure you add this.

▨ *Travel Expenses Related to Interviews* – If this candidate is not local, you may fly the candidate in or reimburse for mileage. Don't forget hotel costs or meals if you need to have him stay over for a night.

▨ *Internal Interviewing* – Make a list of all internal employees who will be interviewing the candidate. Log how much time they spend during this process. It may only be one interview, or it could be multiple. Keep track!

▨ *University Career Fairs* – Whether you are traveling a distance or locally, some of your normal travel expenses may be needed – hotel, airfare or mileage, meals, parking, etc.

▨ *Background Checks* – Most organizations run a background check. Your human resource department can help give you an amount to use here.

▨ *Employee Training* – You will need to estimate the number of employees who will go through training. You will need to estimate the number of hours they will spend in training. You will need to use a salary estimate. We like to use the midpoint of the salary range for this job. Convert the annual salary into an hourly rate based on your organization's standard and multiply by the number of hours you logged.

▨ *Internal Training by Subject Matter Experts (ISMEs)* – You will need to estimate the number of ISMEs and the number of hours each ISME will spend on designing your curriculum, developing it, teaching it, evaluating its effectiveness, and improving it. Most of the curriculum ISMEs will be from the quantitative and technical proficiency skill sets. You will need to use a salary estimate. We like to use the midpoint of the salary range for this job. Convert the annual salary into an hourly rate based on your organization's standard and multiply by the number of hours you logged.

▨ *Off-the-Shelf Vendor Training* – Vendor training costs can be widely variable and take different arrangements. Before you can decide what type of arrangements might be best for your organization, you need to quantify two important pieces of information: (1) How many people will need to go through the initial training programs? (2) How many people will annually go through this program based on hiring that accounts for typical attrition patterns? The typical types of arrangements are: (1) a fixed cost per training program per employee; (2) a fixed cost sliding scale per annum covering "x" number of employees; (3) a variable contract that contains a fixed amount, plus "y" amount times "x" number of employees.

- *Custom External Training* – Here is where you can be creative. You find the off-the-shelf training does not meet your needs. You have outlined the type of training, or in the case above, curriculum that you are looking to deliver. You can explore different options on delivering this content. For example, you can approach an off-the-shelf vendor to develop this content. Remember when we discussed the importance of university partnerships? You could partner with a university to develop the program. You can use consultants. You could partner with other local organizations in some type of collaborative solution. Estimating the costs here is very similar to the type of costs using off-the-shelf vendors, except you will be paying a premium.

- *Academically based Certification Programs* – These are university programs that closely match your curriculum's goals and objectives. Sometimes, these types of programs will fall under an educational benefit offered by your organization.

When hiring an employee, we will use the following formula, regardless of the position (ISME, leaders, business analysts, analytical roles):

Hiring Costs = Salary + Benefits + Sign-on bonus* + New employee productivity costs + Human resources + Advertising* + Third-party recruiter* + Employee referral bonus* + Employee relocation* + Travel expenses related to interviews* + Internal interviewing* + University career fairs.*

* if applicable

Now that we have a standard definition for hiring costs, we can examine the formulas to estimate costs for each of the buckets we described above.

Phase I: (1) upskilling current employees using internal training = Internal Training by Subject Matter Experts (ISMEs) + Employee Training + Hiring Costs.* (When you try to understand the costs here, the first question that comes to mind is, "Do you have an official training department?" If you do, that's a positive. You have a team of employees who can create all the steps from creating to delivering the curriculum. The next question that should immediately come to mind is, "Does our internal training department have ISMEs that can develop, teach, and improve this specialized analytics curriculum?" Will you have to hire ISMEs to join the training program? Or will you count on ISMEs from other parts of your organization to use part of their time to participate in the training program?)

Phase I: (2) upskilling current employees using external training = Employee Training + Off the Shelf Vendor Training* + Custom External Training* + Academically-based Certification Programs.*

There may be a situation when upskilling employees your decision is to use some internal training and some external training. In this situation, please make sure you account for employee training internally and externally. That formula would look like this: Internal Training by Subject Matter Experts (ISMEs) + Employee Training (internal estimate) + Hiring Costs + Employee Training (external estimate) + Off-the-Shelf Vendor Training* + Custom External Training* + Academically based Certification Programs.*

Phase I: (3) hiring new employees (leaders and business analysts) = Hiring Costs.

Phase I: (4) hiring new employees (analytical roles) = Hiring Costs.

Phase II: (1) continuously keep employees current = Employee Training (internal estimate) + Internal Training by Subject Matter Experts (ISMEs) + Employee Training (external estimate) + Off-the-Shelf Vendor Training + Custom External Training +

Academically based Certification Programs. The internal and external training program costs here are related to keeping the material current or adding new material.

Phase II: (2) hiring new employees (leaders and business analysts) = Hiring Costs.

Phase II: (3) hiring new employees (analytical roles) = Hiring Costs.

BUILDING A RESOURCE LIBRARY

One last thing to consider now that you have determined the skills and job roles required to execute your analytics strategy successfully around the people pillar is keeping them engaged in continuous learning. This will improve your likelihood of sustained success. Many of the people who will be part of your analytics team will be have traits around curiosity and continuous learning.

You can feed their appetite a number of ways, through online learning from coursera.org to building a great in-house resource library. One of the most cost-efficient ways is through the building of a resource library. Where do you start? A successful technique is to ask your staff for their recommendations. You will be surprised by their responses. Many staff members will go out and research numerous titles and bring back many to choose from. The most important insight here is they will let you know what is "hot," as well as what is inspiring them.

Below are examples of books that would make a start to a great library:

Analytical Books

- Foster Provost and Tom Fawcett, *Data Science for Business: What You Need to Know about Data Mining and Data-Analytic Thinking* (Sebastopol: O'Reilly Media, Inc., 2013)
- John D. Kelleher, *Fundamentals of Machine Learning for Predictive Data Analytics: Algorithms, Worked Examples, and Case Studies* (Boston, Mass.: MIT Press, 2015)
- Thomas H. Davenport, *Enterprise Analytics: Optimize Performance, Process, and Decisions Through Big Data* (Upper Saddle River: Pearson FT Press Operations Management, 2014)

▪ Jason Burke, *Health Analytics: Gaining the Insights to Transform Health Care* (Hoboken: John Wiley & Sons, Inc., 2013)

▪ Rob J. Hyndman, *Forecasting: Principles and Practice*, (OTEXTS. COM, 2014)

Storytelling/Communication Books

▪ Cole Nussbaumer Knaflic, *Storytelling with Data: A Data Visualization Guide for Business Professionals* (Hoboken: John Wiley & Sons, Inc., 2015)

▪ Alberto Cairo, *The Truthful Art: Data, Charts, and Maps for Communication* (USA: New Riders, 2016)

▪ Stephanie D.H. Evergreen, *Effective Data Visualization: The Right Chart for the Right Data* (Thousand Oaks: SAGE Publications, Inc., 2017)

▪ Reid Hastie, *Rational Choice in an Uncertain World: The Psychology of Judgment and Decision Making* (Thousand Oaks: SAGE Publications, Inc., 2010)

Technical Books

▪ Jez Humble, *Continuous Delivery: Reliable Software Releases Through Build, Test, and Deployment Automation* (Boston: Addison-Wesley Signature Series (Fowler), 2011)

Business Books

▪ Phil Simon, *Analytics: The Agile Way* (Wiley and SAS Business Series) (Hoboken: John Wiley & Sons, Inc., 2015)

▪ General Stanley McChrystal, *Team of Teams: New Rules of Engagement for a Complex World* (New York: Portfolio/Penguin, 2015)

▪ Patrick Lencioni, *The Five Dysfunctions of a Team: A Leadership Fable* (San Francisco: Jossey-Bass, 2002)

▪ Stephen Bungay, *The Art of Action: How Leaders Close the Gaps Between Plans, Actions and Results* (Boston: Nicholas Brealey, 2011)

▪ Michael Lewis, *The Undoing Project: A Friendship That Changed Our Minds* (New York: W.W. Norton & Company, 2017)

■ John Doerr, *Measure What Matters: How Google, Bono, and the Gates Foundation Rock the World with OKRs* (New York: Portfolio/ Penguin, 2018)

When searching for books, we often search for specific subject matters. We knew we would need some books on data mining, predictive analytics, and forecasting since our initial focus was on projects that would use these techniques. Many of the storytelling and communication books came from presentations seen at analytic conferences. Some of the business books are recommended reading by Cleveland Clinic leadership. Some books come from peer recommendations. Don't be shy to ask your peers. Start a library today; it can be one of the best ways to feed curiosity and learning!

CONCLUSION

The following is an excerpt from Mayor Michael Bloomberg's Commencement speech at University of Michigan in 2016:

> If you have the luxury of more than one job offer – now or in the future – don't pick the one that pays the most; pick the one that teaches you the most and don't worry if the people around you seem quicker or smarter. You can't control that, but you can decide that you're going to outwork them.[9]

This quote is telling because it really gets to the heart of what data and analytics people are all about. People in these job roles have insatiable appetites for knowledge. It takes time to train and hire the right staff. Investing in people is a necessity to increase your competitive advantage.

People arguably can be called an organization's most important asset. In healthcare, we can absolutely make that statement. People are also an important part of your overall data and analytics strategy. On your journey, you will make decisions about differentiated

[9] https://www.mikebloomberg.com/news/mike-bloomberg-delivers-commencement-at-university-of-michigan/.

roles with specific skill sets, how many of these differentiated roles you need, and how to structure your data and analytics program. All of these decisions should align with your organization's mission and help deliver value to many facets of your business, from clinical care to operational metrics to financial performance.

We will leave you with a final quote: "I am convinced that nothing we do is more important than hiring and developing people. At the end of the day, you bet on people, not on strategies." – Lawrence Bossidy.

In the next chapter, we will focus on the importance of process. We will discuss how the traditional process workflow is changing from data collection to analysis to decision-making. We will exchange ideas on how agile has adapted itself into the analytical world from the software world. We will share some useful cases.

CHAPTER 3

Process

"Never tell people how to do things. Tell them what to do and they will surprise you with their ingenuity."

— George S. Patton

Process improvement is a journey that can only be completed success-fully with the right tools. Think about climbing Mount Everest. What tools do you need to climb Mount Everest successfully?[1]

Climbing Equipment

- Accessory cord or pre-cut prussiks
- Ice axe
- Crampons
- Carabiner system
- Alpine climbing harness
- Belay device
- Trekking poles
- Ascender

Footwear

- High-altitude all-in-one boots
- Camp boots
- Insulated camp booties
- Light hiking boots or trekking shoes
- Wool or synthetic socks
- Liner socks

Technical Clothing

- Baselayers – top and bottom
- Heavy baselayer bottoms
- Midlayer top
- Trekking pants
- Softshell pants
- Softshell jacket

[1] https://www.alpineascents.com/climbs/mount-everest/gear-list/.

- Hardshell pants
- Hardshell jacket
- Insulated synthetic hooded jacket
- Insulated down parka
- Expedition down parka
- Expedition down pants
- Down suit
- Insulated synthetic pants

Handwear

- Lightweight liner gloves
- Softshell gloves
- Insulated shell gloves
- Expedition mittens

Headwear

- Climbing helmet
- Buff
- Sun hat
- Balaclava system
- Wool/synthetic ski hat
- Facemask
- Glacier glasses
- Ski goggles
- Nose guard
- Headlamp

Personal Equipment

- –40F Down sleeping bag
- –20F Down sleeping bag
- Small pack
- 55-Liter climbing pack
- Inflatable sleeping pad

- Foam pad
- Spoon
- Mug
- Bowl
- Knife
- Pee bottle (1–1.5 liter)
- Pee funnel (for women)
- Water bottle parkas
- Water bottles
- Thermos
- Trash compactor/contractor bags
- Camera
- Large duffel bags
- Toiletry bag
- Water purification tools
- Sunscreen
- Lipscreen
- Running shoes
- Small personal first-aid kit
- Medications and prescriptions
- Base camp comforts
- Hand and toe warmers
- Food

Traveling

- Travel clothes

This is quite a daunting list. Nonetheless, you would never consider the process of climbing Mount Everest without the right equipment. The same holds true in business. A well-defined process is needed to run a successful business, particularly in healthcare where our lives are possibly at stake. Organizations have processes that have been in place for years and, many times, have not changed. Why? Perhaps a couple of reasons. One may be around having the right tools for making the process change. Another could be the culture and behavior of the people. We are going to examine some methodologies that can help drive insights to drive process change in your organization, as well as examine the importance of changing the culture. These methodologies are "ways of thinking" and are not magic elixirs.

Before we examine the tools, let's discuss culture. What is it? Can you describe it? Does it support your analytics process and strategy?

WHAT IS CULTURE?

Every organization has a driving culture. Whether your organization is 100 years old or newly formed, it has an underlying set of ideas, values, and behaviors that employees embrace, like work–life balance, daily work practices, innovation, employee engagement, employee celebrations, teambuilding, etc. In due course, you develop, consciously or unconsciously, rules and patterns that you follow and are reflected in everything you do. A few companies that come to mind as having outstanding corporate culture are SAS, Zappos, and Southwest Airlines.

In 2015, we knew we had an underlying culture in Cleveland Clinic's Enterprise Analytics Division. The quandary was that we could not describe it in a coherent, fluent statement. We examined what views drove our Enterprise Analytics culture. We wanted to know what underlying values were important and reflected how we wanted to work with one another to accomplish our work more effectively and efficiently.

We did an exercise where we asked our employees what they thought our culture stood for. We collected over 780 sticky notes (a lean tool called Crawford Slip Method: see the definition later in this chapter) asking for each sticky note to describe a value that would make employees happy, engaged, and love to come to work. When completed with the Crawford slip method, we found these sticky notes collected into 10 core values. These collective values would serve as a foundation and framework from which we would make daily decisions and manage our project workloads.

The 10 values that represent our department and that reflect and support our larger set of corporate values are:

1. quality,
2. service,
3. integrity and ethics,
4. teamwork/collaboration/communication,
5. humor/fun,
6. innovation/creativity,
7. passion/hard work and drive,
8. compassion,
9. continuous improvement, and
10. continuous learning.

We defined what each of these values meant to Enterprise Analytics.

During our culture exercise we realized that part of our values is geared toward keeping up with the pace of change. Whether the healthcare industry is in the news or not, it is changing daily from the delivery of services to collection of data to performing analytics. It is important to stay ahead of the game in the healthcare industry by striving to improve current processes and individual skill levels to maintain a competitive advantage in the marketplace.

When you think about defining your culture, once you can describe it, you can then sustain, change, or influence it. You can read many ways to sustain, change, or influence culture; however, we believe it must come from within. From your employees to your senior management, they must all be aligned and embrace the values that represent your department. Even today as you experience employee turnover, those prospective employees need to be a cultural fit. If not, you are fighting against sustainability and causing disruption of the corporate values.

WHAT IS DESIGN THINKING?

Design thinking at the core is delivering a practical solution to drive better outcomes by understanding how someone makes decisions.

The team works with the customer or end user to design, prototype, and test solutions.

The team gathers information that is needed to make a decision. Through meetings with the customer, they develop a deep understanding of the end users' challenges and organize the information to create a meaningful decision flowchart that can be translated into a prototype decision-based tool. Typically, you are prototyping some type of dashboard or end-user output. These prototypes can easily be deployed, tested, and iterated. Ultimately, through the cycle of prototyping, testing, and iteration, a final product is delivered to the customer or end user that significantly improves their decision-making process.

WHAT IS LEAN?

Lean is a methodology that teaches your team how to do the work right. Doing the work right is centered on becoming more efficient and effective. It provides a toolkit and processes to understand your current state and how to make improvements. If focuses on eliminating waste and optimizing process. Normally, you think of lean in the manufacturing sector but it has a place in healthcare, too.

Think about patients waiting in the emergency department or waiting for a radiology or laboratory test. Using Lean to understanding current patient flows and employee workflows through these different services can lead to improved waiting times and increase patient satisfaction.

How about transactional processes? Think about your data. Even with our advances in technology, you still cannot ignore processing the data your organization will ultimately use. There are only so many hours in the day you can devote to getting your data ready for organizational use, so making sure you are running at peak efficiency and optimization takes priority. Lean helps reach those objectives.

WHAT IS AGILE?

The typical software development definition of *agile* is an approach that utilizes self-organizing, cross-functional teams where requirements and solutions evolve through the collaboration between their customer or end user. It uses sprint planning to release product versions quickly, instead of waiting for the finished product. This allows for flexibility of the final product design as the customer or end user uses the release versions and informs the agile team of improvements on the fly.

We recommend watching the following videos of Spotify's engineering culture as a great primer. They can be found at https://labs.spotify.com/2014/03/27/spotify-engineering-culture-part-1/.

DESIGN THINKING, LEAN, AND AGILE DEFINITIONS

Following are definitions around terms you will see throughout the book that Cleveland Clinic has either adopted, explored, or implemented. Some of these terms may adhere to the typical definitions within design thinking, lean, and agile. Some of the terms below may have slight variations to the typical definition and are how we are using them at this point in our journey:[2, 3, 4]

■ *A3* – A problem solving method that allows you plan, do, check, and act, also referred to as PDCA. There are essentially eight steps that are repeatable, if necessary, to ensure the anticipated outcome. See the template example, Figure 2.4. They are: (1) problem statement; (2) current condition; (3) goal; (4) analysis; (5) select countermeasures; (6) action plan; (7) implement; and (8) follow-up. The first step is to define the problem statement by asking questions like, "What needs to change?" or "Why should it change?" Second is understanding the current condition. Digging into the current condition requires exploring questions like, "Where do things stand today?" "What is the actual symptom that the business feels requires action?" "What metric indicates that a problem exists?" "What metrics will be used to measure success?" Third is defining a goal. Simply put, "Where do we need to be?" "What is the

---

[2] https://www.leanproduction.com/top-25-lean-tools.html.
[3] https://www.cognitiveclouds.com/insights/key-principles-of-user-centered-design/.
[4] Phil Simon, *Analytics: The Agile Way* (Wiley and SAS Business Series, 2017).

specific change you want to accomplish now?" Fourth is the analysis to understand how the process works today. Doing exercises like process mapping and waste identification. Getting to the root cause(s) of the problem. Fifth is developing countermeasures or alternatives that can be considered to reach your future state or goal. During this step, you will be evaluating among different options and deciding what criteria will be used to pick a recommendation. Steps (6) and (7) are the planning and implementation activities. You will put in writing, at a minimum, what tasks will be required, identify responsible party(ies) for each task, and establish target completion dates. This ensures accountability. If a task is at risk of not being completed on time, you can understand why and adjust as necessary. The last step is follow-up. During this step we are measuring and evaluating our recommended countermeasure that was implemented. We are ensuring standardization so it is repeatable. During this step we want to know if the actions we put in place have the desired impact.

- *Backlog* – User stories that are not in the current sprint.
- *Crawford Slip Method* – A method that allows for the collection of individual ideas. You give everyone a pad of sticky notes. You set a time limit. Everyone participates by putting one idea per sticky note. You collect all sticky notes. You place all sticky notes together. Then you sort into similar topics or themes.
- *Daily Huddle* – These are 15-minute meetings that basically ask three questions:
  - What did we accomplish yesterday?
  - What are we planning to do today?
  - Are there any roadblocks?
- *Epics* – These are projects that will be completed over many sprints. Epics can be as short as a month or longer (within the scope of the project). This usually contains multiple user stories, like phases of a project.
- *Gemba Visit* – This is simply a customer visit. All or some members of the team go to where the customer does the work. It is an opportunity to understand how they work. You can actively

listen to problems and occasionally ask questions to clarify how the work is being done. This visit is not to offer solutions.

- *Just-Do-Its* – These are small tasks that do not need planning. They are normally part of your backlog and when time allows, teams just do them.

- *Kaizen* – A process where you proactively look to achieve incremental improvements.

- *Kanban Boards* – A way the team conveys where user stories or tasks are during a sprint. Normally, you will have columns like: to do, in progress, testing, completed. You can have more or less depending on how you want to define the way the work moves through your process. We give teams the liberty to decide on what columns they will use.

- *Key Performance Indicators (KPIs)* – These are metrics that are designed to track and understand how the organization is performing.

- *Minimally Viable Product (MVP)* – This is the product delivered to the end user based on the minimum usable features defined by the end user and delivers value to their process. This is normally not the final product. It is important to document the different values to be gained fully so that you can prioritize the values and come to consensus with the end user over the values that need to be addressed in the MVP. The MVP will ultimately be driven by alleviating pain points by building processes to support daily work, creating work efficiencies by simplifying and streamlining information delivery, providing leadership with actionable insights to improve performance, or some combination of those values or others.

- *PDCA* – An iterative approach to continuous improvement. Plan (establish plan and expected outcome), Do (implement), Check (collect data to verify expected outcome), and Act (assess and repeat).

- *Process Mapping* – This is the exercise that produces a diagram of what we do in our business. It helps drive a common understanding of how the process works, from steps in the process to pain points/breakdowns to inputs/outputs to customers.

▣ *Root Cause Analysis* – Looks to identify the underlying problem so that corrective action eliminates the "root cause" of the problem. Normally, the "Five *Whys*" approach is used that gets you incrementally close to the actual root cause.

▣ *Scrum Teams* – Have three roles: a product owner, a scrum master, and the team itself. The product owner is responsible for owning the portfolio of work. The product owner needs to keep the team informed of the end users' requirements and objectives, as initially defined or as the change, help determine priorities, and help the team manage potential throughput, that is, understand the number of different projects that will be running simultaneously to produce minimally viable products and the amount of different work that can be delivered upon. A scrum master is a servant leader who champions projects, acts as an agile coach, and is a team facilitator. They are responsible for making sure the teams adhere to agile methodologies, can help clear roadblocks, understand team dynamics to help prevent "in-fighting" that can lead to destructive work environments, and provide guidance. The team is comprised of different roles and decides how the work will get done. Its focus is on maximizing the team's productivity. This is not necessarily the same as maximizing the productivity of individual members. An individual who takes to heart a task is truly "theirs" and does not seek help can hinder a team's chemistry and productivity. It is the team collaborating together to complete their tasks that is truly efficient.

▣ *Sponsorship Meeting* – This is a meeting normally held bi-weekly or monthly. The key leader(s) who are sponsoring the project(s) and key members of the scrum team meeting to review the completed sprint(s), backlogs, and upcoming sprints. Sponsors and key members of the scrum team can adjust priorities and requirements during this meeting, review MVP or enhancements, etc. It is an important informational meeting to understand progress. It can also be used to discuss whether the project is meeting expectations.

▣ *Sprint* – This is the number of specific tasks or user stories that will be done in a defined period of time. Normally, sprints are weekly, bi-weekly, or at worst case, monthly. Normally, anything longer than bi-weekly makes sprint planning difficult. Sprint objectives should have milestones of projects or delivering new capabilities to the end user. There are times when the objectives are internal to the project in nature and showing sustained progress to the end user is imperative.

- *Sprint Planning* – This meeting can take up to two hours. The goal of this meeting is to define the current sprint and re-prioritize the sprint backlog and adapt to changing requirements.

- *Standard Work* – A document that describes best practices around a process. This document should be easy to update and is "live." Since standard work is part of the lean process, it goes to say that standard work should always be improving.

- *Tasks* – These come from user stories. Normally, these tasks can be completed with the sprint cycle. Tasks are usually labeled. You will see labeling ideas using T-shirt sizes like XS, S, M, L, XL. Some will use points. The key is to understand what timeframe your labeling means. If you are using T-shirt sizes, does XS mean one hour, S mean four hours, M mean one day, L mean three days, XL mean five days? If you use points, is one point worth one hour or does it represent two hours? You need to realize what will work for you in understanding how to estimate the time to complete a task. This is critical to sprint planning.

- *User Persona* – This helps you understand your end user. It is a profile to help you understand who they are and what they do. Think of it as a LinkedIn profile on steroids. You not only understand the educational background and professional experience, but also you understand a typical workday, their goals and obstacles, and what types of data and performance metrics they work with daily to make decisions and what visualizations resonate with them.

- *User Stories* – Numbers of user stories can make up an epic, or they can be standalone stories. Normally, these user stories can be completed within a sprint.

CREATING A DATA MANAGEMENT AND ANALYTICS PROCESS FRAMEWORK

When we started our agile journey at Cleveland Clinic, our Enterprise Analytics department had numerous brainstorm sessions around what would be our guiding principles. To date, we have landed on the following way we are developing our teams and the way we work. It is centered around three principles, as shown in Figure 3.1.

The three principles are: (1) Design Thinking; (2) Lean; and (3) Agile. Integrating these three methodologies into our daily work, regardless of analytical projects, standard processing work, or ad hoc work, allows our team to develop and release deliverables more quickly and more cost-efficiently, and increases end user engagement and satisfaction.

Design thinking is about understanding how your end user works. Using Gemba visits with your end user will help you understand how they make decisions or perform their daily work so that you can deliver a product that they will use. Too many times, analyst thinking was used. That is, analysts designed the solution and how it would be used. There was always conflict around the end user. The end user could not use the solution that was developed effectively by the analyst. From an analyst point of view, it was intuitive, because it was built on how an analyst did their job. Making this subtle yet important change to understand how the user of the solution works has delivered solutions that work for the end user and adoption of these solutions does not seem to be as challenging.

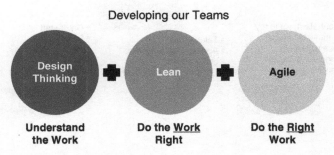

Figure 3.1 Process Framework
Source: Cleveland Clinic.

Using lean principles is about doing the work right. Think about how you were trained to do your work. It started somewhere in the primordial work ocean of deliverables. Someone was asked to deliver a solution. At the time the solution was developed, sometimes 20+ years ago, a process to "get the job done" was created. End of story. Just wash, rinse, repeat.

Really? Nothing has changed since then? People? Technology? Data? The way we worked, no matter how far in the past, from days to months to years, there is no manner to improve? That's where lean principles upset the work paradigm. By instilling the Cleveland Clinic Improvement Model as a culture and not just something to do, all employees are given proper guidance and methodologies to do the work right. Answering the question, "What matters most?" leads to the right behaviors and right results.

Everything we do has a process. Sometimes we fail to realize this, but think of something you do daily. How about getting ready for work? Guess what, there's a process. You might be asking how? Think about it, you can create a process flow of exactly how you get ready for work.

I bet your process (Figure 3.2) would look similar, though not necessarily identical, and would reflect your efficiencies. You probably started with a process that, over time, evolved into the most efficient

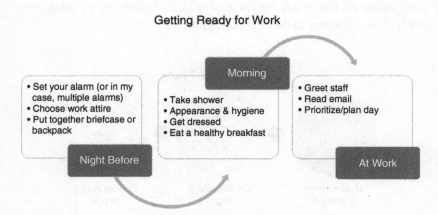

Getting Ready for Work

- Set your alarm (or in my case, multiple alarms)
- Choose work attire
- Put together briefcase or backpack

Night Before

Morning

- Take shower
- Appearance & hygiene
- Get dressed
- Eat a healthy breakfast

- Greet staff
- Read email
- Prioritize/plan day

At Work

Figure 3.2 Getting-Ready-for-Work Process
Source: Author.

way to prepare for the workday. Why? Maybe you were trying to do too much in the morning, which did not allow you to eat a healthy breakfast. Through lean principles, you discovered the pain points that were keeping you from eating a healthy breakfast. Now, you choose your work attire and put your briefcase together the night before to free up the time to eat. Simple, right? Not so fast.

There is plenty that can go into the process change. Not following a systematic approach can lead to pitfalls and problems. Developing a culture of improvement leads to a method of analyzing and understanding your work so that you can make improvements. There are plenty of tools that can help you.

Let's go back to the example above, getting ready for work. A perfect tool to help solve any pain point that may be occurring would be the A3 tool. While this may seem like overkill for what we might simply think of as a mundane task, "getting ready for work," the A3 tool when used properly allows you to understand the whole process from soup to nuts and create the "right" process flow that works for you. Later in this chapter we will explore how A3 was used to create a solution for our contracting efforts.

Using Agile makes sure we are focusing on doing the right work. We continuously have discussions on exploring different ways to implement Agile. We learn each time we have explored different concepts of Agile. Through these learnings, we continue to see improvements to throughput. This statement taken from the Spotify website says it best: "This is a journey in progress, not a journey completed, and there's a lot of variation from squad to squad. So, the stuff in the video isn't all true for all squads all the time, but it appears to be mostly true for most squads most of the time."[5]

I'll simplify it in five words: "Do what works for you." Implementing agile concepts rigidly is not always the best decision. We have found that understanding Agile as a whole will help you test certain constructs. The constructs can be team composition or different techniques. When you think about team composition, are you building self-containing teams that have all the skills you will need for the breadth of projects assigned, a "scrum team"? Or are all of your

[5] https://labs.spotify.com/2014/03/27/spotify-engineering-culture-part-1/.

resources aligned in centers of excellence (COE) teams from which you pluck the amount of resources that would be required from each COE team for a project to create a team and then assign a project? Or is it a hybrid approach that could have some core team members and then, as needed, certain skills are brought on to the team to complete specific tasks? Is it some other structure? Will every one of your teams obey the definition of a scrum team? Should it? By structuring and piloting different structures, your teams will provide the necessary feedback to understand what works for you. Buying-in to the teams' structure is one principle for sustainment.

Let's not get caught up on nomenclature in this next discussion; instead, the emphasis is on how the team works. Whether we call these next items tools of the trade or methods or any other clever descriptive technique, it is more important to focus on the idea that these methods help the team focus on completing the work agilely. Teams will have many methods at their disposal. They will experiment with each tool; some they will use, others they may not. We have found the following methods vital to completing the work, keeping the end users informed, and prioritizing projects. It may take time to see what methods your team embraces and they need to settle in on what methods they will use. Whether you use some or all of the techniques below, finding the methods that consistently work for you will allow your team to develop a rhythm and allow them to reach optimal throughput sooner. We have found the following methods have the most impact to getting the work done:

- Backlogs
- Daily Huddle
- Epics
- Kanban Boards
- User Stories
- Tasks
- Sprints
- Sprint Planning
- Sponsorship Meetings
- Just-Do-Its

Let's examine how this works. First and foremost, you will have a sponsor that needs some work done. In the meeting with the sponsor, you gather requirements, expectations, deliverables, etc. You get an understanding on what the MVP will be for that sponsor and what the potential final product looks like. Now that you have the work, you go back and pull together your scrum team. Remember, your scrum team is what works for you. You may not have a product owner, or a scrum master. You may have team members who play those roles. Nonetheless, you bring back the project to the scrum team. Time to do your sprint planning. During this initial sprint planning meeting, you are creating epics, user stories, tasks, backlogs, times for daily huddles, sponsorship meeting schedules, and your Kanban board. At the end of all the initial work, you are ready to create your sprint.

We use the word *tasks* in the following paragraphs interchange-ably with *user stories* and *epics* to understand the work, but they still represent different ideas. Your initial sprint needs to prioritize all of the tasks. This initial sprint will allow you to understand what tasks can be completed over the next sprint cycle. Whatever you cannot complete goes into the backlog. One of the important parts of sprint planning is to identify just-do-its. As you will soon realize during these sprints, there will be some free time. Since all of your tasks are estimates of time to complete, you will undoubtedly find that some tasks are completed ahead of schedule. This will create opportunities for just-do-its.

"Just-do-its" are tasks that are in the backlog and can be grabbed and completed when time becomes free. Not every time tasks are com-pleted ahead of schedule should you look for just-do-its; you still need to understand dependencies of all the tasks in the sprint to determine if you can grab a just-do-it. If you are unsure if grabbing a just-do-it will impact your sprint, you can mitigate whether you should grab a just-do-it during your daily huddle.

Now that the sprint planning has been defined, how you man-age your sprint cycle is a daily event. This is where your daily huddle comes into play. These quick meetings confirm alignment: you under-stand what was completed, what's next, report roadblocks, allow for the planning and grabbing of just-do-its, and, most importantly, allow for an understanding if a sprint is "at risk."

Normally, the Kanban board is used during these huddles. As the sprint comes to a close, it is important to have a sponsorship meeting. These meetings are important for a number of reasons. These meetings are also reasonably short and, at most, should be 30 to 60 minutes. In these meetings there are a number of objectives that need to be addressed. First should be a report on the recent sprint. This is an opportunity to help the sponsor understand what is going well, and what challenges the team is facing. They can weigh in on any challenges to help provide guidance. An example might be some of the tasks are taking longer than estimated, potentially putting the MVP at risk to its targeted completion. Keeping sponsors informed can alleviate the stress of missing a deadline.

Armed with the challenges, sponsors can help prioritize or adjust other milestones that could potentially get the MVP back on track. Simply put, keeping sponsors informed generates the right dialog to keep focused. In connection with the previous thought, the sponsors review the backlog, add to it, remove from it, and re-prioritize it. This gives the team guidance for their next sprint cycle. In some instances, these meetings may need to extend to 90 minutes or two hours. The extended meetings are usually required when you have a product showcase. These showcases can show capabilities, elicit immediate feedback, and help the sponsor "see" how the product is developing. Not only during the regular sponsorship meeting, but the inclusion of product showcases can lead to another important discussion: Should the project continue?

When you are using traditional process methods, you are delivering a project when it is complete. This can lead to bad execution of deliverables, mainly a bad product that is not what the end user wanted. Why? Projects change over their lifespan, user design is only contemplated at the beginning or, in some cases, not at all, and agile methods are not used, which complicates flexibility. More importantly, the immediate understandings that are created in these sponsorship meetings can help modify product requirements or flat out cancel a product if it is not delivering the intended value. We should not be disheartened with scrapping a product where there is no value add. In fact, this actually adds to satisfaction scores for the team.

Imagine no sponsorship meetings that could provide feedback and direction, and the project just went to completion and then was not used or scrapped. The team perceives their work as wasted and will wonder what other ongoing work will suffer similar fates. Having these sponsorship meetings is highly motivating for the team as they get immediate feedback, require changes, and, most importantly, leadership participation. Now you are back to your sprint planning cycle and the process repeats.

Now that we have examined the three principles that we use to develop our teams, let's summarize a few key takeaways. The most important takeaway is "Do what works for you." We cannot stress this enough. Success is not simply measured on adhering to strict user design principles, lean methods, and agile concepts; instead, it is measured by the sustainment. Sustainment can come in many forms. We see sustainment as a combination of the three principles that deliver value from throughput to choosing the right tools to manage your work to team engagement in defining the way it will work.

Another takeaway is understanding what it means to "do what works for you." We landed on the following basic principles and best practices to guide us:

- Make sure the user community saw a minimally viable product (MVP) early, typically no longer than 90 days, always targeting 30 days.
- Make sure we continue to deliver enhancements or capabilities at regular intervals (two weeks).
- Flexibility to incorporate changing requirements immediately.
- Teams or squads would have daily huddles.
- Teams or squads would have two-week sprint planning huddles.
- Teams or squads would maintain and continuously add to the backlog.
- Allow teams or squads to use whatever user design, lean, agile, and scrum methods work for them.

The last takeaway is sustainment of this process leads to increased ingenuity and innovation. Happenstance? We think not. The increased complexity of business problems requires teams to continuously use the three principles to find solutions to enhance and augment process and the daily changing business requirements. It becomes embedded and part of the team's DNA. Ingenuity and innovation are byproducts when you understand the amount of data and the overall complexity of the business solution, from the daily support, streamlining information delivery, and providing leadership with timely insights to improve business performance, whether it be clinical, operational, or financial.

A final thought: just implementing this three-way principle framework approach does not guarantee successful results. Success and sustainability of this framework is a four-way street. Success cannot come from a top-down approach, nor can it come from a bottom-up approach. It cannot be successful across the organization if all departments are not engaged. It cannot be successful by just "turning-on" the methodology. It is about "trial and error," "blood, sweat, and tears," and "elbow-grease." Use whatever metaphor you want. It is hard work. Success is around sticking with good times and bad. It is pertinent to always be transparent.

CHANGING THE ANALYTICS JOURNEY

Most of us can relate to the traditional process workflow. In the new age of big data and advanced analytics, this process work has evolved and will continue to evolve. We will examine the steps of the work flows and give some examples of projects and how each of these steps are evolving.

Generally, you need a framework for your analytics process. We must trust that allowing your people the freedom to innovate will always produce the best outcome, not only short term, but long term as well. Understanding the framework gives you the governance guiderails needed to ensure consistency between projects and the expectations of the analysts.

We will explore two forms of process change. The first will be the traditional project lifecycle and how that has evolved in the world of digital transformation and data science. The second will be the introduction of agile methods and how we apply those methodologies. Finally, we will discuss how the merger of these two forms of process change has increased deliverables and increased customer engagement and satisfaction.

WHAT IS THE CURRENT PROCESS?

Healthcare has lagged other industries in the use of "data science." If you ask 100 people, you will probably get 100 different answers. Let's just agree that data science in the context of this book is where we are using data sets (whether they are considered small or large is inconsequential) combined with algorithms to produce insights that satisfy the end users' goal of improving clinical, operational, and/or financial decision-making. This next discussion will examine the process workflow consisting of three components – data, insight, and action. We will scrutinize what a traditional workflow looks like and how that is evolving into the future state. Many healthcare organizations can relate to the traditional process workflow pictured in Figure 3.3.

In the data component, there were usually two processes. The first is problem definition. We find one of the biggest barriers to solving the business problem is accurately defining what the current state is and how the desired outcome will improve the business problem. This is where the A3 process can play a substantial role. Business problems that are more transactional in nature can absolutely benefit from the A3 process, like transforming the process for populating your data warehouse. These types of transactional problems can take a few weeks to get through adequately because of the complexity of understanding and mapping the process. You are using methods like

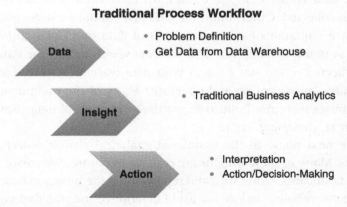

Figure 3.3 Traditional Process Workflow
Source: Cleveland Clinic.

process mapping, root cause analysis, and Crawford slip that require time commitment to doing it right. We find you cannot just use these methods in one 60-or 90-minute meeting. It is a series of meetings to make sure everyone on the team understands and agrees that you have accurately mapped the process. Other business problems that require a more analytical answer, like producing a forecast to inform an operational meeting or producing a financial model to inform a contract negotiation, can usually get through the framework of the A3 process in a shorter time frame. Normally, you do not need to do process mapping, root cause analysis, or Crawford slip in the same way you would do it for a transactional problem. We cannot emphasize enough that this is about using a framework to ensure consistency in addressing and understanding where you are today and where you are going tomorrow.

The second process is getting data from your data warehouse. Depending on how your data warehouse is set up and the complexity of your data relationships, you normally have defined views that everyone can use, rather than giving access to the data tables. Normally, it is a matter of using one of your technology tools, like SQL, OLAP cubes, or Excel, to connect to the data. You understand the criteria defined by your business problem and query the data and return results. In this traditional data gathering approach, there would potentially be roadblocks. The biggest roadblock was around not having the data available. In some cases, the data was in a source system, just not collected. Other times, the data just did not exist. Sometimes, there are limitations based on amount of data that needs to be collected or that is actually stored in the data warehouse. If the data was not collected or did not exist in your data warehouse, the question was, How can we collect and integrate? Many of the traditional data warehouses were not built to ingest the new types of data (unstructured text, streaming, etc.).

The next phase of the traditional analytical process workflow is insights. Many of these insights are reactive in nature. We create traditional dashboards, scorecards, and reports using the historical data from the data warehouse. Below is a list of descriptive statistics that you are probably using daily to help make business decisions. You may not be calculating specific statistics below like skewness or kurtosis, but understanding its definition is still helpful in providing analytical context:

- *Mean (Average)* – Sum all of the numbers in your list and divide by the number of data points.
- *Median* – This is the middle number in your range. You arrange the numbers from lowest to highest. It is the middle number. If you have an odd number of data points, it is the middle number. If you have an even number of data points, you average the two middle numbers.
- *Mode* – This is the number that appears most frequently.
- *Measures of central tendency* – The statistics mean, median, and mode make up this concept and can help describe the center of the distribution.
- *Variance* – It measures how far your numbers are spread from the mean.
- *Standard deviation* – It measures the dispersion of a set of data. A low standard deviation indicates the data points are close to the mean while a high standard deviation means the data points are spread out over a wider range. Regardless of the number, one standard deviation mean it covers approximately 68% of the data, two standard deviations cover approximately 95% of the data, and three standard deviations cover approximately 99% of the data.
- *Percentiles* – This is a measure indicating the number of observations that fall below a given percentile.
- *Range* – This is the difference between the lowest and highest value in your data.
- *Interquartile range* – Represents the data that falls between the 25th and 75th percentiles.
- *Skewness* – This is the measure of asymmetry of a distribution. Negatively skewed distributions have a longer left tail; positively skewed distributions have a longer right tail.
- *Kurtosis* – This is a measure of the shape of a probability distribution.

■ *Frequency distributions* – Can be a list, table, or graph that displays the frequency of your data set. Sometimes you are bucketing your data into ranges (like different height ranges), bucketing into Likert scale variables (like strongly agree, agree, neutral, disagree, strongly disagree), or you can have multiple groupings (like gender by age bands).

With these, you are commonly using the following visualization techniques:

■ *Bar/line charts* – A way to visualize categorical data graphically using bars or lines relating two variables.

■ *Box-and-whisker plots* – A graphical representation where the box represents the interquartile range and the whiskers can represent several possible alternatives, most likely the minimum and maximum of all of the data points.

■ *Scatter diagrams* – A way to visualize two variables. It is a way to identify if there is any relationship between two variables.

■ *Histograms* – These represent the distribution of numerical data by creating bins or buckets of a single variable to count. They give you a rough picture of what the distribution will look like.

■ *Control charts* – A way to show if a process is in control. The charts show upper and lower control limits and, when the data is outside those limits, the process is considered "out of control." You create detection signals that when the process is out of control, some action is required to put the process back in control.

The problem? Whether we are looking at operational metrics or financial metrics, these data and traditional business analytics are reactive in nature. We can look at capacity statistics for a hospital or hospital system over the past day, week(s), month(s), quarter(s), or year(s). While it is informative in nature, can it be used to plan? What if we want to understand how our costs or revenues are performing? We can look at operating statements daily, weekly, monthly, quarterly, etc. and all of the traditional business statistics to help us understand. These high-level analytics like averages and standard deviations, ranges, etc. give us an understanding of the past. The past is not indicative of the future. It is an input to help predict when applying business judgment for the future.

These lead to the action phase. This is where we are interpreting and deciding on actions to take. What normally happens in this phase are questions arise and we answer them by going back to the historical data. While historical is important, should it be the only data we use to inform us?

This leads to the new process. How are analytics evolving? It is by combining the past with the future that provides you the most comprehensive view of the business. It is that competitive advantage you gain by using data, proactive decision-making techniques, and business acumen to drive value in the decision-making process. But what does this new process look like?

It has been noted by Thomas Davenport that your organization's competitive advantage increases with more sophisticated analysis. Logically, that makes sense. When you think about what sophisticated analytics means, it is the use of prescriptive and predictive analytics and the use of machine learning to drive insights and actions that were not once seeable.

Figure 3.4 illustrates what Thomas Davenport was driving at.

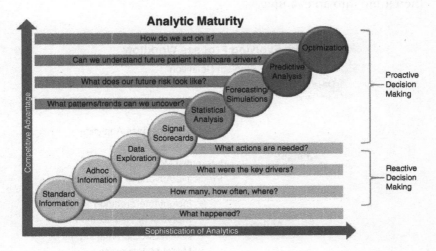

Figure 3.4 The Analytics Maturity Curve

Source: Adapted from *Analytics Maturity Goal: From Reactive to Predictive*, SAS Institute, Inc.

What needs to be done here is really understand the work you have accomplished and the queue of work that is waiting and truly challenge the output or desired outcome. Are there new techniques that can be used to drive better decision-making and understanding instead of just "the number" that is constantly reconciled, challenged, and debated?

Not all new techniques will require deep learning methodologies or the "shiny new technique." It is most important to clearly define a new way of decision-making by understanding which techniques can help.

This competitive advantage takes the traditional process workflow and transforms it into the following evolving process workflow. It incorporates the importance of understanding historical business performance, i.e. the new way we use data and the analytics that can provide forward-looking business scenarios. Overall, this is a much more informed way to make business decisions.

Under this new evolving process workflow as shown in Figure 3.5, the three stages remain the same. There is a data stage, an insight stage, and an action phase. What is enhanced is how each stage is evolving. Let's take a quick look at how each stage has morphed and then jump into an example.

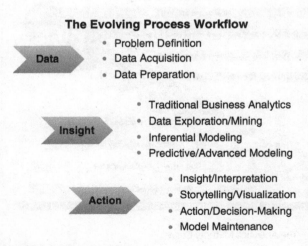

The Evolving Process Workflow

Data
- Problem Definition
- Data Acquisition
- Data Preparation

Insight
- Traditional Business Analytics
- Data Exploration/Mining
- Inferential Modeling
- Predictive/Advanced Modeling

Action
- Insight/Interpretation
- Storytelling/Visualization
- Action/Decision-Making
- Model Maintenance

Figure 3.5 Evolving Process Workflow
Source: Cleveland Clinic.

In the data stage, one constant remains. It is still the most important step in the process. It is the problem definition. The problem definition does not dramatically change. We are still responsible for defining the problem in a way that is up to date, complete, and understood by all users. Our opportunity here is to broaden the solution to the problem in a way that we can incorporate new predictive models. These models can help inform short-term to long-term decision-making. It doesn't matter if we define short term as anything less than a year, or less than six months, just like it doesn't matter if long term is defined as greater than one year or the next three to five years. The overarching theme of "Do what works for you" applies everywhere. Replacing "Get data from data warehouse" from the traditional method is now done in two steps – data acquisition and data preparation. These two improvements center around using the data differently. Think of this as your information portal. You are expected to deliver trusted, standardized information to your enterprise. This allows your business analyst to produce content for decision-makers, giving the analytical people the ability to go after the data in a way that is required for their solution. With the advancement in technologies, the amount and kinds of data that can be collected and made available continue to increase. It is giving them access to the core tables so they can build the appropriate processes, data sets, and data transformations necessary. In the current data landscape, we are collecting all kinds of structured and unstructured data. When there are data elements that are not currently available, the ability to get the data incorporated into your data warehouse is less intrusive. There is a process to collect data from wearables or streaming devices, social media, or public data, like weather. Even data we collect from our source systems is not perfect. There is always human error. There are no perfect data warehouses. Everyone has "data issues." It is this new capability of data acquisition and preparation and the tools and technologies available that allow us to progress to the next stage of analytics evolution.

In the insight stage, we have intensified what we call analytics. This is where technology and analytics meet to create this new competitive advantage. Not only are we continuing to do the traditional business analytics; we are also evolving the analytics to include data exploration, data mining, and predictive and prescriptive analytics. It is that analytic nirvana your organization should be striving for, where you are able to anticipate the decision-making requirements and produce them effortlessly. While we might be exaggerating by using the term effortlessly, we truly mean that the amalgamation of new technologies and analytical capabilities allows you to do things that were once thought impossible, or at least difficult and time-consuming to conquer.

The insight phase is where the analytics are executed. This stage includes what we will call analytics workbenches and advanced analytics laboratories. The analytics workbench is the core for your business analysts. The analytics workbench is where most of the traditional business analytics lie. The business analysts can produce your traditional business analytical content for consumption by decision-makers. The advanced analytics laboratories act as a playground for your data scientists, giving them the flexibility to explore structured and unstructured information from all available data sources to produce content for consumption by your organization. The advanced analytics laboratories give your data scientists the capability for data discovery, developing advanced analytical processes, and performing experimental design theories. You can build prototypes of your predictive models and test how these predictive models can be deployed or embedded into daily workflows or decision-making processes.

In the action stage, this is where a new frontier of interpretation takes center stage. It is the ability to take these results from the insight stage to tell a story and use new visualization techniques and bring to light the insights and interpretation necessary from these complex predictive models to drive improved decision-making. Part of the action stage is predictive model maintenance and management. We call it model maintenance since your predictive model's performance directly impacts the ability to make decisions. It really houses your predictive model's playbook. Without a playbook, you are flying blind in the decision-making process. This is the documentation required for your organization to understand the model, the model's performance, and the model's monitoring and maintenance criteria. If decision-making is compromised because your models are not delivering their intended performance, you will need to take some sort of action, whether it is re-training or transitioning to a new model, suspending the current model, or retiring the model.

What should be in your model's playbook? We believe your playbook should have the following sections:

- *Project Name and Title* – This section should be a current version number and the last time the model was updated. Always keeping a history of the versions is a great way to understand how your model has changed over the lifetime of its use.
- *Summary* – A brief summary of the objective or outcome.
- *Problem Definition/Objectives* – This should be your high-level executive summary. Your executives or senior leadership should be able to understand who the sponsor is, who the lead analyst is, who the audience is, what decision is the predictive model helping to make (operational, financial, clinical, target population, etc.), goals of the model, its output, performance and operationalization expectations, and model maintenance expectations/plan. Brief description of the problem to be solved, its significance, and gap in existing knowledge being addressed by the solution. State the business/medical problem that the model is trying to solve. Some of the information that should be clear in this section is as follows:
  - Sponsor
  - Lead analyst of the current version
  - Intended consumer of predictive output
  - Question answered or decision influenced by the predictive output
  - Goal of the predictive analytic project
  - Intended model(s) to be developed
  - Performance expectation, including accuracy threshold requirements
  - Brief description of operationalization/automation plan, including:
    - Model selection (if applicable)
    - Score processing
    - Automation and reporting
    - Brief description of workflow integration

- Brief description of model performance tracking
- Plan for recalibrating
- How often do we evaluate new inputs, etc.

- *Analytic Strategy/Approach* – A brief description of analytic plan and relevant requirements and/or modeling assumptions. You describe the analytics approach to be taken. What methodologies and why these methodologies are appropriate for solving this problem. What is the rationale for taking this approach?

- *Design* – Outline and discuss the study size, eligibility criteria, what time periods will be used, predictors, outcomes, validation, results, and conclusions.

- *Outcome* – Clearly define the outcome of what is being predicted or prescribed.

- *Limitations* – List any limitations and discuss their importance.

- *Data Sources and Model Features* – Document your data sources for the model, specific data engineering or transformations that occur (handling NULLs, log transforms, etc.), learned model features (predictive outputs of one model that subsequently are included in another model as a feature variable).

- *Data Modeling and Assessment* – Document the software being used, any data preprocessing steps, describe model methodologies, the model training, model testing, and model evaluation (include model settings/parameters).

- *Final Prediction Model(s)* – Document the final model being used. Its equations, interpretation, including human-interpretable explanations on how the model derives results, and what features are included to determine conclusions.

- *Results Summary and Model Validation* – Summarize your final model by showing your model's validation.

- *Production and Automation* – A detailed production automation workflow, operational system integration plan, and organization plans for communication, workflow changes, or enhancements, and roll-out details.

- *Performance Monitoring and Maintenance* – Document how your model is actually performing over time. You should have some key performance indicators or thresholds to understand if your model is degrading. What is your transition plan, model suspension plan, or model retirement plan?

■ *References* – Finally, don't forget to summarize and cite any references consulted.

We cannot stress enough the best practice of developing a playbook template for your organization. This template should be required for all new analytical models you create. Yes, we are notorious for ignoring the importance of documentation. The pace at which we are asked to deliver new analytics is not slowing, yet it would be negligent to skip this part. This playbook will lead to predictive model adoption quicker through some of the following reasons:

1. It is not a black box. Anyone in your organization can read the documentation. They should be able to ask questions. How else will your analytic maturity grow?

2. Your organization's confidence in consuming the predictive model increases because everyone can understand through the documentation all of the work related to the analytic strategy and methods used, limitations of the predictive model, outcomes of the predictive model and performance modeling.

3. It ensures transparency. It can be peer reviewed (which we recommend as a best practice) and we believe peer reviews only lead to better models. Creative discussions and challenges among your model builders about methods and strategies, design, model outputs, etc. can only lead to improved results. In our opinion, if you cannot have these peer review discussions, it means you are probably leaving something on the table.

4. Can withstand employee attrition. Yes, the impossible has happened. The creator of the predictive model has left your organization right when the model is starting to degrade. This allows your remaining analytics staff the ability to take that model and make the necessary model enhancements or retirement types of decisions.

Let's take a look at an example. Providers of healthcare services continue to be confronted with business problems from shortage of resources to fiscal challenges created by contract terms for managing patient populations to long-range healthcare services demand planning. Being able to understand the financial risks associated with how your contracts will perform over the life of the contracts and how your revenue mix will impact financial margins can play a large role in your planning process. This seems like a fairly simple problem to solve. The traditional approach would be to take a snapshot of encounters for that contract from a time period in the past. Using that snapshot, you would apply the contracted rates to those encounters and derive the revenue for a contract year. Each of those encounters also has an associated cost. You may apply a simple adjustment to the costs based on your business acumen, and nonetheless, you have a cost estimate also. You now have two "numbers," revenue and costs, and can imply profitability. Let's assume you have a three-year contract. The second and third years of the contract will also have revenue rates. You take those rates and use the same encounter set. You do the math and there you have it. Three revenue numbers, one for each year. For costs, you may apply assumptions to what you believe your costs will be over the next couple of years. You apply those sets of assumptions to the encounters and, once again, you have three costs numbers. Now you can use the three revenue and costs numbers to produce an estimate of how the contract will perform over a three year-period, end of story. Not so fast! Now you are asked to produce a worst-case and a best-case scenario. You have your underlying model so now you can just go to your assumptions, tweak them to represent the worst case and the best case, recalculate the three numbers, and now you have it: an analysis that has a worst-case and a best-case scenario and, sandwiched in between, your initial analysis. After everyone has a chance to review the three-year forecast, they may ask you to run the numbers through a different set of encounters to produce a different set of results to consider. Easy enough, you can just pull your new encounters, plug them into your model, and produce new results. Again, three more sets of numbers to compare. You can do this simple financial model for every contract and produce an overall financial plan for three years.

What does this number really represent? What is the real decision they are trying to make? How important are those three yearly numbers? How much risk is in the current process? All three questions are very complex and hard to answer. What if you are tasked with caring for an attributed population? That is, the healthcare provider is responsible for the total cost of care for patients that are assigned to them. Let's use a hypothetical number of patients, 100,000. These 100,000 patients are not going to use the exact same amount of healthcare resources year-in and year-out. How many times a patient will see a physician will depend on how they are feeling. In fact, every aspect of healthcare services will vary. How can you improve this process to produce an analytic that can be consumed and used in a more insightful manner? You think to yourself, there has to be an easier way to produce results that can inform leadership with insights and risks to understand to improve decision-making.

Now let's examine how this process may look with our new analytic process. When you think about the purpose of the calculation, are you not trying to calculate what you believe will happen over a time period in the future? Do you think the same identical encounters will occur during the future time periods? Of course not, yet we have been conditioned to calculate the "number" and use that as a basis for decision-making.

A common technique to consider is Monte Carlo simulation. When you think about all of the variables in play and the risk inherent in just a "number," why not use this simple technique to enhance your decision-making capability? Can you really make a sound business decision with all of the ambiguity and risk inherent in just a single number? Using this technique, you can create a distribution of possible outcomes and adjust your business plan accordingly. By controlling the underlying distributions and assumptions, you can produce scenarios around assumptions you control the input to. Why not take advantage of the business acumen (which, coincidently, is one of those capability pillars we discussed in the previous chapter)? There is so much business knowledge in your organization that can inform all of the new methodologies and techniques you can employ.

Before delivering any results, your team sets up a plan to execute on Monte Carlo simulations. Now, this is not the only way to do this, but a way to start thinking about what types of flexibility you will need and how to construct your model. One of the first key inputs is to talk to various parts of your organization to tap into that business knowledge. First and foremost, you are probably delivering this model to your contracting team. They are tasked with understanding how the terms of their agreements will affect revenue generation. During their conversations, they are tasked with communicating both to internal and external organizations. Your analytics team's tasks are to collaborate with your contracting team to understand what metrics are key to communicating, in other words, what matters most. Externally, is it in terms of Medicare payments? Total revenue generated by the contract? What about internally? Depending on how your organization is structured, you could be asked to report on many different types of dimensions in aggregate, by service line definition, or by specific healthcare services classification systems. For instance, you may be asked to report inpatient services using Major Diagnostic Categories (MDCs) or diagnosis-related group (DRG) or for outpatient services using Ambulatory Payment Classifications (APCs). We could go on and list many different dimensions of reporting that would give your internal team the necessary information to understand the risks to their business plans. The point is, you need to understand the different types of reporting requirements meticulously to make sure your information is structured properly.

From there, your start to understand, as consultants love to say, "what levers can be pulled." In other words, what types of requirements you are putting into the contract, if any. This could be as simple as multiyear contract inflators, or specific rate schedules over the life of the contract. Are you implementing any specific types of products that you expect to drive utilization? It is these types of business requirements that your team needs to understand so the right inputs can be entered into the predictive model. It doesn't stop there. Next are internal business strategy discussions. What are you strategically trying to accomplish? What do your internal subject matter experts expect in terms of utilization changes? How will new pharmaceuticals, medical devices, and surgical techniques change your business? What other strategic plans can you add to the predictive model inputs to understand what your contract will yield? It is this type of due diligence that can create a predictive model that will generate a competitive advantage in your decision-making.

Now it's time for the exciting part: building the predictive model that delivers the necessary results. It's your team's ability to innovate and deliver a complex predictive model "under the hood" and what your organization will see is a Ferrari 250 GTO. Now, we are not going to get into the specifics of actually building the predictive model, but we offer some thoughts on the model. You will need to consider the types of underlying distributions for the predictive model and how you will effect these distributions over time. Are you creating distributions by specific dimensions, like inpatient versus outpatient encounters? How are you adjusting the distributions over the lifetime of the simulation? Are you making adjustments quarterly? Yearly? Not at all? What types of adjustments are being made? This is basically determined by your due diligence from speaking to all your internal customers. It can be as complex and granular as you desire. You need to consider what you expect the utilization to look like over the contract life. Are you looking at utilization monthly, quarterly, or annually? How are you adjusting the "out years"? Again, all basic types of questions you can explore to determine how complex a model you want to generate. One best practice we like to build is the number of simulations you would like to run. Depending on your requirements, build parameters, and granularity, how many simulations should you run? We believe the analytics team is best suited to answer this question. With today's technology (from in-database processing, referenced in Chapter 4, to cloud solutions, which will be discussed in Chapter 6), space considerations (on-prem or in the cloud) and time (computing time is fast!) are usually not a barrier. You can read many whitepapers or academic papers that suggest running between 5,000 and 20,000 simulations. Our best practice is to run simulations until we see stability that meets certain thresholds. This makes sure that, no matter what size your annual utilization is for the contract you are modeling, the simulations run until this stability threshold is met. When you think about multiyear simulations, we can be talking about results that can generate 50+ million simulation records, and depending on your organization's size, more than 10 billion simulation records could be created that will need to be aggregated.

Now that you have the results of your simulations, it is time to use this new technique to make your business decisions. Once again, your team's creativity and ingenuity can be highlighted. This can take a variety of options. From creating interactive visual solutions to help understand the risk of a specific level of revenue to using storytelling to help tell the story of the contract and its inputs by any of the dimensions available. The information now consumed is an understanding of different levels of potential revenue generation and the inherent risk associated with those levels. You contracting staff now has the ability to have a discussion without having to go back and ask your analytics team to rerun the simple type of models previously used. If your organization decides to plan conservatively, you make use of a revenue number generated at the bottom portion of the simulations. If your organization has strategic planning scenarios and one of those scenarios has aggressive assumptions, you can translate those assumptions into a revenue number in the upper portion of the simulation range and understand the probability that that revenue "could" happen. Now, you are able to change the decision-making conversation into a more constructive business planning process. You can understand the probabilities of hitting certain revenue targets, the probability your revenue target is exceeding your expectations. The Action phase is kicked up a notch now because there is no limit to the artistic way to consume the results. The resourcefulness and inventiveness of your analytics team will be pushed to the limits as the end users become more comfortable with using the new analytics and start to generate more thought-provoking, complex business questions. Many times, questions they were asked in the past could not really be answered insightfully and confidently because of the simplicity of earlier models and were always fraught with caveats. You know what I mean; there were always warnings, and forewarnings to those warnings, that paralyzed organizations from making decisions. Now with these new types of analytics, you can simulate many different assumptions and understand how those assumptions overlap through simulation comparisons to help assuage the fears of those single-number models. You can get to new deep-insight types of questions that will undoubtably come to mind that will increase your level of confidence so you can ultimately make that final decision with an understanding of the risk that used to plague you and eat away at your gut.

A final thought on your process journey. We would like to be able to tell you this journey seems as simple and clear-cut as above. In truth, the journey is intense and invigorating, stimulating your brightest minds to use their ingenuity. We are confident that your brightest minds will not disappoint you or your organization with their ability to provide a deeper understanding of the most complex analytical problems with clever, inventive, and even cunning solutions. However, it is an iterative process that continues to evolve. Do not think of the process as a hamster on a wheel. This is not to dishearten you, but to prepare you for the continuous improvement method that becomes embedded in your culture. Think about continuous improvement as a series of adventures. Sure, your journey will have its peaks and valleys. You will feel like you just summited Mount Everest. There will be times like you are in the Mariana Trench. Not only should you be celebrating those highs, you should be celebrating the learnings from those lows. In time, those lows become less noticeable, because you will be more proactive and not reactive and will be continuously celebrating highs. There is always a sense of satisfaction and goodwill when you are creating and implementing solutions, whether they are analytical or process oriented in nature, before the problems become perceptible.

CHAPTER **4**

Technology

"Data is a precious thing and will last longer than the systems themselves."

— Sir Tim Berners-Lee

We mentioned in Chapter 1 that the healthcare industry is collecting more data than ever before, in all varieties of structured and unstructured data. It was noted that, by 2020, healthcare data will exceed 2.314 zetta-bytes of data and is expected to increase by 48% annually. With all of this data, healthcare organizations are presented with great opportunities and greater challenges. There has never been a greater need for proactive and agile strategies to capture the opportunities and conquer the challenges with technology. Well-understood scenarios are fed by lots of data. The more data you have to draw from to examine dependencies and relation-ships, the better prediction and impact they will make to insight-driven decisions for healthcare. As the inventor of the World Wide Web, Sir Tim Berners-Lee accurately stated, "Data is a precious thing," and with the current landscape of technologies, there is so much healthcare organiza-tions can do to improve performance, economics, and governance.

What strategies and technologies should you consider? A list would include the following:

- Buying more hardware and software
- Process improvement to data management
- Data movement with analytics
- In-database
- In-memory
- Open source
- 3D printing
- Cybersecurity
- Virtual and mixed reality

How should you evaluate the technologies for organizational needs? Another list would include:

- Pros and cons for each technology with desired skillsets
- Costs integrating existing technology with new ones
- Benefits such as return on investment, scalability, and automation

In this chapter, we will focus on the challenges using traditional methodologies of data and analytics and how modern technologies such as in-database, in-memory processing, and open source technologies (Hadoop, Python, R, and Spark) are ideal for overcoming the challenges.

STATUS QUO

Healthcare professionals have shared with us their challenges and frustrations managing data and analytics in a fragmented environment. They are in search of technologies to help them streamline the processing of data and apply the analytics to all the data that are produced, collected, and stored. However, not all technologies can accommodate the specific needs of healthcare since it is so complex and in a disintegrated ecosystem. When we talk to healthcare professionals, these are some of the biggest and most common themes we hear:

- "My data is dispersed all over. Where do I go to get the data for analysis?"
- "How can I integrate the data administration with analytics to make my processes run faster?"
- "My analytical process takes days and weeks to complete, and by the time it is completed, the information is useless."
- "My staff is spending too much time with tactical data manipulation tasks and not enough time focusing on analytical exploration."
- "What I can do to retain my staff from leaving because their work is mundane and no longer challenging?"
- "How do we transform the way we work?"

We, as humans, are creatures of habit. We tend to accept the status quo when a process is working and may not get the attention when it is not broken. There is a saying, "If it ain't broke, don't fix it." This philosophy is very true and relatable when it comes to managing data and analytics in healthcare. Typically, data analysts, statisticians, or data scientists (as mentioned in Chapter 2) access and extract the data from a database or data warehouse to a server or their personal computer in order to analyze data. Traditionally, many healthcare professionals are approaching analytics by moving the data out of databases into a separate analytics environment for processing and then sending the results back to the database. This process was taught and practitioners were trained this way to analyze data to obtain insights. However, users have been sheltered from the fact that traditional approaches to data analysis required massive movement of data out of the database for analytical processing. This process is expensive and slow, due to the input/output of the network. The users have not had to contend with the fact that the habitual approach to analytics has imposed performance limitations as data was moved out of the database and into a separate analytics environment. The outcome from this process creates duplicate data and redundant data in many silos. They may not know where to look since the data is dispersed and not consolidated. Nor have they had to consider the security risks and exposure inherent in moving data from one environment to another. Figure 4.1 illustrates the traditional approach to analytics.

Figure 4.1 shows the common and traditional process and architecture used by many healthcare organizations to manage data and analytics. In this approach, data are collected from a variety of sources across multiple applications. The traditional approach has many moving parts and processes, including lots of data movement and replication. It presents many challenges within an organization – in particular data validation, data quality, performance, economics, and governance. The challenges and frustrations to the traditional process include:

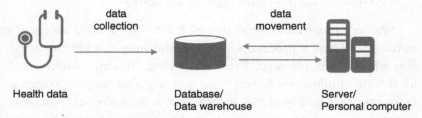

Figure 4.1 Traditional Approach to Data and Analytics
Source: Author.

■ Moving the data through the network can be extremely slow – just imagine transferring terabytes or petabytes of health data across a network that has limited bandwidth. This process can take days and weeks to complete. During this process, you may be negatively impacting your corporate network and the productivity of others within the healthcare organization.

■ Duplicating the data adds another component of cost and data silo to manage – by copying millions and billions of rows of data, there is another data set to maintain and support, which creates a data silo and adds additional costs to the infrastructure (for storage, backup, etc.).

■ Governing the data can be challenging – because data are scattered and collected from many sources to be analyzed, it is cumbersome to govern where the data are being stored, or how they are being used and analyzed.

In a conventional architecture, you have the data management process separate from the analytical application, and they are not likely integrated to streamline the process. Data management is a key element to having effective analysis of the data and the data preparation process within the data management side can be very time-consuming and labor intensive. Having separate processes and disconnected technologies can be costly and not very economical.

Applying the analytics where the data reside and leveraging the power of the database eliminates costs, time, data quality, and security issues associated with the traditional approach by simply processing the analytics in the data warehouse.

IN-DATABASE PROCESSING

In-database processing is defined as the integration of data analytic functions into the data platform such as a data warehouse or database. The concept of in-database processing is innovative. In-database processing was introduced in the mid-1990s, when database vendors such as Teradata, IBM, and Oracle made it commercially available with analytics vendors such as SAS, Fuzzy Logix, and SPSS. The in-database capabilities were still in their infancy and did not really catch on with customers until after 2010. The concept of migrating analytics from the analytical workstation or personal computers and into a centralized enterprise data warehouse sounded promising and too good to be true. Like anything new and innovative, industries such as healthcare were very wary of how in-database processing could work within their practices, architecture, and cultures. In addition, healthcare professionals were questioning what capabilities were present that would add value to their organization toward the adoption of the technology.

The need for this technology has become more evident as the amount of health data grows and becomes more complex. In the healthcare sector, the ability to collect and analyze data continues to grow at an alarming rate, largely due to the expansion and use of the Internet and mobile devices in the healthcare sector. With the amount of unstructured data being collected, the need for change from healthcare organizations has accelerated where performance gains of hours to seconds can make a difference in the decision-making offered by insights delivered by analytics that can be life or death. In addition, as more healthcare organizations rely on data and analytics to respond to important business challenges, the questions they ask have become more complex, which in turn mandates more sophisticated technologies and even more precise results. This insurgence of complex health data is one of the primary reasons for in-database processing – an enabling technology to gather, process, and analyze data efficiently and effectively.

In-database processing refers to the seamless integration of advanced analytics into the data platform functionality. Many organizations in financial, retail, and even government leverage this technology because it offers significant performance improvements over the traditional methods. Since its inception and increasing commercial availability, many business analysts have adopted in-database processing and have been able to realize the valuable business benefits. Figure 4.2 shows the in-database approach to integrating data management and analytics.

With in-database processing, healthcare professionals have the ability to explore the data, prepare it for analytics, develop complex data models, and score the model – the end-to-end capabilities within the database or data platform. By doing so, it removes the need either

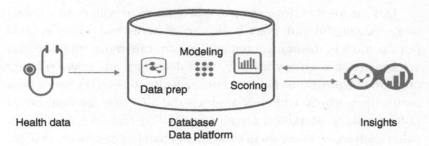

Figure 4.2 In-Database Processing Approach
Source: Author.

to move or extract the data to a different environment. This makes an in-database analytics approach faster, more efficient, more productive, and more secured than the traditional method. In-database processing delivers immediate performance, scalability, and governance improvements because data never leaves the database or the data platform. One of the main advantages of using the in-database method is eliminating the movement of data, which is accomplished by integrating the analytical functionality with the database.

By leveraging the in-database analytics capabilities, healthcare organizations can now make business decisions faster and that were not previously possible. By executing predictive or advanced analytics directly in a database, analysts can perform critical drill-downs and deep analyses that were previously not possible or practical. In addition, the in-database approach allows organizations to analyze more data faster, more accurately, and more cost-effectively than ever before in even the most complex, data-intensive healthcare industry.

Innovative and leading-edge organizations have realized that effective use of analytics enables them to outperform their competition and improve key processes such as patient care, product development, pricing, risk assessment and management, advanced research, and sales ultimately to increase the bottom line. It has become a common philosophy that the more advanced your analytical capabilities are, the better equipped healthcare organizations will be to structure and fine-tune successful business strategies for insight-driven decisions. These insight-driven decisions will increase profitability, productivity, efficiency, and even brand recognition.

This means that, for example, a healthcare provider can conduct more meaningful and exact healthcare analysis and create optimal pricing models. Insurance companies can run more effective risk assessments, proactively identify fraud detection, and develop better preventative programs. Pharmaceutical institutions can enhance their innovative portfolio with new products and offer new medications for faster recovery. Marketers are able to conduct real-time direct campaign analysis, enabling them to adjust or abandon campaigns in order to maximize returns on their marketing spend.

Cost of In-Database Processing

The value of in-database processing is quite clear but justifying the investment can be challenging. We often hear there is a lot of interest, but healthcare executives are concerned about the investment or costs to adopt and implement this technology. To adopt in-database processing, there will be some investment in software, hardware, and training the staff to a new a technology that affects the processing of data and analytics.

From the software perspective, there are technology vendors ranging from open source, small boutique startups to visionary market leaders. The open source vendors are starting to integrate with some of the database vendors to offer low-cost in-database processing capabilities. With open source, there is a large and growing user community to leverage free sample code that is easily accessible. However, this type of software can be limited to analyzing large, complex data because it is memory bound and is single-threaded processing for linear performance. Niche or small-boutique vendors are also entering the in-database solution area. They offer another low-cost alternative with more modern user interface for organizations whose staff prefer the nontraditional, line-by-line coding technique. However, the software may not have the depth and breadth and may not be certified as a standard in industries such as healthcare, insurance, or pharmaceutical. Finally, the visionaries or market-leading vendors offer the most robust and mature in-database solutions. Not only do they offer the depth and breadth of in-database functions, but they also deliver proven methodologies, integrated consulting services, and documented best practices. Professionals in healthcare can easily adopt these solutions with minimal disruption to their existing process or code to apply in-database processing.

As the name implies, in-database processing requires the database vendors to offer the hardware and software for the database to host the data for data management and analytics. Most database vendors that offer in-database solutions are visionaries and leaders. There are a select few open source companies that have started to work with the analytic vendors in the last couple of years. However, the database vendors have developed mature, high-performance technologies to enable the heavy lifting of data for analysis. Because in-database processing can impact the performance of the database, it may require additional hardware purchases to handle the additional capacity for executing analytics. In considering in-database technology, vendors may ask for the following details to configure the right solution:

- *What size is the data to be processed in-database?* Whether it is small (in the gigabytes) or large (in the terabytes), in-database processing can impact the performance of your production environment. Some healthcare organizations have a development or testing environment in the form of a data lab or sandbox to test before moving it into production. This best practice minimizes the impact of your production environment. Consider the largest data set that you are dealing with to apply in-database processing.

- *How many users will have access to the in-database capabilities?* If your healthcare organization is laser focused on having one department (such as the research group) only to have in-database technology, then the licensing and purchasing of the in-database solution can be minimal. However, if it is intended for enterprise-wide usage, then a bigger investment is needed in both software and hardware to accommodate the needs of the number of users for your business.

- *How many concurrent sessions may be running?* In-database processing may be used in many concurrent or parallel sessions at either an enterprise or departmental level to prepare the data and/or run the analytics. Depending on the size of your organization, consider giving one or two departments access to in-database capabilities first to show its value before enabling it throughout the enterprise. Consider setting priorities to more critical tasks that take a long time to process. You can also use a scheduler to arrange concurrent sessions for execution.

In-database processing will require some retraining on how users handle, manage, and analyze health data. As you select the vendor, consider how the users will need to transform the way they do things. Try, if possible, to select a solution that will minimally disrupt the current data preparation and analytic process. In addition, healthcare professionals will want to reuse existing code since it has been certified. If they are able to leverage the existing code and make minor tweaks, it will minimize the learning curve and disruption to the culture within the company. Acceptance and adoption will increase when change is minimal.

Depending on your healthcare organization's needs for in-database, the investment can be minimal. Selecting the appropriate in-database solution will make a big difference in value, adoption, and success.

IN-MEMORY PROCESSING

In-memory processing is another innovative approach to analyzing large amounts of health data. In-memory analytics is a method in which all the data used by an analytic application is stored within the main memory of the computing environment. Data is lifted into random-access memory (RAM) for analysis. Since the data can be kept in memory, multiple users can share data across various applications and the calculation is extremely fast, in a secured and parallel environment. In-memory processing also takes advantage of multi-threading and distributed computing, where you can distribute the data and complex workloads that process the health data across multiple clusters. Vendors such as SAS and Teradata are collaborating to offer in-memory processing. SAP, Spark, and other technology vendors also provide in-memory analytics.

There are significant differences between traditional and in-memory processing. The first and most significant difference between the traditional and in-memory approach is *where the data is stored* for analytics. Today, with the powerful hardware available commercially, healthcare organizations can fully take advantage of in-memory processing power instead of constantly transferring, meddling, or shuffling data residing on the disk. In the case of in-memory processing, the persistent storage is the data platform, but the data is read into memory when needed for analytics. The second difference and biggest advantage compared to traditional processing is *speed*. In-memory processing allows users to keep the data in memory and run iterative processing or jobs without having to go back and forth to the disk each time. The end users can quickly get answers without worrying about the infrastructure limitations for analytical experiments or testing. In addition, data scientists are not restricted to a small sample of data. They have all of the data and can apply as many analytic techniques and iterations as desired to find the answers in near real-time.

Figure 4.3 shows the in-memory approach to integrating analytics with data. In-memory processing is not only associated with queries, data exploration, and data visualization, but is also used with more complex processes like predictive analytics, prescriptive analytics, machine learning, and artificial intelligence. For example, regression, correlations, decision trees, and neural networks are all associated with in-memory processing.

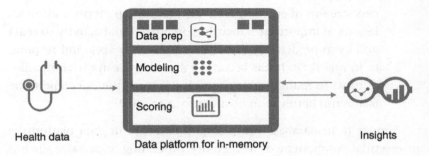

Figure 4.3 In-Memory Processing Approach
Source: Author.

In-memory analytics help to solve the following issues that challenge the traditional approach:

- *Obtaining immediate business insights from multiple health data sources:* In-memory processing can support complex analytical workloads with parallel scaling for increased performance, as compared to the traditional architecture. What has previously taken days or weeks to analyze via complex analytical models for strategic insights can now be executed in seconds and minutes.

- *Analyzing granular and deeper analytical insights using all of the health data as opposed to working with a small subset:* You can now take advantage of this innovative technology to uncover meaningful new research, mitigate unknown risks for drug development, and drive quality patient care with near real-time insights.

- *Integrating digital health data with new demographics and external audience:* This is the ability to be preemptive in analyzing tweets, postings, and texts. In order to gain competitive advantage, organizations need to discover, analyze, and proactively respond to different, changing, and fast-moving events that occur in volume such as social media. These events of interest are only apparent when they are understood and heard by the dependent parts of the organization. This requires event processing that follows through the organization in contextually relevant data-driven actions. The ability to ingest data and process streams of events effectively identifies patterns and correlations of importance, focusing organizational activity to react and even proactively drive the results they seek and respond to in real time. It has become a directive for many companies not just to maintain but continue to push the envelope to be faster and better with in-memory analytics.

Similar to in-database processing, a database or data platform is an essential component of in-memory processing, especially since it contains a set of health data that is integrated and refined. In addition, in-memory processing allows for more self-service for end users because there will be less dependence on IT to create, maintain, and administer aggregates and indexes of the data. In-memory processing also helps meet diverse and unplanned workloads for healthcare organizations that want to adopt artificial intelligence.

Need for Speed

In-memory processing is becoming the new or next-generation high-performance computing. Many vendors in this space have developed visually rich analytics features with click, drag-and-drop capabilities levering in-memory technology. With easy access to data and analytics, organizations are adopting in-memory processing to develop interactive health data dashboards and explore data without limits. There are a few vendors that offer in-memory for advanced analytics. With in-memory technology, healthcare organizations can now engage their data with blazing speed, resulting in more informed, proactive, insight-driven decisions.

Gartner Research[1] confirms that not only can data be retrieved faster, but in-memory technology performs complex calculations and query results significantly faster than disk-based approaches. This allows users to dissect data and create robust reporting without the limitations associated with traditional business intelligence (BI) tools such as multidimensional cubes or aggregate tables. Near real-time, ad-hoc query capabilities can be extended to even high volume and velocity for healthcare organizations.

Organizations are adopting in-memory processing to solve many issues in conjunction with the traditional approach and seeing the need to improve performance, economics, and governance. The needs are very similar to in-database processing and become the main drivers for many organizations in healthcare and other sectors. Here are some reasons for in-memory analytics:

Complex Analytics Requirements

Traditional IT infrastructures present a number of challenges, and one of them is to overcome the slow query performance supporting complex analytical requirements. It simply cannot keep

[1] Predicts 2019: In-Memory Computing at a Turning Point, Driven by Emerging Persistent Memory Innovation (December 2018).

pace with today's changing and dynamic data management and analytical requirements for fast and accurate analysis. In addition, it is not designed to process complex analytics on terabytes (or beyond) of data efficiently. This is where in-memory processing can help. In-memory processing can solve complex analytics that are often coupled with large data volumes.

Growing Big Data Volumes

Many enterprises are being challenged by a massive explosion of data in their databases and analytics applications. Traditional data is being captured and stored, along with unstructured forms of data files such as emails, notes, images, and freeform text (such as tweets, clinician comments/status, and other social media sources). At the same time, tighter regulations under the Health Insurance Portability and Accountability Act (HIPAA) and the Food and Drug Agency put the burden on healthcare providers and organizations to maintain and store data available for years to come in case of audits or requests from law enforcement agencies. In-memory processing makes access and analysis of large data volumes possible at incredibly fast speed and yields a higher return on investment.

Less Reliance on IT

With the presence of digital transformation and the explosion of web-enabled applications, healthcare organizations are discovering it is becoming harder to manage their data and analytical projects. With the traditional approaches, the queries and reporting are taking too long to execute because it takes too long to manipulate the data. In-memory processing eliminates complicated disk-based shuffling of data. There will be no need to wait for the IT bottleneck to build summary and aggregated tables to be used for analysis from the disk-based data. Business units can be more self-serving with in-memory processing. Self-service has driven a wider adoption of analytics because of the speed it offers to the users throughout the enterprise.

Enhanced User Interface

Vendors have developed very attractive and intuitive interactive data visualization solutions using in-memory technology, which have been adopted as the common front-end interface to analytical applications. With intuitive displays, it is a new paradigm for business analysts and IT users who are not accustomed to the grid style of analysis and reporting offered by relational databases and spreadsheets. Interacting and exploring data using in-memory visualization tools offer very user-friendly tasks such as clicking on a bar chart, line chart, or dragging data onto a scatter plot – and the ability easily to visualize the relationship of their data is a trendy concept.

Departmental Usage

In-memory processing is ideal for departmental applications, as users can analyze the full depth and breadth of health data since there are no practical limits to performing drill-down style capabilities. Organizations who have adopted in-memory analytics are able to facilitate a more exploratory, visual analysis of health data with access to common graphical user interface components such as sliders, radio boxes, and checkboxes offered via the user interface.

Although the need for in-memory processing is still growing, we are seeing huge benefits from organizations that have either adopted the technology or implemented in-memory processing. Here are some business and IT benefits.

Benefits with In-Memory Processing

Depending on the size of the organization and the use of in-memory processing for analytics, the benefits are truly remarkable. Organizations that implemented in-memory analytics see big transformations of their analytical processes, productivity, and culture within IT and business departments. There are tangible and intangible benefits using in-memory processing:

Impressive Performance Improvements

Data analysts are querying and interacting with data in-memory, which is significantly faster than accessing data from disk to execute complex analytics that are data volume intensive.

New Discovery, Interesting Insights

In-memory processing can give business users rapid execution of advanced analytics to deliver new levels of interesting insights to optimize healthcare operations or improve the decision-making process without the IT bottleneck. Sharing new discovery and interesting insights can help healthcare organizations and providers to provide better care and outcomes for their patients.

Widespread Adoption

The most valuable benefit that organizations are experiencing, albeit less recognized because it is an intangible one, is the ease of use which leads to a high adoption rate. In-memory processing allows business analysts and line-of-business managers to build their own reports, charts, graphs, and/or dashboards with very little training or technical expertise because of the intuitive interface that allows users simply to click, drag, and drop data for analysis. This also encourages significantly higher levels of user adoption due to the autonomy and sense of ownership that business analysts and nontechnical personnel have to explore their own data and not feel intimidated by the data and technology. The ultimate benefit is that the transformation shifts away from those who manage the data to the stakeholders who use, own, and analyze the data. In-memory analytics enable users to comprehend and expose their business in new ways and interactively explore big data without limits.

Ease the Overburdened Data Platform

In-memory processing offers the wonderful benefit of eliminating a big chunk of repetitive and expensive (in terms of central processing unit (CPU) usage and disk input/output (I/O)) processing that would normally be time-consuming and add to the burden placed on the database or data platform. With in-memory processing, the analytics engine pulls the data into memory from the data platform when it is needed. This process can be scheduled to populate the data as a batch or incremental load and/or overnight during off-peak hours. Thus, it alleviates the capacity demand by offloading the query from the data platform or database during peak interactive hours of the day. By easing the burden of the data platform, organizations can benefit from delivering faster performance, producing more reports per hour, and free up capacity on the source database servers or data warehouse for other data queries and purposes.

Enabling Departmental Applications

Companies are realizing the value of convenience and availability by setting up a mechanism for departments or workgroups to leverage in-memory analytics. I see two camps: one for the power users and the other for specific departments such as sales or marketing. In one extreme case, customers are setting up environments for power users to conduct high-performance analytics using in-memory technology and limit its use to perhaps the PhD students or statisticians. On the other hand, organizations are realizing the benefit of self-service environment for larger user groups for sales and marketing to operate autonomously using in-memory technology without impacting the data platform workload.

Ad-Hoc Analysis

Ad-hoc analysis is very limited or nonexistent in the traditional approach because it can take a significant amount of time to obtain the data from disk. In-memory analytics makes it possible to conduct ad-hoc analysis because of its infrastructure – data is lifted into memory only when it is needed for analysis. And it is in the true sense of the word, ad-hoc. In-memory analytics provides the ability to lift the data rapidly from the database or data warehouse and users can explore, discover, and build an analytic application to meet a specific task at hand. For example, let's consider exploring the relationship of age groups and recent usage of coupons that are delivered to customers via emails or smartphones. In this case, the analysis is undertaken and then programs can be built to offer more coupons and bigger incentives to the most loyal customers with even deeper discounts. It could be a flash sale or limited offers to attract customers and increase sales.

Now that the benefits are explained, let's examine the justification and how to get started for in-memory processing.

How to Get Started

With any new technology, there are questions and concerns about its capabilities and the value it brings into an organization. Organizations often have an analytics strategy and roadmap in mind before discussing the in-memory processing approach. Keep in mind that analytics tend to be high compute, whereas data management tasks are much more I/O intensive. Here are some things that you should consider justifying to get you started with in-memory processing for healthcare organizations:

Identify a Business Problem

Start by identifying the problem or opportunity. This is often obvious and perceived as a "no brainer," but it can be the most time-consuming and resource-intensive process. Every business has issues or problems but identifying "just" one to perform a proof of value or proof of concept can be challenging. Organizations definitely want to get the "biggest bang for the buck" effort, but not every problem can or should be solved with in-memory technology. It may not be available for run in-memory. However, if your organization is report-oriented and the infrastructure does not facilitate what-if analysis, interactive exploration of data, discovery of data patterns, and new opportunities, then adopting an in-memory technology can definitely be beneficial. Start small and grow/expand as needed once you are able to solve one problem and people will see value with the new technology.

Find Bottleneck Issues

With any organization, there are bottlenecks to any data-intensive process. Are the users expressing grievances about poor query response times? Do complex queries and analytical computations time out before completing? Does poor performance prevent asking business questions or any questions? If so, consider in-memory technology that delivers an integrated data management and analytics for the ultimate user experience. It is critical that the technology does not constrain users but offers flexibility and scalability in terms of data access, analysis, and reporting.

Check and Balance the Expected Benefits

In-memory processing will require some investment from the company in terms of new hardware, new software, professional services, and definitely training. Since an in-memory deployment involves supporting another data structure and analysis, it will need to involve support from IT and business sides to work together. In-memory investments have delivered great value and benefits but they may be hard to quantify and articulate to the leadership team. On one hand, the business side often is not aware of tangible benefits, lower cost of ownership benefits such as minimizing data movement, integrating the platform, and reducing administrative labor that would otherwise be required to make these queries run faster and more efficiently. On the other hand, you may have the IT side that would have to support the hardware maintenance and may not see the intangible benefits of ease of use, access for business analysts, and ad-hoc capabilities, so bringing the two sides together is critical. Organizations contemplating in-memory analytics often would develop a business case to justify the investment. Positioning in-memory analytics with the user communities and types of applications is critical in the cost-benefit analysis and overall analytics strategy.

Seek an Executive Sponsor

Having a senior corporate and executive sponsor for in-memory projects is a must. Many projects are unable to move forward (even after spectacular results) without having a senior management sponsorship. The sponsor provides the financial support and guidance on how to maneuver the political landscape within IT and business sides. In addition, this sponsor can help to identify the business problem that will help to drive innovation and increase the bottom line. Without a sponsor within an organization (albeit specially in healthcare), it is very challenging to justify the investment of new hardware, software, services, and training.

Finally, it is vital that you involve all parties – IT, business users, and sponsors – early in the decision process, as well as throughout the practical side. When they participate in the decision process, I witness higher success rates and on-time, on-budget delivery of tasks.

Requirements

Many vendors offering in-memory technologies offer similar capabilities features, functionality, and infrastructure. However, the success or failure of in-memory processing is dependent on the technology selected to be the delivery platform. Organizations that adopted this technology say that the platform needs to be web-enabled/centric as their primary requirement. Beyond the web-enabled requirement, here are some other essential technology-driven prerequisites to consider:

Integration with Your Existing Technologies

The need for a data platform is still prevalent for in-memory processing. While some vendors convey or advertise that in-memory processing does not require or avoid developing a data platform, this option may work for smaller organizations that have only a single data source or a small system. However, for larger companies that typically have multiple data sources or larger, more complex systems, the data warehouse is still the ideal platform to capture, transform, and integrate the data for analysis. This is where the in-database capability can be part of the overall infrastructure. As you explore and consider in-memory solutions, make sure that they can be integrated with the existing data platform and business intelligence (BI) environments. An in-memory solution normally comes with visualization capabilities and it can tap into the BI applications and data platform to discover data patterns, develop complex data models, and deliver insights to the web or mobile devices for enterprise consumption.

Scale for Fit

Most if not all organizations tend to start small to enable in-memory processing for a specific department. If you fail to scale correctly, the proof of concept (POC) can yield poor performance and underdeliver the promise of in-memory processing. Get a solution architect involved to ensure that the proposed architecture meets the needs of the department and obtain a system that has enough memory to process the data and analytics. Once proven to show value and a positive return on investment (ROI), the vast majority will upgrade to a bigger platform and add more memory to handle additional data for high-performance analyses. Therefore, it is important to select a solution that can scale linearly as you grow. When you add more data, more complex analytics, more analytical data models, and more data, ensure that the technology can scale to support today's and tomorrow's requirements. Therefore, it is critical that you select a solution that can provide enterprise-class infrastructure that enables you to grow and expand.

Data Refresh

Whether you create reports or build an analytical data model, data are extracted from a source system, most likely from a data warehouse. In-memory processing lifts the data directly from the source system into in-memory nodes, and data latency can be a concern. There are service-level agreements where reports or analytics have to be delivered within a specific window of time. Therefore, an in-memory solution will need high-speed connectivity to the data platform so that the data can be extracted ad-hoc or otherwise can be scheduled for incremental data loads during off-peak hours. Having the flexibility to refresh data in near real time for in-memory processing is a powerful benefit for insight-driven decisions.

Data Security

Depending on the vendor you select and the infrastructure for in-memory processing, there is a higher potential risk of exposing high volumes of data to more end users than ever. This raises data security concerns:

- How is the data accessed?
- Who can access the data?
- Where is the data stored?
- How much data is analyzed?
- Who can see and distribute the data and analyses?
- Can the information can be circulated to mobile devices for information sharing?

In recent months, there have been a number of data security breaches globally in both the private and public sectors. Thus, selecting a solution that has heightened data governance and data security capabilities can alleviate major headaches, costly remedies, and public embarrassment. A vendor that has a solution around a centralized data server such as a data warehouse or database is the most secured and enables IT to govern the data in a highly secured environment. With a centralized data repository, such as a data warehouse, in-memory processing can adapt and conform to your organization's data security measures. Another recommendation is to identify the users with certain rights and privileges to access sensitive data and adjust as the employees change their role or job function within the company. In healthcare, the integrity of an organization lies within its security and the sensitive data that needs to be protected from hackers.

Cost of In-Memory Processing

To obtain the increased speed and performance from in-memory processing, there is investment or cost associated with the hardware and software. It depends on the vendor and the architecture that you choose to select for your healthcare organization. Every vendor offers different options when it comes to in-memory technology. On the hardware side, you will likely need a separate server to host the in-memory processing. The nodes that reside in the server should be dedicated for in-memory processing. When sizing the hardware, you should work with the vendor to configure the system appropriately by providing the vendor the following information based on your organization's requirements:

How Many Analysts Will Need Access to the Environment? In this case, the environment refers to the software and the server that supports in-memory processing. As users/analysts access the data from the data platform and lift it into in-memory for analysis, the size of the server should be configured correctly to meet the needs of the number of analysts. We normally suggest starting with 10 users at most to access and test the environment. Once your organization sees the value and robustness of the technology, expand the user base and usage.

How Many Concurrent Analyses Will Be Running?

In-memory processing may be used in many parallel or competing analyses from an enterprise or departmental level. Depending on the size of your organization, consider one or two departments first to have access to in-memory processing and run parallel sessions such as in-memory machine learning and specific domain such as data mining to see the gains in performance. As your organization expands the number of jobs to run, you may consider scheduling these processes and set priorities.

What Is the Volume of Data That Will Be Lifted into Memory?

The amount of the data determines the number of nodes needed in the server. Whether it is in the gigabytes or petabytes, the software and hardware need to be configured to analyze your largest data set. Most of the organizations that leverage in-memory processing are in the petabytes. Keep in mind that the nodes in the server are all dedicated to running in-memory processing. Thus, you will get superior speed and performance for complex, advanced analytics tasks that are data- and compute-intensive because of the dedicated memory.

On the software side, there are solutions that offer in-memory data visualization with deep analytical capabilities. In addition, there are specific domain in-memory processing packages for data mining, statistics, forecasting, econometrics, text mining, and optimization. If a customer is looking for industry-specific in-memory solutions, there are anti-money-laundering, risk, and marketing optimization. Depending on your needs, we advise adopting one solution and testing it out to see if it meets the requirements of your business. Once you have proven it to be successful, you can expand the hardware and adopt additional software packages to extend the use of in-memory processing.

OPEN SOURCE TECHNOLOGY

When we discuss the topic of technology for data and analytics, we must include the availability of open source technologies that are being adopted in healthcare organizations globally. Open source software has existed for over 20 years. Today, open source software is everywhere and includes operating systems, mobile applications, Internet connectivity, data management, and analytics applications. Open source software has enabled new ways of doing business and provided a paradigm shift to sharing code and algorithms for online communities.

Open source software grew in popularity and significance in the era of big data in the early 2010s. The emergence of big data spurred the exploration and adoption of open source technologies to manage the variety, volume, and velocity of big data. Big data comes in many shapes and forms and impacts many industries. Table 4.1 shows the data sources that are considered as big data and the description of the data impacting various industries.

The variety of data encompasses everything from call center voice data to genomic data from health research and medicine. Healthcare

Table 4.1 Data Sources

Type Data	Description
Black Box	Data from airplanes, helicopters, and jets capture voices and recordings of the flight crew and the performance information of the aircraft.
Power Grid	Power grids data contain information about consumption by a particular node and customer with respect to a base station.
Sensor	Sensor data come from machines or infrastructure such as ventilation equipment, bridges, energy meters, or airplane engines. Can also include meteorological patterns, underground pressure during oil extraction, or patient vital statistics during recovery from a medical procedure.
Social Media	Sites such as Facebook, Twitter, Instagram, YouTube collect a lot of data points from posts, tweets, chats, and videos by millions of people across the globe.
Stock Exchange	The stock exchange holds transaction data about the "buy" and "sell" decisions made on shares of different companies from the customers.
Transport	Transport data encompasses model, capacity, distance, and availability of a product such as a car, truck, merchandise, medical equipment, etc.
Traditional (CRM, ERP, etc.)	Traditional data in rows and columns coming from electronic health records (EHRs), electronic medical records (EMRs), customer relationship management (CRM), enterprise resource planning (ERP), financials about a product, customer, sales, etc.

Source: Author.

organizations that learn to take advantage of complex, unstructured data will gain real-time information from sensors, radio frequency identification, and other identifying devices to understand their business environments at a more granular level, to create new products and services, and to respond to changes in usage patterns as they occur. In the health sciences, such capabilities may pave the way to treatments and cures for threatening diseases.

If you are collecting any or all of the data sources referenced in Table 4.1, then your traditional computing techniques and infrastructure may not be adequate to support the volumes, variety, and velocity of the data being collected. Many organizations may need a new data platform that can handle exploding data volumes, variety, and velocity. They also need a scalable extension for existing IT systems in data management, archiving, and content management. Thus, open source software can fulfill these needs with its ecosystem of technologies. Open source technology is not just a storage platform for data; it is also a computational platform for analytics. This makes open source software ideal for companies that wish to compete on analytics in healthcare.

For the remainder of this chapter, we will discuss Hadoop, Spark, R, and Python, as they are the most popular open source technologies in healthcare for business analysts and data scientists.

HADOOP

As your business evolves, a data warehouse may not meet the requirements of your healthcare organization. Organizations have information needs that are not completely served by a data warehouse. The needs are driven as much by the maturity of the data use in business as they are by new technology.

For example, the relational database at the center of the data warehouse is ideal for data processing to what can be done via SQL. Thus, if the data cannot be processed via SQL, then it limits the analysis of the new data source that is not in row or column format. Other data sources that do not fit nicely in the data warehouse include text, images, audio, and video, all of which are considered as unstructured data. This is where Hadoop enters the architecture.

Hadoop is a family of products (Hadoop Distributed File System (HDFS), MapReduce, Pig, Hive, HBase, Impala, Nifi, Mahout, Cassandra, YARN, Ambari, Avro, Chukwa, and Zookeeper), each with different and multiple capabilities. Please visit www.apache.org for details on these products. These products are available as native open source from Apache Software Foundation (ASF) and the software vendors.

Once the data are stored in Hadoop, analytics applications can be used to analyze the data. Figure 4.4 shows a simple standalone Hadoop architecture.

- *Unstructured Data Sources:* The unstructured data cannot be stored in a relational database (in column/row format). These data sources include email, social data, XML data, videos, audio files, photos, GPS, images, sensor data, spreadsheets, web log data, mobile data, RFID tags, and PDF docs.

- *Hadoop:* The Hadoop Distributed File System (HDFS), which is the data storage component of the open source Apache Hadoop project, is ideal for collecting the unstructured data sources. (However, it can also host structured data as well.) For this example, it is a simple architecture to capture all of the unstructured data. Hadoop HDFS is designed to run on less expensive commodity hardware and is able to scale out quickly and inexpensively across a farm of servers.

- *Analytics Applications:* This is the analysis and action component using data from Hadoop HDFS. These are the applications, tools, and utilities that have been natively built for users to access, interact, analyze, and make decisions using data in Hadoop and other nonrelational storage systems. *MapReduce*

Health data
Unstructured data

Hadoop

Analytics
Applications

Figure 4.4 Hadoop Architecture
Source: Author.

is a key component of Hadoop. It is the resource management and processing component of Hadoop and also allows programmers to write code that can process large volumes of data. For instance, a programmer can use MapReduce to capture electronic health record (EHR) clinical notes and other narrative data for comprehensive analysis of a patient's history. In addition, MapReduce can process the data where it resides (in HDFS) instead of moving it around, as is sometimes the case in a traditional data warehouse system. It also comes with a built-in recovery system – so if one machine goes down, MapReduce knows where to go to get another copy of the data. Although MapReduce processing is fast when compared to more traditional methods, its jobs must be run in batch mode. This has proven to be a limitation for organizations that need to process data more frequently and/or closer to real time.

Since the inception of Hadoop, there has been a lot of noise and hype in the market as to what Hadoop can or cannot do. It is definitely not a silver bullet to solve all data management and analytical issues. Keep in mind that Hadoop is an ecosystem of products and provides multipurpose functions to manage and analyze big data. It is good at certain things but it has its shortcomings as well:

- *Not a Database:* Databases provide many functions that help to manage the data. Hadoop has HDFS, which is a distributed file system and lacks the database functions such as indexing, random access to data, support for standard SQL, and query optimization. As Hadoop matures and evolves, these functions will likely be part of the ecosystem. For now, you may consider HBase over HDFS to provide some DBMS functionality. Another option is Hive, which provides an SQL-like interface to manage data stored in Hadoop.

- *Low Data Value:* The frequency at which data are accessed – often described as its "temperature" – can affect the performance and capability of the warehouse. Hadoop lacks mature query optimization and the ability to place "hot" and "cold" data on a variety of storage devices with different levels of performance. Thus, Hadoop is often complemented with a DBMS, to process the data on Hadoop and move results to the data warehouse.

- *Lacks User Interface:* Users who prefer a user interface for ease of use may not find it with Hadoop. This is one big drawback from customer's feedback. However, many vendors are creating applications to access data from Hadoop with a user interface to fill this gap.

- *Deep Learning Curve:* Hadoop has a deep learning curve since it is an emerging technology and subject matter experts are few and far between. Once you have learned Hadoop, the writing of code can be very tedious, time-consuming, and costly. Because it is open source, the reliability and stability of the environment can create issues.

- *Limited Data Manipulation:* Joining data is a common practice to prepare data for analysis. For simple joins, Hadoop offers tools to accommodate those needs. However, for complex joins and SQL, it is not efficient. This process will require extensive programming, which requires time and resources from your organization.

- *Lacks Security:* Hadoop lacks security features common in RDBMSs, such as row- and column-level security, and it provides minimal user-level controls, authentication options, and encryption. In recent years, security has been enhanced to alleviate some of the security concerns.

For the above reasons, organizations should consider integrating Hadoop with a data warehouse. The combination of Hadoop and the data warehouse offers the best of both worlds, managing structured and unstructured data and optimizing performance for analysis.

SPARK

Spark is an open source framework from Apache. It is commonly used for analyzing big data and has a powerful engine for advanced analytics for machine learning (which will be discussed later in Chapter 7,

Future). Spark leverages in-memory processing, which allows queries and analytical computations to run very fast and delivers results quicker to data scientists and business analysts. Spark was developed to augment the limitations of Hadoop MapReduce. Such limitations are scalability, security, near-real-time streaming of data, input/output cost, healthcare analytics complexity, and low latency. Spark is capable of handling petabytes of data at a time where data is distributed across a cluster of multiple servers. It has an extensive set of developer libraries and APIs and supports languages such as Java, Python, R, and Scala. Its flexibility makes it well-suited for a range of use cases as described below.

Data Preparation and Integration

Health data produced by fragmented systems across an institution is rarely clean, integrated, or consistent to simply and easily be combined for analytics and reporting. Extract, transform, and load (ETL) processes are often used to integrate data from different systems, standardize it, and then load it into a system for analysis. Spark is used to reduce the cost and time required for this ETL process.

In-Stream Processing

From log files to sensor data, healthcare institutions are increasingly having to manage and handle streams of data. This data arrives in a steady stream, often from multiple sources simultaneously. While it is certainly feasible to store these data streams on disk and analyze them retrospectively, it can sometimes be critical to process and act upon the data as it arrives. Streams of data related to healthcare transactions, for example, can be processed in real time proactively to identify and deny potentially fraudulent transactions.

Prescriptive Analytics

As data volumes grow, prescriptive analytics approaches become more feasible. Algorithms can be trained to identify and prescribe actions upon triggers within well-understood data sets before apply-ing the same solutions to new and unknown data. Spark's ability to store data in memory and rapidly run repeated queries makes it a good choice for prescriptive analytics. Processing similar queries continually and at scale significantly reduces the time required to go through a set of possible solutions in order to find the most efficient treatment.

Interactive Insights

Since Spark leverages in-memory processing, it can respond and adapt to queries on-the-fly and enables data scientists to test more theories, ask more questions, and explore more data. Dashboards can be built interactively with new data and deliver new insights to healthcare institutions operations.

Since its inception, Spark has been used and adopted in health-care organizations to manage and analyze data for various projects with large volumes of data. EHRs collect and store massive volumes of data. Spark is able to aggregate various sources of data from EHRs, research, and development health data for insight-driven decisions. Traditionally, clinicians use their judgment while making treatment decisions but, in the last decade, there has been a shift toward evidence-based medicine. This involves systematical assess-ment of clinical data and making treatment decisions based on the best and latest information using Spark. Spark is designed to com-bine individual data sets into analytical algorithms effectively. Once executed, the results provide the most robust evidence to develop a treatment. This process alleviates the small sampling of data and allows clinicians to analyze all available data within a population of a particular disease.

Such other use cases are analyzing patient records along with past clinical data to detect which patients are likely to encounter health issues after being discharged from the hospital. This analy-sis can prevent hospital readmittance as clinicians can deploy home healthcare services to the patient, saving on costs for both the hospi-tals and patients. Spark is utilized in genomic sequencing to reduce the time needed to process complex genome data. Traditionally, it took several weeks to organize all the chemical compounds with genes and now it takes just hours using Spark. This use of Spark might not be so real-time as others but delivers considerable benefits to clinicians and researchers over the traditional approach for genomic sequencing.

PYTHON

According to *Harvard Business Review* in 2015, being a data scientist is considered the sexiest job of the twenty-first century. The popularity of being a data scientist around the world is presented with excitement with complex data problems to solve. To break down the role of a data scientist, it is a profession that explores data and interprets the relationships of the data. In simpler terms, a data scientist's role is to analyze all data to deliver actionable insights. Within the complex questions, insights are discovered through mountains of health data across many systems. In order to obtain insights, data scientists often rely on popular programming languages and tools such as Python and R.

Python is a flexible programming language that can do everything from mining data to designing applications. It is popular among recent graduates and academic institutions since it is open source, has no cost for the code base, and can be easily downloaded via the web. Its design value is based on the importance of being simple and producing human-readable code. Algorithms in Python are designed to be easy to read and write for a wide range of users, from beginners to advanced users. Python is a language data scientists and business analysts can use for practically every data management and analytics process (see Figure 4.5) thanks to its versatility.

Health data   Python, R, etc.   Data Analysis   Insights

Figure 4.5 Data Analysis with Python and R
Source: Author.

Many data scientists use Python to help solve their data and analytics problems. As much as 40% of the open source online community is using Python based on a data science survey[2] conducted by O'Reilly in 2013.

One of the strengths of open source technology is the online community filled with brilliant and versatile professionals who collaborate together to promote and push Python and its associated packages forward. Healthcare professionals in data science can find answers to many questions via the python.org website.[2] There are literally tens of thousands of users online and the community has been continually growing over the years. The online user community develops and publishes many types of analytical libraries, even specialized ones for healthcare. You can find all kinds of open source code libraries for solving specific data and analytics problems.

Python is like a Swiss Army knife that provides data management and analytics capabilities. This popular programming language allows users to collect raw data with support for all kinds of different data formats, process the data with its extensive libraries for data analysis (such as Pandas), and explore the data for insights. Using Pandas data analysis libraries, business analysts can easily scan and clean the data. Data scientists can take the data and apply complex calculations such as deep learning models or time series analysis to review weekly admissions to the emergency departments with just a few lines of code from the online community. Python offers the capability to visualize your data in various plots and graphs options. Plots and graphs can be simple or complex depending on your organization's needs.

Python is a powerful, versatile, high-performance language that can be used to solve your data and analytics problems from end-to-end. It is very popular in the data science profession, with a large presence in the online community for accessing and sharing code. It can be learned even if you are a nonprogrammer with its easy to read coding, simple syntax, and ease of implementation. After all, it is open source and free, which makes it appealing for startups and smaller companies.

[2] https://www.oreilly.com/ideas/2013-data-science-salary-survey.

R

R is another open source technology and is a programming language dedicated specifically to solving statistical analysis that originated out of the academic community. R is even more popular than Python within the data science community (although the gap is rapidly closing). In the same survey[2] as referenced above, 43% of data scientists use R in their profession compared to 40%. Unlike Python, it is not a Swiss army knife that has uses outside of statistical analysis. R was developed for and specializes in solving data science problems as it was created by computer scientists. Because it is so specialized, there is a steeper learning curve and it can have more complex syntax and less human-readable code when compared to Python.

Among organizations with data scientists, R really shines and stands out when it comes to developing statistical data models and visualizing the results. R has an environment with a variety of statistical and graphing functions ranging from time series to classification, the majority of which are available from a single location on the Internet. In the role of a data scientist, building regressions models and testing for statistical value of results is a common task. R is very well suited for developing those models, from bell curves to Bayesian analysis to time series analysis. There are many online contributors to R code and libraries which can you get started using and leveraging R.

R can also collect raw data from most of common data sources, albeit not as robust as Python. The R community is working on developing modern packages for R data collection to address this limitation. Adding new columns of information and transforming the data is readily available within R. Exploring the data with R is one of the biggest strengths since it was built from ground up for statistical and numerical analysis for large data volumes. Data scientists can easily access libraries to build probability distributions, apply a number of statistical tests to the data, and utilize advanced data mining techniques. Like Python, R has the ability to display and visualize the data with its suite of scientific packages for visualization and graphical displays. You can save these files in various formats (such as jpg and PDF) to share the results with your organization.

R is another programing language within the open source portfolio of technologies. It is free and purposely designed for data analysis. Users can freely install, use, update, clone, modify, redistribute, and resell R. Very popular among the data scientist community, R is sometimes called the "golden child" of data science. Its commercial applications are growing over the years and organizations are adopting it for its versatility.

R is also considered the best language option for complex, resource, and data-intensive calculation and it can be used on high-performance computer clusters. R has a large, vibrant population of contributors estimated to be 2 million users who are very passionate and dedicated, interacting on discussion forums. With more than 2,000 free libraries published, there is code covering a number of statistical use cases.

OPEN SOURCE BEST PRACTICES

Here are some best practices (dos and don'ts) based on our experience. Keep in mind that best practices will continue to grow as the technology matures into the mainstream and is adopted. Here are some for you to consider now:

Start Small and Expand

Every organization has many projects, and you rely heavily on technology to solve your business needs. You have probably heard you should focus on a project that gives you the biggest bang for your buck. For open source technology, identify a small project with an immediate need. Too many times projects fail in organizations due to the level of complexity, lack of resources, and high expenses. Selecting a small project to get started allows the IT and business staffs to become familiar with the interworking of this emerging technology. The beauty of open source is that it allows you to start small and add/expand as you go.

Implement Change Management

These open source packages are updated frequently, as are the support for packages and libraries. As these are community developed code, there may be a lack of regression testing undertaken with each new release. So, when a new base package or library is released, it will frequently not work the way the previous versions did or not work at all. This lack of testing is a major problem if there are models in production that rely on these packages. Before any new packages or updates are applied, there needs to be an extensive regression testing within the organization to ensure that the models continue to work as expected.

Monitor the Infrastructure

The open source technology is an ecosystem and there are many parts with multipurpose functions. These moving parts relate to the data and management level and it is recommended to monitor the infrastructure. By monitoring the infrastructure, you can detect problems before they occur and know problems immediately when issues arise such as disk capacity or failure.

Adopt a Data Integration Process

The process of integrating data is very critical. Open source technologies can store all data, both structured and unstructured. You can populate the data and you can define the structure at a later time. Ensuring that the data are standardized, named, and located up front can help to make it easier for analysis. The integration process enhances reliability and integrity of the data.

Implement a Multiple Environment Infrastructure

Build multiple environments (development, test, production) infrastructure. Not only is this a common best practice but it is also vital because of the nature of open source and its nature of instability. Each project within the open source environment is constantly changing and having a nonproduction environment to test upgrades and new functionality is critical. Having one environment such as production only tends to pay the price when the issues arise and upgrades are not successful.

Leverage the Open Source Community

Every project has its hiccups. When things go wrong, you have a local or online community. The open source community consists of millions of users globally and there is a very good chance the problem you are having is just a quick click away using online search engine. The open source ecosystem continues to mature and the community is a great resource to resolve your issues.

There is no question that health data is either too voluminous or not structured enough to be managed and analyzed through traditional means and approaches. Open source technologies can complement your traditional architecture to support the structured and unstructured health data that you are collecting. With new approaches and technologies to manage complex health data, it has prompted organizations to rethink and restructure from the business and IT sides. Managing data has always been in the forefront, and analytics has been more of an afterthought. Now, it seems inevitable for health institutions to bring analytics to the forefront along with data management. Organizations need to realize that the world we live in is changing, and so is the health data. It is practical for healthcare organizations to recognize these changes and react quickly and intelligently to evolve in a global economy. In the healthcare sector, the new paradigm is no longer stability – it is now agility and discovery to bring healthcare into and beyond the twenty-first century. As the volume of health data explodes, organizations will need a platform to support new data sources and analytic capability. As the industry evolves, the open source architecture will develop into a modern information ecosystem that is a network of optimizing insight-driven decisions, communicating code, and results, and generating new, strategic value for healthcare. Regardless of the technology, clinical judgment is a key component that is always needed in healthcare and will not go away in our lifetime.

5

Unifying People, Process, and Technology

"It doesn't make sense to hire smart people and tell them what to do; we hire smart people so they can tell us what to do."

— Steve Jobs

In order for an organization to be a leader in analytic maturity and create a competitive advantage, you need to develop an analytics strategy. An organization cannot just throw technology at the problem and expect to "win." It should be a strategy around four pillars. The pillars are around data, people, process, and technology and we covered each of these pillars in the previous chapters. Each one of these pillars will play a crucial role when executing your strategy. The order in which you address each of these pillars is based on your organization and the support you have from senior executives. Ultimate success is executing on all four pillars and is a journey which may take years to complete.

In the 2000s, healthcare work was usually completed in siloes. Figure 5.1 shows the traditional silos or domains organizations typically worked in, and healthcare institutions are no exception. The operational silo is where business intelligence usually existed. They were responsible for data mining, querying, reporting, delivering decision-making dashboards around various business needs, from utilization

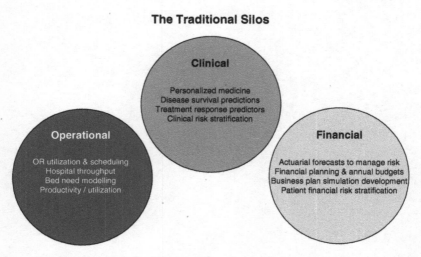

The Traditional Silos

Clinical

Personalized medicine
Disease survival predictions
Treatment response predictors
Clinical risk stratification

Operational

OR utilization & scheduling
Hospital throughput
Bed need modelling
Productivity / utilization

Financial

Actuarial forecasts to manage risk
Financial planning & annual budgets
Business plan simulation development
Patient financial risk stratification

Figure 5.1 Traditional Work Silos
Source: Author.

and scheduling to throughput and productivity. The clinical silo housed caring for the patient, from personalized medicine to chronic disease management to clinical risk stratification. The financial silo is where financial planning, budgeting, service line management, and business planning existed. Each of these silos may have had their own tools, technologies, and data warehouses to accomplish the tasks of turning raw data into insights and getting actionable information to decision-makers.

In this constantly changing healthcare landscape, the work that used to be housed in those traditional silos does not vanish and continues to get more complex. There is still work that belongs in those three domains driving operations and continuity in healthcare. Figure 5.2 illustrates how the work in the traditional silos of clinical efforts, operational management, and financial responsibility becomes more integrated and requires the three traditional silos to work together as the complexity of caring for patients transitions into population health management activities.

This converging work requires changes to culture. Whereas traditional work silos created a sense of ownership for their work, a new sense

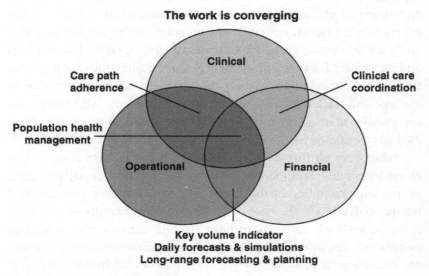

Figure 5.2 The Work Is Converging
Source: Author.

of ownership is now evolving, one where the mindset changes from individual ownership to group ownership. When you think about care path adherence, it is operational ownership creating the necessary operational workflows in the systems and the clinicians creating comprehensive treatment plans. Both have ownership with their respective expertise, but need to own the work jointly to ensure efficiency and success. Operational and financial metrics cannot be measured independently. As emphasis on care delivery and payment models develops, it requires a confluence of operational metrics and financial metrics to succeed in these new models. Clinical care coordination brings together clinical and financial owners to help solve limited resources on both sides to make sure we are able to treat all patients. All three of the silos or domains eventually unite in the body of work called population health management. There is no one single owner. It requires coordination between clinical, operational, and financial owners to improve healthcare outcomes. Data, people, process, and technology needs to create a comprehensive platform where clinical, operational, and financial data are connected seamlessly for enterprise consumption. Your enterprise data platform along with the right analytical tools will create opportunities for clinical, operational, and financial efficiencies. Some of the characteristics of a successful population health management program are leveraging data and analytics to produce real-time or near-real-time insights for clinicians and operations for specific patient segments, addressing care gaps and throughput. In addition, disease management solutions are able to manage and track costly chronic conditions, promote well-being, and successfully manage growing financial risk–based contracts and bundled payment models.

What does all this have in common? It is a culture change. It is about leveraging data, people, process, and technology daily to get a deeper understanding of the health of populations we manage. It is where analytics is at the core of keeping patients healthy and treating those patients who are sick or have chronic diseases. It is capturing, integrating, and interpreting data from all available sources. It is about predictive algorithms that surface opportunities for intervention and prevention. There is plenty of hype and excitement that artificial intelligence (AI) will solve all of our healthcare issues. We are using *AI* as if it were a verb or an action that can be easily taken. As we continue to solve problems facing healthcare daily, we seem to say, "Let's AI it," as if we can just throw some algorithms at the problem and it will vicariously solve our healthcare issues. We would like to think it is the thoughtful use of augmented intelligence, that is, human judgment and knowledge combined with AI to improve clinical decision support, operational planning, and financial outcomes. It requires new skills, knowledge, and talent pipelines for our existing and future analysts and leaders. The promise of AI is high but not everything is best solved with AI.

The culture change is about valuing data as an asset, collaboration between teams, or a team of teams approach to prioritize resources and projects that will use analytics to drive positive return on investment. Cultural change also means having leadership that is passionate about using analytics daily and developing analytical talent throughout the organization. It means we will take many approaches with trial and error to achieve success.

First, data will be treated as an asset. The data hygiene cycle will create "clean" data through two avenues. The first avenue will be around the development of enterprise standards, that is, cataloging, metadata management, and development of a business glossary. This ensures that all of an organization's caregivers understand the technical information surrounding the data, from the data definition to the source to calculations to data reliability to how the data should be applied. The second avenue will be a three-prong approach using information security, data quality, and master data management. Information security will make sure the data is accessed according to HIPAA compliance standards. Data quality will ensure rules-based checks are made to ensure only cleaned data that passes is available for analysis. Data stewards will focus on tactical processes to correct the data at the source. Master data management will create the "golden" records for critical domains identified by your organization. Examples of these critical domains are patients, providers/physicians, location and reference tables. This will provide a single point of reference for these critical domains and ensure consistency in analytic endeavors. Scorecard dashboards will sit on top of this three-prong approach to help the organization understand the data's grade.

Second, we will take a team-of-teams approach to solve problems. The team-of-teams approach is a cultural shift that combines adaptability and agile using small teams to harness the power of your organization. It's about the continuous cycle of changing and assessing and changing rapidly. This helps teams realize there is no perfect solution, since none exists, and delivers minimally viable projects that are enhanced over time. The book *Team of Teams* by General Stanley McChrystal is a great read for those looking to get a more thorough understanding. We will leverage sponsors who will be engaged in using analytics and who see the value added in using analytics, whether it be clinical predictive algorithms to help produce positive outcomes, operational forecasts and simulations to optimize operational metrics, or financial predictive models to create long-range financial plans. The sponsors will be a positive voice and commit to sharing success with the organization and help create opportunities for others. This team-of-teams approach ensures collaboration as a shared effort. The analytics and technology teams, along with the team associated with the sponsor, will work hand-in-hand from data to intelligence to action. The collaboration will make sure we're focused on delivering the most valuable work and service to the organization. We will bring the end users closer to the process. Everyone involved will have accountability.

Third, leadership will play a lead role. The characteristics that will emerge are their support and awareness in building analytical capabilities, and that they demonstrate fact-based analytical decision-making, challenge others in the organization to follow their lead, and are not afraid to push the limits. Building analytical capabilities does not require you to "know the math"; it requires awareness of techniques and tools that are being used to solve particular business problems and the limitations they present. Leaders will demonstrate their fact-based analytical decision-making using outputs from the analytical projects they commission or those that are created by the analytics team. As stated by W. Edwards Deming, cited in Chapter 1 of this book, "Without data, you're just another person with an opinion." Leaders using these analytics will challenge those who question if using these new analytics is worth the change management involved or those unsure if a project would benefit from these new analytical capabilities. Leaders should push the limits of the analytical team. They should challenge the team to be innovative and create new analytical ways to solve problems knowing that experimentation will also have some failures. They realize that failing quickly can often lead to new innovation and breakthroughs.

Fourth, the organization needs to be committed to developing analytical talent. This doesn't mean you go out and hire PhDs or talent with advanced degrees. There are three ways to accomplish this. First, yes, you will hire some really smart people, either by creating positions or hiring them through attrition. Second, you need to invest in your current workforce. This is through internal and/or external tools, education, and training. Third, you will work hard to make analytics intuitive through better visual tools, representations, and data exploration approaches and will commit to educating and training caregivers in these approaches:

- Building analytics libraries for them to use.
- Creating learning opportunities through internal analytical training classes covering a wide variety of analytics techniques that are used consistently in your organization by those analytic subject matter experts.
- Giving them access to third-party learning.

Fifth, you need to develop new talent pipelines through enhanced internships and updated job descriptions. The healthcare industry is lagging in this area. Creating internships where students come in and participate in analytic solutions gives them a bond to healthcare. This can create a positive feedback loop when the students return to school. Creating meaningful work is the best word of mouth on college campuses. Another tactic is to create updated job descriptions. As colleges and universities continue to create analytics and data science majors, the organizations that fail to keep current job descriptions will lose out on talent acquisition attempts.

The following four case studies will highlight the cultural change discussion above. The case studies will be dealing with each part of unifying people, process, and technology individually and then a final case study will talk about each part in synchronization. This is not to say that each case study could not address unifying people, process, and technology. The goal is to focus on each part individually to understand its importance. Throughout each case study we will describe the problem being addressed and we will give a few facts about the models used and the size, but it is not about the model itself. The first case study will discuss when people are important. When we speak about people, we are talking about the sponsorship and the role they play that leads to a successful outcome. Our second case study will focus on the process. During this case study we will talk about how the analytics professional can utilize the analytics playbook and how an advanced analytics checklist can help scale using analytics for your organization. The third case study will discuss what technologies might come into play in order to create "real-time" analytics. The final case study will give an example of when people, process, and technology are harmonious toward the quest for intelligence.

PEOPLE USE CASE – DELIVERING PRIMARY CARE PREDICTIVE RISK MODEL

Reducing costs of delivering healthcare is probably the number-one challenge that is being addressed throughout the healthcare ecosystem. Efforts in many types of population health initiatives, from primary care services to chronic care delivery to reducing prescription drug costs, focus on reducing utilization without rationalizing, and costs to continue delivering the best, most cutting-edge healthcare in the world.

The undaunting task facing every provider organization is not caring for their patients; it is the magnitude of patients requiring healthcare services. Trying to balance patients who need chronic care services, like cancer or asthma, patients who just need services because they are currently fighting a cold or flu, and patients who are just seeking well-care visits, or who are not in immediate need of healthcare services because they are young and consider themselves healthy, results in challenges to optimizing physician resource time. Understanding the risks of their patient population is one way the Cleveland Clinic is addressing this challenge. Through true population health management efforts, Cleveland Clinic created a primary care predictive cost risk model to help improve patient care. The expected outcome of the model would be to assign a risk score to each patient to help physicians, nurses, and care navigators with four important functions: (1) help prioritize patients who have care gaps, those services that are critical to maintaining proper health, like A1c, blood pressure, mammograms, etc.; (2) identify high-risk patient lists to schedule patients for visits to try and keep them from developing costly healthcare complications; (3) schedule patients who are healthy for well-care visits to help keep them healthy, or catch potential healthcare issues before they develop; and (4) provide a score so that when that patient comes for a physician visit, the physician would understand the relative risk for that patient to incur substantial costs for healthcare services in the future.

There are industry algorithms to calculate a risk score for patients who are associated with some type of population health total cost of care model. In these situations, it is partnering with the health insurance companies to understand the claims data from all the different health providers a patient utilizes. The problem Cleveland Clinic was trying to solve was calculating a risk score for all patients, regardless of insurance status. This meant creating a credible model that would score more than 1.8 million patients currently and that number of patients is expected to continue to grow. Over three years of data were used to train the model. More than 300 different variables, from claims data to electronic medical records (EMRs) to Hierarchical Condition Categories were used. We are currently working on a new version of this model. As we discussed earlier in the book, the amount and types of data continue to grow and that logically leads to the exploration of model improvements. We digress; back to understanding how the people play an important and significant role.

In order for this model to be considered credible, our population health team addressed the importance of every patient having a risk score. Once the decision was made that every patient was to receive a risk score, there were a number of decisions regarding where to place this risk score in the clinical workflow and how it would be used. For all of these types of decisions, we needed a clinical sponsor as well as physicians, nurses, and care navigators underneath the clinical sponsor. This clinical sponsorship team would provide two important matters: (1) clinician validation that the model is performing to high credible expectations and (2) where to embed the risk score in the daily clinical team's workflow that would allow actions to be taken to improve the quality of care and reduce overall total cost of care.

Clinical validation is an important step in the model building process as well as model acceptance. We can build a model using a variety of techniques from random forest to stepwise regression to neural networks to ensemble modeling. None of these techniques matters unless we procure clinical validation behind them. Just letting analysts loose to build models using claims data was fruitless and would lack of support of any risk score the model would deliver. In our discussions with physicians, the physicians agreed that claims data, both internally and externally, would add value to the model. What really added to the credibility of the discussions was the physicians' constant insights into what EMR data they believed should be tested. For clinical variables, we discussed the importance of transforming the clinical variables using transformations like minimum value, maximum value, most recent, etc. Not only did we discuss what variables were evaluated; we also discussed how to handle missing values and outliers to produce the best model. Being able to show the importance or nonimportance of EMR data as an emerging variable in the final model as the model evolved allowed for important conversations between physicians and analysts, and added to the physician comfort level. Throughout the model building process, we brought the model building progress back to the physicians. We recognized that engaging the physicians in the model building process would not only accelerate model acceptance, it would allow for discussions between the physicians and analysts building the model that would eliminate confusion and inconsistencies in interpretations.

When the model was ready, we could not just run the model, create a score for each patient, and load it into the workflow. We needed to take a sample of patients and get physicians to validate the model. Throughout the validation process, we continued to discuss the most important variables that were being used. We asked a number of physicians to review by hand the patient, their score, and their EMR. However, just giving the patients the score would not give the physicians any magnitude of risk, either. The validation came by assigning the patients one of three classifications. The patients were classified as (1) low risk, (2) medium risk, or (3) high risk. For each patient's classification, we asked the physicians to give the patient one of three outcomes: (1) agree with the model, (2) disagree with the model, and (3) undetermined. Once we received the results, not only did we start to understand the patients who were marked levels 2 and 3 by the physicians, but we also needed to understand those marked level 1. It was important to understand from the physician's perspective why these patients were assigned that specific outcome. Meetings were held to make sure all the necessary feedback was clearly understood. By working with the physicians, the organization began to have conviction in the model and could then understand tweaks to the model and how these would affect the classifications. By now in this new age of analytics, it is understood that all models have some misclassification rate. Blindly not understanding the misclassification rate will erode model acceptance by the organization and could potentially misguide patient care.

The next set of people who are important to any analytical model deployment are the ones who will be using the model's output. Depending on the type of model, you may need to deploy the results in your EMR in an operational decision support system, a financial decision support system, or create a new "home" for the output. Depending on the model, the analytics team and end users have decided on the frequency of the model's output. Is this a model that runs daily, weekly, monthly, etc.? In this case, the model's output would need to be updated monthly. Even on a monthly basis, the expectation needs to be set on the day of the month that the model will update. If the model is supposed to execute over the weekend or on a holiday, will the run date for the model be moved to the next business day? What happens if there is a failure in the process? All of these questions require people to make decisions so that the appropriate workflow, scheduling, and execution can occur. In some cases, there may be a need to store historical results of the model's output. The importance of your model's playbook comes into play here as it is people who will document and make sure the details are there to ensure successful production automation. In this use case, we are updating the model monthly and it was decided the monthly history of the output would not be stored at this time. Other important considerations that would need to be planned for during this process are the need for a pilot and whether it will scale. Is there a testing period before release to production? Where does that testing reside? It is the importance of the people building and maintaining these models, deploying these models into production systems, and using the models to make sure they are in sync to ensure they are meeting end user compliance expectations.

Now that it is understood how the model's output will be used and where it should reside in the workflow, a team of people will be required to make sure the requirements are gathered and documented to coordinate the production automation workflow. This includes making sure all aspects of the workflow are vetted with the development team to make sure the hosting systems, execution of the model, and the operational system integration plan complete as planned to make sure the model output reaches its destination. Creating a communication plan is critical to understanding how error-handling and/or failed job processes are handled. In a worst-case scenario, the model's output is not updated as scheduled and the previous model's output remains in place with the appropriate communications to the end user. The notifications should be able to communicate effectively and succinctly what failed and mitigation timelines. Keeping the end user updated with information will allow the analytics team and development teams freedom to troubleshoot and fix the issues without the need to support phone calls from end users who were expecting the updates from the model. This stage of the workflow is critical and should not be rushed. Once a model is ready, there is always eagerness to move these models into production. In the lifecycle of analytics projects, do not let the return on investment of the project hasten the due diligence and attention to workflow details. It is important to start realizing the value to the patients as quickly as possible; however, a lack of focus from the people on the technical details in implementing the model can cause further delays.

During this implementation phase, there are three stages:

1. Known knowns
2. Known unknowns
3. Unknown unknowns

How do you mitigate known knowns? Depending on the complexity, one team may not be able to complete their task until another team has finished theirs. You can plan and communicate around this risk. There are also known unknowns that need to be considered. There may be other priorities this project is competing with. You do not know if this is a risk yet, but potentially it could become one, so you can plan for contingencies. Then there are unknown unknowns. These are the risks that just pop-up: something that even the best planning may not catch. These risks can be minor or major and will be dealt with when they arise. It is important to make sure communication channels are established between the analytics team, the development and implementation team, and the end user to handle questions/issues that may arise, and that there is accountability in the playbook with the details around the people at each of the implementation stages and management of timelines during this stage. This is all reliant on people. Don't let failures at this stage jeopardize this model or future models.

Finally, the model is in production and being used. There is the team that will monitor and maintain the model and process. Since there has been a thorough playbook built by the analytics team, with the help of all other stakeholders, from the clinical team to the technical team, there is a common understanding of what model maintenance will look like. Model maintenance will include plans around removing the model from production if necessary and how the work would be completed that relied on model output, to transitioning to a new version of the model, and to retiring the model. As the use of analytics continues to grow, some models will not be required or could be incorporated into other models and/or should be retired. The analytics team needs to discuss with their end user what types of decision criteria will be used for model retirement or replacement. There will also be instances where the analytics team will initiate improvements to the model before degradation starts. One thing is known: models will degrade over time and the people building the model and using the model will need to have a documented plan to understand if the model just requires retraining, if it should be transitioning to a newer model, or for retiring the model. This plan should have built-in timelines to ensure end user workflow will not be disrupted or alternatives can be implemented. By incorporating the correct monitoring measures, there should be ample time that degradation alerts can be communicated and discussions between the analytics team and the end users can plan on the next steps. There should never be a surprise when you come into work and a model has been removed from production. During this stage, it is important for the analytics to have a clear plan in place to understand fully any analytical model's lifecycle.

This case study is a perfect example of how a team of teams works together to help patient care. The importance of people at every stage of the analytics process cannot be underestimated, misjudged, or undervalued. Each member of this process plays an important role and every subject matter expert needs to have a voice. There will be successes. There will be issues or problems. People are the resource that will bring ingenuity and innovative solutions. The importance of model sponsorship and the right team of "model validators" underneath ensures organization acceptance. The success of the project will be judged on the following objectives from the "model validators":

1. Does it work as designed? Did we assign a risk score to each patient identified? Yes.
2. Do end users use it to help prioritize patients who have care gaps, identify high-risk patient lists, help schedule patients who are healthy for well-care visits, and provide a score to help clinicians understand relative risks? Yes.
3. Does it meet the overall goals of the project to reduce healthcare costs and keep people healthy? To be determined.

We are accomplishing the first two of these. Reducing overall healthcare costs is a longer-term measure, not just something that will be judged a success over days, weeks, or months. It may take years to understand. We are confident that this proactive approach to population health will meet this objective and reduce healthcare costs.

PROCESS USE CASE – RATE REALIZATION MODEL

This case study will focus on process and the improvements advanced analysts can make to a seemingly simple insight, improving service line decision-making. A frustration that can encumber decision-making is having to make adjustments to data that lack accuracy and could impact the right decision. Managing service lines in an organization requires two important numbers: accurate revenue and costs to derive profitability. Most organizations can accurately determine the cost of their service lines. However, when it comes to revenue, that can be a bit complicated. We need to understand the "realized revenue" in order to derive true profitability and make business planning decisions. What is "realized revenue"? Many organizations are tracking two revenue numbers: (1) some type of model revenue from contracts; and (2) actual payments that are being received from government plans, commercial payers, patient payments, etc. The "realized revenue" is considered the revenue that is ultimately reported once a patient's account is closed or paid in full. It includes insurance payments, patient payments, and write-offs for contractual obligations, bad debt, or charity. In many instances, it takes months, even occasionally years for accounts to be considered paid in full. You might wonder how you can make business decisions if paid-in-full account data is months old, or longer?

The answer lies in developing a model that can predict this "realized revenue" for open accounts and deliver it on a timely basis into your decision-support data. Cleveland Clinic created a champion model tournament that uses eight different models with at least nine different techniques and 40 variables to produce "realized revenue" for every account that is open. Sounds simple enough, right? As the model was tested, validated, and being prepared for production, it was agreed that the model would be run weekly. That means, as new accounts are processed and moved into the decision support system, those new accounts that required a "realized revenue" would need to use the modeled revenue number as a proxy until the next model run. This model revenue number is normally overstated but was not considered material since it was only affecting one week's worth of data.

Now that you have a little background on the model and how often the model is being run, let's discuss the process required to get this model into production. Just like in any process, there was a problem that needed to be addressed. We needed to improve service line decision-making through predicting "realized revenue" for open accounts. The current status was that users of the data had three options to choose from: (1) use modeled revenue; (2) use payments as they were received and posted; or (3) make adjustments to modeled revenue or payments using their own judgment or history. Each of these options was not optimal. The first option would most likely overstate revenue. The second option would most likely understate revenue. The third option would just give you a number between options (1) and (2) and was reliant on end user judgment. If the end user left the organization or the service line area, a new end user would have to step in and apply their judgment. That could lead to all kinds of questions about how you made the adjustment instead of focusing on making a decision. The goal was to create a model that would produce realized revenue.

Next came the model development lifecycle. It started the process of data discovery and mining efforts to understand the different sources of data available, the number of different variables that could be considered in the model, and the amount of data that would be available for train and tune the model. Once this step was completed, the next steps in the process were to pull the data, prep the data, and transform the data for the model. This process flow that needed to be built had to deal with the complexities around handling missing data, imputations of some data elements, how to handle outliers, and log transformations of certain data elements. Next came model training and tuning. We utilized a four-step approach. First, we created a model hierarchy that needed to be followed. There were eight different models in the hierarchy. Second, we used a machine learning approach to evaluate different techniques. We used over nine different techniques for each of the eight different models and 40 variables from three different data sources. Third, we used a champion tournament to select the weekly winner. Fourth, we monitored model performance for degradation and enhancement opportunities. The final step in the model lifecycle was to validate the model to make sure it was reproducing results within acceptable limits (e.g. predicted "realized revenue" was between model revenue and actual payments).

Now that the first version of the model was created, it was time to move the model into production. We divided this into three steps. The first step is documentation. Even though we list this step here, it was really started at the beginning. If you remember, in Chapter 3 we discussed the need for a model playbook. This step is essential and is required before a model goes into production. Next is the production step. This step requires a workflow integration flowchart or diagram. The flowchart displays the steps that need to be completed in the correct order to ensure the technical folks have the roadmap necessary to move the model from your development area, to your Q&A area, and finally to your production area. This includes quality data management rules and signoffs before the data is migrated to your production area for end user consumption. The final step in the process is model management. This is also defined in your documentation step, but is the visual way of understanding model performance. In this case, we store weekly information for tracking average squared error (ASE) at various levels and use different control charts to signal potential issues, to identify degrading prediction errors, to determine periodic retraining efforts, and to help investigate data anomalies. An ASE of zero means your model has perfect accuracy, which we know is virtually impossible. In this case, we have expectations to minimize the ASE of the analytical model and strive to make sure the model performance adheres to certain thresholds.

This process would not have been successful without the efforts of and support of a multidisciplinary team. Having a good working team with strong project management certainly played an important role in the success of this project. During the model building phase, it was the collaboration between enterprise analytics and subject matter experts from revenue cycle management and revenue and reimbursement departments that helped inform, test, and validate the models. During the implementation and post-implementation phases it was the teamwork between enterprise analytics, business solutions (developers), and processing (data reconciliation) departments to get the data ready and available in the decision support system for the end users. The final piece of success comes from end user adoption. During this process, it was transparency with the end users and areas that were affected by the change. It is about change management before the results go live, letting them know change is coming, and creating educational opportunities to ease the stress before production goes live. Educational communication can come in many forms, from webinars to in-person townhalls to one-on-one department sessions. A successful tactic you can employ once you go live is to hold "office hours."

Remember, back in school there were times when you were shy and would not ask a question in front of the class or, once the class was over, your questions finally dawned on you? The perfect opportunity to get your questions answered was to visit your professor during his "office hours." Staffing some open "office hours" is a great way to eliminate stress once the model goes live.

TECHNOLOGY USE CASE – POPULATION HEALTH MANAGEMENT APPLICATION

When we discuss "real-time" analytics, it can be used in the context of various situations. "Real-time" could mean having a model at the edge and using it with a patient to help inform during a patient visit, or produce financial outcomes based on asking questions during a meeting. "Real-time" could also mean having a model that can produce results within a few hours so that actions could be taken. "Real-time" could also mean having a model run daily that can produce results used within a decision support system. This case study will explore "real-time" in having a model that can produce results within a few hours so that actions could be taken by leveraging the right technology.

Patients in population health management programs are becoming a larger part of the fiscal responsibility of the organization. Current long-range planning methods did not have a method for understanding the impacts of these patients. We set out to build an application that would allow the organization to collect assumptions to drive models that would provide impacts that could be incorporated into long-range planning assumptions.

Technology was an enabler for this project. We were armed with a technology solution that would allow the team to be innovative and stretch the limits of analytics. The first step in this case study was a two-day brainstorming session around the functionality we wanted the application to have. The team laid out six functional elements that we wanted to be able to model:

1. Rate and charge changes
2. Movement of services

3. Shared savings simulations
4. Volume changes by location/payer
5. Volume changes by location/institute
6. Narrow network product simulations

The output of the application needed to be a 72-month rolling projection. It would also need to produce output that could be reported on by various dimensions, like location, type of service, service line, payer, etc. The output also needed to produce outcomes that could help the healthcare organization understand the risk of the assumptions for any given element or combination of elements. The team also had an extensive list of data requirements from our own data warehouse to third-party data to public data that would be used to help seed distributions and provide utilization guidance. The minimally viable product that was used during this initial case study excluded the third-party data and public data. Those enhancements remained in the backlog. Subsequently, a new demand model is in development that is using those enhancements.

The team decided to produce a two-stage model. The first stage would produce the necessary 72-month rolling forecast. Once the forecasts were completed, the second stage of the model would produce simulations for each month of the 72-month period. This would require plenty of computational power and storage requirements.

We will give a little background about each of the functional elements. Rate and charge changes would require the pricing assumptions during the 72-month period by payer by location by date. This would drive the revenue calculation requirements. Movement of services would require assumptions driving services from one or multiple locations to one or multiple target locations. Assumptions would be date driven. As services would move, an option to "backfill" vacated services with similar or different services was required. Shared savings contracts needed various inputs from population selection (commercial business/Medicare business) to the number of members in the contract to medical loss ratio targets and other inputs to calculate contract performance for only those members. Volume changes by location/payer would require assumptions around the shift in volume from one or more payers to one or more target payers by location by date. Volume changes by location/institute would require assumptions around the shift in volume from one or more institutes to one or more target institutes by location by date. Narrow network product simulations would require inputs on membership, utilization, and cannibalization rates.

As you can start to see, the complexity of the model just in handling the inputs becomes challenging. Add to that the complexity the simulations needed to account for. We would start with a bank of encounters. In this case, an encounter is an inpatient stay, starting at the admission date and running through the discharge date. The bank is made up of historical encounters, and in some cases is adjusted to present time revenue and cost metrics that describe the probabilistic interpretation of what types of encounters we will see during any month. This bank could be adjusted throughout the 72-month forecast, if necessary to account for changes in the distribution over time, either by industry thought leaders or internal input.

Put this all together and you have a model that is producing billions of rows of data. Being able to leverage in-memory and in-database technologies makes this type of project achievable. The key to this project was understanding that no decision was going to be made by changing parameters in a meeting, examining the results, and making a decision on the spot. The complexity of the interactions does not warrant this type of decision-making. This was a situation where we wanted to be able to collect and run a set of assumptions and produce output that would be available for the teams, like financial planning to be able to start consuming within hours. We would not have been able to produce results within hours in a traditional data warehouse setup. Being able to deliver results requiring large computational scale requires innovative approaches like in-memory and in-database technologies.

Don't let technology be the solution. First and foremost, let your team try ground-breaking pioneering approaches that stretch the limits of analytic capabilities for one-of-a-kind competitive advantage models based on the requirements laid out. This will lead to the appropriate technology solution.

INTEGRATING PEOPLE, PROCESS, AND TECHNOLOGY – ENHANCING CLEVELAND CLINIC WEEKLY OPERATIONAL MEETINGS/CORPORATE STATISTICS DASHBOARDS

We wanted to use this current case study as a great example of unifying people, process, and technology. While this case is currently in process, it shows the importance of unifying data, people, process, and technology. Over the course of time, organizations evolve the way they measure their business. Cleveland Clinic is no different. Cleveland Clinic is currently using the concepts discussed in John Doerr's *Measure What Matters*. It describes a system that involves defining objectives and uses key results to understand performance. An important concept in this type of goal-setting system is the transparency of these objectives and key results throughout the organization. It is important to understand how we were performing yesterday, a week ago, a month ago, etc. It is just as critically important to understand how we think we will be performing tomorrow, a week from now, a month from now, etc.

The organization was confronted with two difficult challenges it was looking to solve. The first one was to help alleviate the burden of preparing for operational meetings. The preparation for these operational meetings was labor intensive across those departments. It involved collecting, preparing, and analyzing data from different data sources, from actual volume to budget information to different analytics across various metrics, and compiling them into a format that could effectively run operational meetings on a weekly basis. The goal of providing leadership with actionable intelligence was to improve performance, which would also drive four additional secondary outcomes. First, we needed to build a process to support daily and weekly operating meetings. We would have to understand and build a process flow to support data collection to model output to data integration into dashboards. Second, we would simplify and streamline information delivery. We needed to be able to deliver data in a format that could easily be digested into new dashboards to run meetings and also be available for downloading by end users. Being able to download information from the dashboards would support additional analytics and visuals from ad hoc requests that would not be handled by the agreed upon meeting visuals. Third, this process would continue to ensure alignment and consistency in reporting of corporate statistics and financial performance management. Lastly, we would be leveraging enhanced statistical methodologies that would support our business cycle.

The second challenge was around producing forecast estimates for the corporate statistics dashboards. The current logic around producing these forecast estimates was rudimentary. It wasn't until using objectives and key results that brought to the forefront the need to revisit the forward-looking information on this dashboard. This is where the harmonious interactions between many departments, the building of a process, and the use of technology produces a pleasant piece of music. The information that was to be produced looked to solve relatively short-term time horizons, in this case a forecast that could help inform our business over the next two months.

We will discuss how we are successfully tackling these two challenges and understand how each of the objects is satisfied by unifying data, people, process, and technology.

Let's talk about data first. Without data, there would be no information. Believing that we can forecast the future is simply impractical. Think about the behaviors that influence your models. Take weather forecasting, for example. When you listen to a weather forecast, there is likely a "chance of," "a percentage for precipitation," or "a range in temperature." What weather forecast is 100% accurate? Answer: since I am not a meteorologist, I will safely guess, virtually none. Think of the complexity of how weather forecasting is done. It requires taking observations of weather-related inputs, like temperature, barometric pressure, humidity, wind speed, wind direction, solar radiation, precipitation, etc., from land-based and sea-based reporting stations, normally hourly from automated reporting stations around the world, and processing this information into their computer models. You get the point: an extremely complex set of inputs are then modeled using many different forecast models using a complex set of mathematical relationships to produce results.

While your forecast models are probably not relying on taking global observations hourly, you are still challenged with the complexity of influencing behaviors and inputs that need to be defined. Part of understanding what data needs to be collected is knowing what problem you are trying to solve. As explained in our case study, we are looking to produce forecasts to alleviate operational challenges as well as producing daily forecasts for our corporate statistics dashboards for short-term planning. Armed with this knowledge, we were able to start exploring the data to prepare for our model. In this case, it wasn't necessary to collect data hourly. Nor was it necessary to collect data weekly or monthly. By collaborating with the decision-makers and end users, we were able to understand that having input data daily would be necessary to create the forecast models required to deliver outcomes successfully. We were able to leverage an extensive daily history of data to build forecast models for performance measures like surgeries, admissions, evaluation, and management (E&M) visits. The key data features of these models include data like operational case volumes, same data add-ons and cancelations, volumes by types of service settings like inpatient and outpatient, location types like hospitals and ambulatory surgery, clinical institutes like heart and vascular, neurology, digestive disease, cancer, etc., scheduled and filled slots, holiday schedules, national conference schedules, and unusual occurrences or events identified internally.

Let's explore people and process from a couple of different perspectives. As this project evolved, we knew that there would be two ways to think about the analytics. Back in Chapter 2, we discussed the importance of producing and consuming analytics. In Chapter 3, we examined the importance of a process framework around understanding the work, doing the work right, and doing the right work. In this project, we are producing a forecast, which we call the science of forecasting, and consuming the forecast, which we will call the art of management. Let's delve into what we mean by the science of forecasting. Believing that we can forecast the future with 100% accuracy is simply impractical. Think about the behaviors that influence your models. Whether your forecast models are simplistic in nature or use an extremely complex set of inputs to inform many different forecast models using a complex set of mathematical relationships to produce results, there is a science to forecasting.

While your forecast models are probably not relying on taking global observations hourly from approximately 1,200 weather stations, you are still challenged with the complexity of influencing behaviors and inputs that need to be defined and understood. The science is to produce an accurate forecast. In this case, "accurate" is based on the ability to take action and will be discussed momentarily in the art of management. The science required is twofold. First, the analysts will create one or more models. Some examples of the different models that are created are Auto Regressive Integrated Moving Average (ARIMA) with intervention and causal variables (ARIMAX), unobserved components model (UCM), and exponential smoothing models. These models are included in a champion tournament daily, where the best performing daily model's results are used. Second, the analysts will be tuning existing models or creating new models by identifying, improving, and/or eliminating inputs that do not add significant value to the final forecast model. More inputs are not necessarily better. This continuous improvement process around the forecast models will take into account the model's responsiveness to new inputs. Understanding the incremental benefits of improving your forecast models compared to the costs related to maintaining the models needs to be considered. Comparing the model's incremental performance gains while minimizing the people resources required to maintain the models needs to be clearly understood so they can be deployed on other projects. Some levels of accuracy may not be achievable and we often pursue those unrealistic levels leading to the consumption of resources that could be deployed elsewhere. There may also be costs related to collecting existing data or new data. Does the data exist in a format the models can consume? What resources would be required to make the necessary transformations from development to production? If there is new data that could possibly be tested, what resources are required to build data pipelines? Do you need to setup a process to incorporate the new data into the models? Analysts building the forecast models need to take into account the monthly seasonal effects and day-of-the-week cycles. The analysts will take into account unusual events or anomalies to understand if the noise created by those events should be modeled. The analysts will continue to evaluate new methods to add to the champion tournament. The last science aspect we will discuss is the measurement of the models. There are many outputs you can collect on forecasting performance. The analytics team needs to balance metric performance that can be understood by the end users, as well as more complex measurement techniques that the analytics team finds value. The analytics team tracks some performance metrics that are simpler conceptually and easier to interpret. Some of the most popular metrics in this category are:

1. Mean absolute percentage error (MAPE) expresses the accuracy by converting the difference between your forecast and actual results as a percentage. You calculate this measure by taking the sum of the difference between your forecast and actual results and divide by the actual results for every point and then divide this value by the number of points in your defined period, in this case, a two-month period and then multiply this result by 100 to make it a percentage.

2. Mean absolute error (MAE) examines the average of the absolute difference between your forecast and your actual results over a defined period of time. Since our forecast is for two months, we calculate the most recent MAE for the two-month period.

3. Coefficient of (multiple) determination or adjusted R^2 gives you some information about the goodness of fit of your forecast model. It provides a measure of explainability through how well your actuals are replicated by the model based on the proportion of total variation of outcomes explained by the model. The closer this value is to 1, the better the fit. This calculation is a little more involved and is provided for you in most forecast model performance outputs.

These metrics do have their drawbacks and educating your end users on how to use them is important. This will be discussed in the art of management below. The analytics team will store these metrics as well as other model performance metrics after every forecast run. This will allow us to build visuals over time and create alerts to help in monitoring the forecast model's performance. This will allow the team to monitor continuously and make improvements to the champion tournament.

Let's continue the discussion around the art of management. In the art of management, it is not about using the forecast exactly as it is predicted. The forecast model is constantly fed with new data, producing new forecasts with constantly changing predicted values and ranges. It is using these ever-changing forecasts that leads to what we like to call the "art of management."

Let's go back to our weather forecast example. Think about all of the forecast outputs they are projecting: temperature, precipitation, humidity, wind speed and direction, and the duration of forecasts, from 12 hours and 24 hours to 3-day, 7-day, and 10-day or more forecasts, and this is just scratching the surface. How we consume these forecasts is based on the expectations of how we will use them. Let's discuss how we might use a weather forecast over the next 24 hours. The weather forecasting models can get the high temperature or low temperature correct, but maybe not during the hour they forecast. Think about how you want to consume the model. If your concern is making sure you have the correct clothing for the day, you are certainly interested in the high and low temperature range, as well as when those temperatures will occur. Think about how close you really need the forecast to be. If the forecast models are predicting a high temperature for the day of 80 degrees Fahrenheit, as long as the forecast is within your tolerance to influence your decision in changing your selection of outerwear for the day, you most likely do not think about the forecast if the actual high temperature for the day comes in at 78 degrees, 80 degrees, or 83 degrees Fahrenheit. The critical interest in the weather forecast model is if the model predicts a high temperature of 80 degrees Fahrenheit and the actual high temperature is 50 degrees Fahrenheit. This would surely alter your outerwear choices for the day.

Sure, it would be easy just to use the "science of forecasting" and blame the model if decisions do not pan out. We don't need a complex forecast model with elaborate data and processes to get an improved forecast. We need to understand our business process and the inputs that we can use to build a reliable model. Let's think about why we are producing a forecast. It is so that we can enact change. The forecast is produced to guide us in answering the following types of questions:

- Can we make a decision?
- What decision are we trying to influence?
- At what point would you take action?

■ What is the acceptable range of outcomes at various volume sizes?

■ Do we understand the forecast bias in adjusting our decision-making process?

As you can see from the above questions, we have not included questions like:

■ How accurate is the forecast? What is the MAPE?

■ What is a good level of accuracy? What is the MAE?

■ Should we change the forecast based on recent data anomalies?

Why? The goal is to provide leadership with actionable intelligence from the forecast to enact change that will improve performance. An important piece in the art of management is educating the users on how to use the forecast, from the end-user preparing for the operational meetings to the senior leadership that will be using all of the information prepared to ultimately make a decision. It is to not focus on specific forecast metrics to determine "should we use the forecast." Each of these metrics has flaws and needs to be understood in context so that "forecasts are not thrown out."

Let's take a look at the forecast metrics we defined above to help understand in context how they should be considered. Depending on what level of aggregation you are reporting the metrics on can cause confusion and apprehension in using forecasts. No matter what level of aggregation you are reporting on, all metrics are correct. The metrics can be used in different situations. The mistake often made is comparing them to one another. Misusing these metrics can lead to focusing on questions like:

■ Is the forecast usable?

■ How can we improve the forecast?

■ Why doesn't this metric apply to all forecasts?

■ Is the forecast right?

George Box, one of the greatest statistical minds of the twentieth century, said, "All models are wrong." This is going to be true of your forecasts, but understanding that they are useful is vital to consuming the forecast. The art of management is not using the forecast metrics to guide your discussion. It is important to understand what these metrics are telling you and how to use them in your decision-making process. Let's examine the mean absolute error (MAE) and the mean absolute percentage error (MAPE). Understanding how these two metrics can work together is important so as not to influence judgment on the trustworthiness of forecast models. Always keep in mind that the objective is to assess whether we can use the forecasts to enact change through the decision-making process.

As outlined above, we are producing forecasts for different metrics. For this discussion, we will compare and contrast the MAE and MAPE with the surgical volumes and evaluation and management visits forecasts. Since the case study is around our weekly operating meetings, we are calculating the MAE and MAPE on a weekly basis. Again, the forecast is daily and we are producing a two-month forecast. Defining the time periods for metric comparisons and contrasts is important. We could have discussed the daily, bi-weekly, or monthly MAEs and MAPEs; however, using the metrics at those aggregation points would not translate well into the process we are solving for the weekly operational meetings. We are calculating weekly MAEs and MAPEs for different dimensions, namely facilities and institutes for planning purposes and we will focus the discussion around institute comparisons to take out the dynamic of our organizational structure.

For simplicity, we will use the hypothetical values in Table 5.1 to guide our discussion. We needed to educate the end users not only on the MAE and MAPE calculations themselves, but on how to interpret the values and use them by institute and across institutes and across metrics. The MAEs and MAPEs for these metrics are volume-related and have different implications.

We will closely examine Scenario 1 for both weekly forecasts. What do they have in common? One can easily see the MAEs are identical for each independent forecast. Would you feel comfortable using the forecast for surgical volume or E&M volume? If so, what institutes would you consider using it for? Without focusing on anything else, you might be inclined to consider the surgical forecast as more accurate since the MAEs are 10 times lower than the E&M forecast. However, within each forecast, the MAEs can tell a

Table 5.1 Surgical and E and M Forecast Model Performance

	Average Weekly Surgical Volume	Scenario 1		Scenario 2		Average Weekly E&M Volume	Scenario 1		Scenario 2	
		MAE	MAPE	MAE	MAPE		MAE	MAPE	MAE	MAPE
Institute A	1500	20	1.3%	125	8.3%	20,000	250	1.25%	1,000	5.0%
Institute B	500	20	4.0%	15	3.0%	5,000	250	5.0%	750	15.0%
Institute C	100	20	20.0%	50	50.0%	2,500	250	10.0%	100	4.0%
Institute D	25	20	80.0%	2	8.0%	1,000	250	25.0%	100	10.0%

Source: Author.

different story. Some MAEs give you the confidence that your fore-casts will provide actionable intelligence. Now, focus your attention on the MAPEs for each forecast. What story does that tell? Certain institute forecasts provide a percentage error that one feels com-fortable in using. One thing you will notice is that there is no total for the forecast models. One reason is in the way in which we are using the forecast models. We are making operational planning deci-sions at the institute level and the overall performance tends to be less important for the overall process. This comes back to the ques-tion of should you target a specific metric in order to use a forecast? Should we arbitrarily set an accuracy objective? What would happen if you set an objective of 5% accuracy or you need the forecast to be within a certain volume? The nature of forecasting can set unreal-istic expectations of model performance. Does that mean we cannot use the surgical forecasts or E&M forecasts for Institutes C and D in Scenario 1?

Let's transition to Scenario 2 before we tie this table back to the important concept of the art of management. At first glance, there are no commonalities between the forecasts. The MAEs are all dif-ferent, as well as their respective MAPEs. What would happen if you set an objective of 5% accuracy or you need the forecast to be within a certain volume in this case? Could we only use Institute B's surgical forecast and Institutes A and C's E&M forecasts? All of the questions explored above in Scenario 1 can be asked of Scenario 2 performance results. The one common thread that can be weaved together in Scenario 1 and Scenario 2 is going back and revisiting why we are producing a forecast. It is so that we can modify our current operational plan. Remember those questions related to the art of management?

- Can we make a decision?
- What decision are we trying to influence?
- At what point would you take action?
- What is the acceptable range of outcomes at various volume sizes?
- Do we understand the forecast bias in adjusting our decision-making process?

Do the MAEs and MAPEs give you specific guidance? Should you rely solely on those metrics across institutes and metrics? The answer is no. It's about working together; analysts, end-users, and senior leaders need to understand fully the implications the forecast will have in the operational meetings and how each of the questions above plays a role. Each question above should not be thought of in a silo nor should you only consider a combination of questions. You should not rely only on MAEs or MAPEs or Adjusted R^2s. This is a continuous collaboration and education effort that goes both ways between the analytics team and the operations team. The analytics team is constantly educating the end users on model performance metrics and how those metrics should be consumed to influence the decision-making process. The operations team is constantly educating the analytics team around anomalies, communicating planning, intervention, and/or process changes to enhance the forecasts. It is these five driving questions that we constantly keep at the forefront to make sure our forecasts are actionable.

The ultimate question is, can you make a decision? This is not about MAEs or MAPEs. This is not about changing the current plan. This is about the forecast providing support and intelligence in the decision-making process. Forecasts are not produced so we can make a change, they are produced to provide insight into *should we make a change*. Is the forecasting providing intelligence into volumes that will lead to new actions that you would not have considered yesterday or a week ago or two weeks ago, or whatever the timeframe? The forecasts should be engaging the interactions between the analytics team and the operations team to understand the underpinnings of the forecast models to make sure the forecast models are producing actionable insights. It is not productive for the end users to set MAPE or MAE tolerances. Trying to set general MAPE or MAE guidelines is self-defeating. All models are different and have unique characteristics driving them and to apply general accuracy measures to each model creates unrealistic expectations of performance. Focusing on these measures alone and not the entire spectrum will put you on the hamster wheel to nowhere. The question, "Can you make a decision?" seems pretty simple to answer. Isn't it yes or no? In reality, it is quite difficult because it is not about the MAEs or MAPEs. "Can you make a decision?" is the driving question that has multiple sub-questions that need to be understood and considered to incorporate into the models. The key takeaway for this question is to make sure you consider those important sub-questions driving the process of making a decision. How do holiday and physician staffing levels play a role? What are the financial performance targets we budgeted for? What unusual events did we or can we account for? How are seasonal cycles affecting the model? This is the art of management that drives successful collaborations between teams to produce a forecast that will allow senior leaders the confidence in decision-making.

What decisions are we trying to influence? Collaborating with end users to understanding staffing decisions? More, operational metrics? Are we looking to move scheduled surgeries or visits? Are there optimization consequences involved?

At what point would you take action? Forecasts become less reliable in the future. Forecast errors in the short-term are less than the longer-term forecast. Let's say it is September 1 and you are using the forecast and it has predictions out through the end of October. Are you starting to plan for the end of October or are you more worried about the projects for the middle or end of September? As you continue to close the timeline and end-of-October forecasts are revised, do you change your decision-making process? That is, at what point would you start taking action? Are we starting to make planning decisions two months out and as it gets closer?

Do we understand forecast bias and should we make adjustments? Not all forecasts produce consistent forecast bias. Some models may systematically over-forecast; some models may systematically under-forecast. Some of the bias could be data-related. That is, is the most recent data weighing heavier or lighter in the forecast? Some of the bias can be human-related, that is, setting weights for inputs based on gut feel. Let's assume we are talking about adjusting for holidays. What weights should we use? We can categorize the holidays into major or minor and assign a number that will influence major holidays differently than minor holidays. What do we consider major or minor holidays? Who makes that determination? How do we educate on forecast bias and how do we adjust our decision-making process? How will forecast bias change over time?

Could we do more harm than good by trying to adjust for bias? In general, if you understand bias, you can account for it by changing the forecast routinely. This is the art of management that makes sure forecast bias is successful.

One thing a forecast does not have is human business knowledge. Some might argue that a forecast has human business knowledge. It does to some degree. It has variables and information from business cycles, processes, etc. that we can translate into use in the model. The thing the forecast models do not necessarily reflect timely and accurately are changes in business processes or that "gut" intuition that management has. The forecast has business knowledge incorporated into it, like holidays, vacation schedules, school breaks, insurance benefits, etc., but sometimes up-to-the-minute business knowledge trumps the scientific forecast. Maybe there was a process change or a recent uptick in the flu that has not been accounted for in the model yet. There will be those times when the forecasts are projecting lower or higher numbers that will cause you, the decision-maker, to pause and alter your decision. It is understanding those biases that allows your judgment to guide you.

During this project, we are continuing to use the Cleveland Clinic Continuous Improvement model. As we think about Figure 3.1, we can focus on the challenges of understanding the work through engaging with our end users, doing the work right, and doing the right work.

Understanding the work through engaging with our end users was not just a 30-minute meeting with the outcome of "We would like you to produce a forecast so we can run our operations meetings." It meant setting up a reccurring set of check-ins during the project to make sure requirements were gathered, enhancements were made, and deliverables were tested. It allowed the team to understand the product needed to run the weekly operations meeting. Consistent end user engagement builds trust, understands the end user's pain points, and allows you to manage expectations when deliverables cannot alleviate those pain points, thus offering opportunities to brainstorm solutions or bring critical decisions to the sponsors.

Doing the work right is giving the team the freedom to deliver an innovative solution that incorporates the steps outlined in Figure 3.5,

the evolving process workflow. It allows the team to use lean principles to build a process flow from data collection to running the forecast models to integrating output from model with other data sources,
like the budget data to create a meaningful data set that can be used
to run the meetings delivering actionable insights to improve performance. At the time of this writing, the team was in the final stages
of coding an automated solution that will run daily that will allow a
championship tournament of all the forecast models created and to
deliver the best result. This automated solution will include the final
steps of incorporating the data from these weekly operational meetings into our corporate statistics dashboards.

Doing the right work was a by-product of understanding the work.
This gave the teams a backlog of enhancements and a task list that was
managed through weekly huddles. It gave the teams a forum to share
accomplishments, discuss what was working and what wasn't working, discuss outputs of the forecasts for reasonableness and reliability,
discuss priorities, and inform the analytics team of interventions of
process changes to consider.

Finally, it is no secret that having a technology platform with analytics at the core is what makes this possible. The complexity of the
requirements of this case study, the amount of data transformation
involved throughout the various processing stages, the amount of data
coordination between forecast models, the amount of data coordination between forecast output and other data sources, and producing
output that can be used by visual means would have definitely been
a challenging task in a traditional data warehouse environment. Projects like this will only grow in size and complexity and being able
to use technology as an enabler and not a solution will lead to success. Whether you have the ability to use in-memory processing,
in-database processing, vendor or open source solutions, or a cloud-
based solution, technology is going to play a key role in delivering
a computation platform to handle the next generation of analytical
solutions. As we think about enhancements to our weekly operating
meeting that could include weather data and change data capture,
that vast amount of data will require a technology solution to be able
to leverage all of these data sources.

CASE STUDY TAKEAWAYS

The success of any project requires a shared sustainability effort between all teams. The analytics team will have responsibilities and the weekly operating team will have responsibilities. Some responsibilities will be daily in nature, some will originate from meetings, and some might be initiated from process changes. The analytics team needs to deliver with a daily production model. This requires constant monitoring of the process to ensure it can run to meet processing deadlines. When the process "breaks," the team needs to respond and understand what went wrong and make the necessary adjustments in coding and scheduling on a timely basis so forecast data does not become too outdated. Continuous education is a key element. We need to educate end users on the inputs and outputs and how the models work to make sure they are making informed decisions. It will require continuous monitoring of the forecast models for the following four reasons:

1. To deliver dynamic model recalibration
2. To understand important model key performance indicators
3. To communicate to key stakeholders changes or interventions potentially impacting results
4. To explore new features

The weekly operating team would be required to interpret the results in context for the meetings. They would need to identify and investigate data anomalies with the appropriate facilities and/or clinical institutes to provide context back to the analytics team. This important responsibility enables the analytics team to make sure forecasts are tuned properly if necessary. The team would need to help the analytics team, based on planning and intervention methods. Clearly articulating and communicating interventions or process changes will enable the analytics team to incorporate those events to enhance the forecast.

The final sustainability effort is held jointly. It requires regular check-ins across all levels of the organizational hierarchy. The cadence of these check-ins will differ, depending on what level you are talking about. For example, senior-level executives will probably need a check-in at most quarterly. Check-ins for the end users and analytics staff will be more often, bi-weekly to even weekly. These check-ins are important because they create a feedback loop to dynamically enhance the forecasts. It creates collaboration opportunities around model tuning and education of model features. Even during this first round of forecast model building, the interaction and feedback between all teams continues to produce a list of data enhancements to be explored. A couple of examples are weather-related data like temperature, snowfall (being in the Midwest, travel can be difficult on occasion), pollen, etc. and seasonal flu data from the Centers for Disease Control.

CONCLUSION

Unifying people, process, and technology is a strategy that requires enterprise-wide support. It cannot be successful without leadership that sponsors (and funds, depending on your organizational model) the projects. These projects require people, process, and technology to be integrated and to work together. In our experiences, success is dependent on a team-of-teams approach – from the analytics team to the development team to the end users. Having the right framework surrounding people, process, and technology will provide you with the roadmap for success. It requires a cultural change that needs to be applied daily. Strategies are not implemented overnight. It is a change that takes time. Only your organization will know its timeline. Every journey seems to start out slow. Be patient. Be innovative. The quest for intelligence is rewarding. Don't let a disappointment or two derail you. Disappointment is always going to be a part of the journey. Finding engaged leaders where you can turn projects into success stories is the necessary fuel to keep the strategy burning. The same can be said for the front-line caregivers. Those delivering the analytical solutions and seeing the fruits of their labors in action is also fuel to keep the strategy active.

CHAPTER **6**

The Future in Healthcare

"An investment in knowledge always pays the best interest."

— Benjamin Franklin

Healthcare organizations continually evolve and technology plays a significant part in this evolution. In Chapter 4, we shared details on technology that is available and being adopted by many healthcare institutions, as well as by other industries.

Up to now, you have read and learned what some of the latest technologies can do in the area of data management and analytics for healthcare. In-database and in-memory processing can be applied to analyze massive amounts of data quickly and efficiently. These technologies are complementary and can be augmented with the traditional process to optimize the data management and analytics processes. Organizations with Hadoop are integrating an existing data platform such as a database or data warehouse to analyze big data. In addition, open source technologies such as Python, R, and Spark are being adopted and implemented to augment analytics in healthcare. These innovative technologies enable insight-driven decisions improving healthcare for you and me today and in the future.

So, what's next in healthcare for data management and analytics? What are some focus areas in the next three to five years that will take healthcare management to the next level? How will healthcare advance into the next generation with data and analytics? Many of these questions will be answered in the next few sections.

CLOUD

Clouding computing is a trendy and very popular innovation across many industries. It is talked about everywhere in businesses large and small. The global cloud computing market is growing at a fast pace and is expected to reach US$623 billion by 2023.[1] In an article from CIO, 96% of organizations[2] are either already using, or want to use, cloud computing as a part of their operations. It is an ideal technology for

---

[1] https://finance.yahoo.com/news/global-cloud-computing-market-outlook-115300653.html.

[2] https://www.cio.com/article/3267571/it-governance-critical-as-cloud-adoption-soars-to-96-percent-in-2018.html.

data management and analytics due to the data explosion phenomenon, specifically in the healthcare industry.

Because cloud computing has become mainstream, there is a lot of confusion as to what it is and whether it is anything new that we are or are not yet doing. In the simplest terms, cloud computing is a technology that allows you to store and access databases, servers, programs, and a broad set of applications over the Internet instead of your personal computer or on-premises data server. Cloud computing providers own and maintain the network-connected hardware and software for applications ranging from data integration to business analytics and operational reporting. Cloud computing allows consumers (like you and me) and organizations to use programs and applications without a large upfront investment in hardware and spending a lot on the heavy lifting of managing and maintaining that hardware. Instead, businesses can provision exactly the right environment and size of computing resources you need to enable analytical capabilities within departments or across the enterprise. You can have access to the cloud around the clock, year-round, anytime and anywhere, and only pay for what you use.

When discussing cloud computing, let's illustrate it with an applicable example that is easy to understand. One that is relatable to many users is email, regardless if you have gmail (Google mail), Hotmail (Microsoft mail), or Yahoo email, etc. All you need is an Internet connection; type in your login ID and password into the application and you can start crafting and sending emails with text and pictures. The server and email management software is all on the cloud and is entirely managed by the cloud service provider: Microsoft, Google, Yahoo, etc. The consumers (you and I) get to use the software and enjoy the many benefits such as accessibility and ease of use without having to manage any systems.

Traditional on-premises deployments of data warehousing, reporting, and analytics remain a key strategy for many organizations and the move to cloud computing offers an alternative and modern approach. In an article from *Forbes*[3] from 2018, nearly half of organizations are planning to migrate their business intelligence, data warehousing, and

---

[3] https://www.forbes.com/sites/louiscolumbus/2018/08/30/state-of-enterprise-cloud-computing-2018/#77408c02265e.

data analytics applications to the cloud in the next 12 months to three years. Cloud computing is providing IT departments with the ability to focus on delivering services and avoid the tedious tasks like procurement, maintenance, and capacity planning. As cloud computing has grown in popularity, several different models and deployment strategies have emerged to help meet specific needs of different users.

In another report, *Forbes*[4] reported that healthcare is ranked fourth behind the manufacturing, high-tech, and telecommunications industries being pressured by executives to move to the cloud. We believe the cloud initiative in healthcare will escalate into second or third since there is a real need for a single, unified system of records about the patient.

The cloud computing services market growth would be dependent on the global demand for technology services, which in turn depends on the state of the global economy. Currently, the growth is driven by demand in developed countries in Western markets such as North America and Europe. Less well-developed nations are slow to adapt to the cloud concept, and are expected to drive the growth toward the latter part of the decade. The emerging economies pose restrictions on cloud computing due to lack of infrastructure availability and technical know-how. Selecting the right type of cloud computing for your needs can help you strike the right balance of control and benefits.

Cloud Deployment Options

There are various deployment options for you to choose from to support the type of cloud for your organization. Of all cloud deployments, private and public cloud computing are the most popular. Recent research indicates that public cloud adoption is increasing and surpassing the private cloud option. According to "Cloud Computing Trends: 2019 State of the Cloud Survey,"[5] an overwhelming 58% embrace the hybrid cloud strategy, which is a combination of private and public clouds. There are four deployment options: public, private, hybrid, and community:

---

[4] https://www.forbes.com/sites/louiscolumbus/2018/08/30/state-of-enterprise-cloud-computing-2018/#77408c02265e.
[5] https://blogs.flexera.com/cloud/cloud-industry-insights/cloud-computing-trends-2019-state-of-the-cloud-survey/.

Public Cloud

Public clouds are open to the general public with cloud infrastructures that are owned and managed by the cloud service provider. A public cloud deployment is established where several businesses have similar requirements and seek to share infrastructure such as hardware or servers. In addition, it can be economically attractive, allowing users to access software, application, and/or stored data. In addition to the economics, the public cloud can empower employees to be more productive even when away from the office.

Private Cloud

Private clouds are only accessible to the users or partners of a single organization with dedicated resources. Private clouds can be built and managed within an enterprise data center that includes software and hardware. They also can be hosted by a third-party provider and managed either on or off premises (on-premises can be at the company's location). Customers seeking to benefit from cloud computing while maintaining control over their environment are attracted to deploying a private cloud. Private clouds simplify IT operations, on-demand access to applications, and efficient use of existing underutilized hardware.

Hybrid Cloud

Hybrid clouds are a blend of private and public clouds. Customers can choose to create a bridge between public and private clouds to address increased demand for computing resources during a time period such as end of the month or specific peak shopping time such as the holiday season. A hybrid deployment is a way to connect infrastructure and applications between cloud-based resources and existing resources that are not located in the cloud. The most common approach of a hybrid deployment is between the cloud and existing on-premises infrastructure, connecting cloud resources to internal system for additional performance and flexibility.

Community Cloud

Community clouds are comparable to private clouds but targeted to communities that have similar cloud requirements, where the ultimate goal is to collaborate and achieve similar business objectives. They are often intended for academia, businesses, and organizations working on joint projects, applications, or research, which requires a central cloud computing facility for developing, managing, and executing cooperative projects. Community clouds share infrastructure between several organizations from a specific community with common concerns and can be managed internally or by a third-party and hosted internally or externally. The costs are distributed across fewer users than a public cloud but more than that of a private cloud to share the saving potential.

Cloud Computing Benefits

Businesses can glean the many benefits that cloud computing has to offer. These benefits include cost savings, simplified manageability, high reliability, and strategic focus:

Cost Savings

The most significant cloud computing benefit is cost savings. Regardless of the type and size of the business, keeping capital and operational expenses at a minimum is always a challenge to endure and a goal to achieve. Cloud computing can offer substantial capital costs savings with zero in-house server storage, application requirements, and supporting staff. The off-premises infrastructure removes the associated costs in the form of power, utility usage, and administration. Instead of having to invest heavily in data centers and servers before you know how you are going to use them, you only pay for what you use and there is no initial invested IT capital. It is a common perception that only large businesses can afford to use the cloud. On the contrary, cloud services are extremely affordable for smaller and medium-sized businesses.

Manageability

Cloud computing offers enhanced and simplified IT management and maintenance capabilities through central administration of resources, vendor-managed infrastructure, and guaranteed service level agreements. The service provider maintains all of the IT infrastructure updates and maintenance and resources to support the architecture. You, as the end-user, can access software, applications, and services through a simple web-based user interface for data management and analytical needs. There are no more infrastructure investments or time spent adding new servers, partitioning silos. With the cloud, you basically have access to unlimited storage capability and scalability.

Reliability

With a managed service platform, cloud computing offers high reliability and high-performance infrastructure. Many of the cloud computing providers offer a service level agreement which guarantees around-the-clock service with 24/7/365 availability. Businesses can benefit from a massive pool of IT resources as well as quick failover structure. If a server fails or a disaster occurs, hosted applications and services can easily be relocated to any of the available servers within the cloud as backup.

Strategic Focus

Cloud computing can alleviate the technological annoyances. There is no IT procurement to deal with and the high-performance computing resources give you an edge over competitors to focus on being the first to market. Cloud computing allows you to forget about technology and focus on your key business activities and objectives. It can also help you to reduce the time needed to market newer applications, products, and services, and even become more strategic in focus for your business. Focus on projects that differentiate your business, not the infrastructure. Cloud computing lets you focus on your own customers, rather than on the heavy lifting of racking, stacking, and powering servers.

Disadvantages of Cloud Computing

However, there are some drawbacks and disadvantages to cloud computing, including security and cyber-attacks, possible downtime, limited control, and interoperability of technology:

Security Risks

Customers of the cloud are most concerned about security. Although cloud service providers implement the best security standards and industry certifications, storing data and important files on external service providers always opens up risks of exploitation and exposure. Using cloud technologies means you need to provide your service provider with access to important business data that is sensitive and needs to be protected at all times.

Public clouds heighten security challenges on a routine basis. The ease in procuring and accessing cloud services can also give malicious users the ability to scan, identify, and exploit loopholes and vulnerabilities within a system. For example, in a public cloud architecture where multiple users are hosted on the same server, a hacker might try to break into the data of other users hosted and stored on the same server.

Outages and Downtime

As cloud providers take care of a number of customers each day, they can become overwhelmed and may even encounter technical outages. This can lead to your business processes being temporarily interrupted. Since you access the cloud services via the Internet, you will not be able to access any of your applications, servers, or data from the cloud if your Internet connectivity is offline.

Control

Since the cloud infrastructure is entirely owned, managed, and monitored by the service provider, the customer has little or minimal control of the systems. The customer can only control and manage the applications, data, and services but not the backend infrastructure itself. You use what is negotiated and provided.

Interoperability and Compatibility

Although cloud service providers claim that the cloud will be flexible to use and integrate, switching cloud services is something that has not yet completely developed. Organizations may find it difficult to migrate their services from one vendor to another in case you receive a better cloud service package. Hosting and integrating current cloud applications on another platform may disrupt interoperability and support issues. For example, applications developed on Microsoft Development Framework (.Net) might not work properly on another platform like Linux. The availability of containers and microservices from vendors such as Kubernetes,

Microsoft Azure Container Service, or Google Container Service can help with enhanced interoperability and compatibility.

There is no doubt that businesses can obtain huge benefits from cloud computing. However, with the many advantages, there are also some disadvantages. We personally recommend that you take the time to examine the advantages and disadvantages of cloud computing, and select the cloud provider that suits your business needs. Cloud computing may not be appropriate for every business but should be considered in the near future for data management and analytics.

SECURITY

Information security is at the peak of interest for many organizations, specifically in healthcare. Protecting information and patient data has been in practice for many years and is not a new concept. Regardless of the business and industry that you are in, data breaches can happen and can occur without any warning or notice. In the entertainment sector, the cyber-attack that happened to Sony accessed the company's internal servers giving access to internal financial reports, top executives' embarrassing emails, private employee health data, and even new, yet-to-be-released movies and scripts. This information was leaked and placed on the Internet for public consumption. In the government sector, the US Office of Personnel Management (OPM) was hacked and exposed personal records, including names, addresses, Social Security numbers, and background checks on millions of people. Among the details of this data breach were copies of millions of sets of fingerprints. In the financial industry, a cyber-attack seized data from millions of customers of Wall Street giant J.P. Morgan Chase, revealing names, addresses, and phone numbers of millions of household and small-business accounts. Finally, in the healthcare industry, Anthem, Inc. experienced a very sophisticated external cyber-attack, which resulted in the theft of personal information such as medical ID numbers, Social Security numbers, income information, and contact details from millions of customers and subscribers. As a result, 2.5 billion personal records from cyber-attacks were exposed in the past five years.

Data is a strategic asset as mentioned in the previous chapter and should be protected by all means necessary. Using analytics to detect anomalies for IT security is a common practice. For example, in the financial services sector companies such as Visa, MasterCard, and American Express have used data and analytics to detect potentially fraudulent transactions based upon patterns and pattern recognition across millions of transactions. In the public sector, the government agencies have been using data and analytics to uncover terrorist threats and fraud in social programs and detect insider threats, as well as in other intelligence applications. Although big data brings opportunities for businesses, it is also being exposed to malicious use from hackers. With additional data sources, hackers are finding new ways to strike corporate IT systems, abusing the big data opportunities for data breaches and cyber-attacks.

The topic of security is very relevant to recent massive data breaches and cyber-attacks. Security has become a main concern of many executives, particularly for chief information officers (CIOs) and chief security officers (CSOs) due to recent security incidents. In many of these cases, the cyber-attacks have led to very costly data breaches for Anthem, Inc., J.P. Morgan Chase, Sony Pictures, OPM (Office of Personnel Management), and Target. These types of cyber-attacks are costing businesses US$400–500 billion annually. With such costly measures, IT spending around security is on the rise. The analyst firm Gartner anticipates and predicts that the world will spend over US$170 billion on information security by 2022.[6] Another report from Markets and Markets indicates that the cybersecurity market will grow to US$170 billion by 2020. As expected, industries such as aerospace, defense, and intelligence continue to be the biggest contributors to cybersecurity solutions since they have highly classified and sensitive data.

Not only do these data breaches and cyber-attacks affect businesses, but they also affect you and me as consumers, customers, and subscribers to these businesses. If our personal information is exposed, we are at high risk for fraudulent activities such as identity theft, credit card misuse, and false claims on insurance. Unfortunately, many

[6] https://cybersecurityventures.com/cybersecurity-market-report/.

organizations are simply not prepared and lack the right analytics-based approach, strategy, process, technologies, and skill sets to deter and prevent cyber-attacks. Since companies and other organizations can't stop attacks and are often reliant on fundamentally insecure networks and technologies, there is a need to adopt smarter defensive strategies. Compared with traditional security methods and efforts for preventing cyber-attacks, big data with new data sources brings additional complexity for analysis. New approaches and new ways of thinking about cybersecurity are beginning to take hold by better capturing the various data points and leveraging advanced analytics. Organizations are aggressively looking at data management and analytics for detecting fraud and other security issues by using advanced algorithms to mine historical information in real time. They are responding far more quickly, using platforms that alert security staff to what is happening, and what may likely happen, and quickly help them take action in terms of predictive analytics.

In addition to technology enablement with tools and solutions, all businesses big and small must acknowledge the new cybersecurity realities and requirements by adopting and modifying their practices to embrace an early detection methodology with rapid response and coordination strategy. The historical dump-and-analyze approach has proven ineffective because the needed data history is not typically stored or analyzed in a timely fashion. New approaches are required to leverage and evaluate data in a way that can determine what data is and isn't important to support cybersecurity-based behavioral analytics. In the current approach, information security is really based on correlating data and events designed for monitoring and detecting known or past attack patterns – "what is happening" or "what has happened." This strategy and tactic has some gaps:

Data Type Restriction

Most systems leverage a relational database and therefore require that all of the data aggregated be integrated and predefined prior to loading. The requirement to predefine the data and control how the data is sent for analysis can restrict the volume and variety of data that can be collected and analyzed. This also requires significant time managing the data system for end users as they keep up with updates and change revisions. All of this results in unwanted limitations on the types of security data that analysts see and what they can do to analyze or apply analytics to this data once it becomes available.

Detection of Incidents

As mentioned earlier in the Hadoop chapter, the database is ideal for certain data types and structures. Combating security breaches and preventing cyber-attacks requires constant streaming of data such as location, physical security information, role, and identity. Leveraging the database to include these additional data points requires the process of predefining the data before analysis can take place, which may result in delayed analysis due to integration and customization of the data. These data points and contextual details are essential and can make a difference between offensive versus defensive detection of incidents.

Real-Time Challenges

The system is designed to collect, filter, and correlate log events from security devices to detect issues from all the logs and alerts generated. By analyzing the logs with multiple data points simultaneously, the system could identify the most critical alerts to investigate. In order to analyze events across multiple devices, the data needs to be normalized and stored in a database. However, this design is optimized for detecting alerts but may not be optimized and less effective for ad-hoc queries to examine attacks that use multiple tactics that span across various touchpoints and systems.

Rigid Solution

Regardless of the type of company and industry, no two organizations are identical. Every business has different technologies and unique environments, security processes, databases, and analytical applications. Certain out-of-the-box capabilities and reports are sufficient, but most organizations need to customize their security solution to fit their environment and business needs. This includes adjusting existing correlation and business rules, developing enterprise dashboards and reports, or generating new ones for added business value. Additionally, nontraditional data sources in the form of semistructured data (video, blogs, etc.) are often necessary to tackle advanced threats and the ever-changing world of cybersecurity.

From a recent survey[7] conducted by the Enterprise Strategy Group (ESG), 27% of organizations say they are weak when it comes to analyzing intelligence to detect security incidents. Looking at the current status or what-has-happened model is no longer effective. Multidimensional cyber-attacks are often executed. Hackers are becoming more dynamic and can manipulate different tactics and techniques to gain entry and exit from an organization's network and data systems. In addition, the traditional approach and set of security devices are designed to look for particular aspects of attacks such as a network perspective, an attack perspective, a malware perspective, a host perspective, or a web traffic perspective, etc. These different technologies see isolated characteristics of an attack and lack the holistic picture of security. This makes cyber-attacks extremely difficult to distinguish or investigate. Until the entire event data is combined, it is extremely hard to determine what an attacker is trying to accomplish.

In order to combat security issues, building a strong data management foundation for advanced analytics is critical. This entails getting insights into all activities across networks, hosts (e.g. endpoints and servers), applications, and databases. It also includes monitoring, alerting, and analyzing for incidents, and then coordinating, containing, remediating, and sharing threat intelligence incorporated back into the monitoring, alerting, and response process. The IT and security teams also need the ability to detect attack activities leveraging breadcrumbs of evidence found lying across the entire technology stack (e.g. firewalls, IPS, antivirus, and servers). The universal problem is how to be on the offense instead of the defense and to determine the root cause of incidents quickly so that it can be contained before it can be spread throughout the organization. Of course, the obvious intent is to return insight and intelligence from the analysis back into the data system for continuous security improvement.

[7] https://i.crn.com/sites/default/files/ckfinderimages/userfiles/images/crn/custom/ESGWhitepaperIntelligenceDrivenSecuritywithRSASecurityAnalyticsandR-SAECAT.pdf.

Borrowing a quote from French military and political leader Napoleon Bonaparte, "War is 90% information." In regards to security and the fight against data breaches, this statement is noteworthy and very accurate in today's world. Information that lends to proactive data-driven decisions is critical. Tackling new types of cyber-threats requires a commitment to data gathering and processing and a greater emphasis on analytics to analyze security data. If your organization is looking to embark on or enhance your data security initiative, consider the following shortcomings of your IT system:

Not Collecting and Analyzing All Data Types

Today, the limitation for analyzing cybersecurity is the inability for organizations and cyber-software solutions to leverage all of the data assets. Since multidimensional cyber-attacks most likely navigate a variety of systems, networks, protocols, files, and behaviors, companies need to analyze data across all areas. This means collecting from a wide variety of data sources, including logs, flows, network packets, videos, identity systems, and physical security, etc., and making them available to all members of the IT and security team. Since multidimensional attacks can occur over an extended period of time, historical analysis is vital and must also be incorporated with the new analysis so that analysts can analyze the root cause and determine the breadth of possible cyber-attacks or data breaches. With the appropriate analytical cyber-solution, context is provided so that patterns and anomalous behaviors can be proactively identified that are indicators of fraud, theft, or other security breach.

Inflexible Data Management System

While original data formats and context should be preserved for integrity and governance, the security team must also have the ability to tag, index, enrich, and query any data element or group of data elements collectively to get a wider perspective for threat detection/response. This allows the analysts to add context to the raw data, making it contextually rich and more informative for proactive actions. In addition, enhancing the data can help analysts alleviate some steps in cyber-investigations and become more productive in the process.

Simplify Application Usage

Asking questions and the ability to get responses to these questions in a timely manner is critical to any operation, especially in security. To state the obvious from renowned quality control expert, operations specialist, and profound statistician Dr. W. Edwards Deming, "If you do not know how to ask the right questions, you discover nothing." This quote can apply to any industry but is very appropriate for detecting cybersecurity issues. Any data but in particular security data will remain a black hole if it cannot be easily accessed, analyzed, and understood by the security teams. To accomplish this, applications must provide a simple, easy-to-use interface to access the data and apply advanced analytics to that data. This will empower analysts at all levels to investigate threats quickly and gain valuable insights. Applications should also allow for uncomplicated ways to develop dashboards, queries, and reports to convey security operations to executives and the leadership teams. Thus, applications with data exploration, data visualization, and advanced analytics provide in-depth understanding of the data and track historical trends across data elements.

Businesses face a stark reality when it comes to protecting their important asset, their data. The processes and technologies they employed for the last few years are no longer adequate in a world of ever-increasing change and complexity. Sometimes it is better to take a step back and evaluate the landscape of cybersecurity. This practice will reveal the complex nature of modern multidimensional cyber-attacks and will likely convince them to adopt a more offensive, proactive, and comprehensive strategy. Therefore, a vast improvement in security around cyber-attacks requires a robust analytics solution to transform data into intelligence. This means collecting, processing, and analyzing all data and focusing on the people, process, and technology needed to detect and address the security activities. It also includes responding in a coordinated manner to an incident to investigating and determining root cause by scoping, containing, and analyzing the problem, which then bring the results of the investigation back into the application for proactive prevention and mitigation. This new approach to cybersecurity prevention can be viewed as an end-to-end relationship between data management and big data analytics technologies, along with some consulting services. The technology must scalable, manageable, and easy to use. Having the right technology and infrastructure is only half of the equation. At the same time, a process is needed for an organization to respond by asking the right questions, knowing how to navigate through the data, and leveraging analytics to stop the cyber-attacker in their tracks.

New Targets for Heightened Risks

The database or the data warehouse remains the primary target for hackers to penetrate, access, and attack. Once they are able to enter the system, it is exposing sensitive and critical information about the company and its customers. In addition to misusing the data, cyber-attacks can really disrupt the day-to-day operations of your company. Hackers often demand a ransom payment to restore access and not to distribute the data publicly. "Ransomware" is not new but it is on the rise. This is where hackers use a kind of software that can lock people out of systems until they make a bitcoin payment. For those who are unfamiliar with bitcoin, it is a new kind of open source, peer-to-peer money with no central banks to manage transactions.

As mentioned above, it can happen to any company across industries. However, a number of cyber-attack cases occurred in the healthcare industry, particularly hospitals. Hospitals are most vulnerable since they traditionally spend a very small fraction of their budget on cybersecurity. Aside from having malware and other cybersecurity software, it is also educational to teach a large network of doctors and nurses not to view and click on suspicious links via email. The way hackers get into a system is generally through a phishing attack – persuading any random employee to click on a link or an attachment in an email – or by finding a network loophole. By doing so, it allows its technical systems to be vulnerable to hackers armed with a cutting-edge, ever-evolving set of tools. Most of these doctors and nurses are basic users of technology and are not IT savvy enough to know how to detect suspicious emails and what not to click. As hospitals have become dependent on electronic systems to coordinate care, communicate critical health data, and avoid medication errors, patients' wellbeing may also be at stake when hackers strike. In some ways, healthcare is an easy target since its security systems tend to be less mature than those of other industries, such as banking, retail, and technology. Where a financial-services or technology firm might spend up to a third of its budget on information technology and security, hospitals spend only less than 5% percent.

Hospitals are used to chasing the latest medical innovations, but they are rapidly learning that caring for sick people also means protecting their medical records and technology systems against hackers. Their doctors and nurses depend on data to perform time-sensitive, lifesaving work. Hospitals' electronic systems are often in place to help prevent errors. Without IT systems, pharmacists cannot easily review patients' information, look up what other medications the patients are on, or figure out what allergies they might have before dispensing medications. And nurses administering drugs cannot scan the medicines and the patients' wristbands for giving the correct treatments. When lab results exist only on a piece of paper in a patient's file, it is possible they could be accidentally removed by a busy doctor or nurse and this critical information could simply disappear.

In several US hospital cases where cyber-attacks occurred, a virus infiltrated their computer systems and forced the healthcare company to shut down its entire network, turn away patients, and postpone surgeries. It resorted to paper records, where information was scattered and may not be updated. Hackers were demanding payments in the form of bitcoins to restore the operations of the IT systems.

In addition to the traditional database, hackers are evolving and going after the digital sources such as websites and social medial. According to International Data Corporation (IDC), the premier global market intelligence firm, cyber-attackers are aiming at modern technologies such as social media (Facebook, Instagram, Twitter), mobile devices (cellular phone, tablets, PDAs), clouds (private, public, and hybrid), and finally the Internet of Things (IoT), where a variety of digital devices are connected to the Internet (more on IoT in the next section in this chapter).

Vendors offering cybersecurity are developing advanced solutions, specifically cyber-analytics. At the same time, hackers are also evolving and targeting new sources and target areas. They also look for the lowest hanging fruit of vulnerability (i.e. healthcare and hospitals) to set sights for cyber-attacks. The data landscape for cybersecurity is becoming much more complex and CIOs and CSOs are dealing with challenging tasks to protect all data, prevent attacks, and proactively mitigate these threats. Having the right data management and analytic capabilities for cybersecurity is only half of the equation. The education and cultural perspective may be harder to solve and maintain. Training staff and employees not to leave sensitive data unattended, not to click on links in emails they did not expect to receive, and reporting any suspicious phishing activity is a daunting and enduring task. It takes a coordinated effort of people, process, and technology to be successful at addressing security.

INTERNET OF THINGS

The Internet of Things (IoT) can mean different things for many people and works in conjunction with big data. It is a system of physical objects—devices, vehicles, buildings, machines and others — that are embedded with electronics, software, sensors, and network connectivity so that these objects can communicate through the exchange of data via the Internet. The term was created by a British entrepreneur, Kevin Ashton, back in 1999. IoT is and will continue to generate a lot of data as it represents the connection of the fast-growing physical devices and systems. Data transmitted by objects provides entirely new opportunities to measure, collect, and act upon an ever-increasing variety event activity. According to Gartner, approximately 21 billion connected things will be used globally by 2020. Another staggering statistic is more than 5.5 million new things are connected every day, from sensors on industrial machines to alarm monitoring systems in your homes to GPS location of intelligent vehicles and fitness devices.

IoT spans a broad range of mature and early stage technology from radio-frequency identification (RFID) tags and remote monitoring to autonomous robots and microscopic sensors dubbed "smart dust." A new forecast[8] from IDC predicts that there will roughly 42 billion connected IoT devices that generate nearly 80 zettabytes of data by 2025.

[8] https://www.helpnetsecurity.com/2019/06/21/connected-iot-devices-forecast/.

That means the number of Internet-connected things will be overwhelming to manage and analyze across industries.

A respected US President, Theodore Roosevelt, once said, "In any moment of decision, the best thing you can do is the right thing, the next best thing is the wrong thing, and the worst thing you can do is nothing." Decisions with limited information are a thing of the past. IoT is enabling insight-driven decisions with a wealth of information that has been often overlooked. Connected devices, coupled with advances in data collection and analytics, are giving business managers at all levels more relevant and timely information when they need it than they have ever had before. How that affects the decisions they are making is having a deep and lasting impact on operational and business performance.

The Internet is now embedded into wearables, houses, vending machines, factory equipment, cars, security systems, and more. The connected world can be smarter and has potential to change our personal lives and how we conduct our daily business operations. Here are some examples of how industries can benefit from IoT in Table 6.1.

Table 6.1 IoT in Industries

Industry	Use of IoT
Consumers	Households in the United States collectively have over 500 million connected devices including Internet service, mobile devices, tablets, and monitoring alarm systems, with an average of five smart applications per family.
Healthcare	Smart monitoring systems and wearables for patients can alert family, doctors, and nurses when a critical situation occurs; insulin injection trackers and prescription drugs are adjusted based on real-time analysis of patient's health — all of which can improve patient care and health management.
Manufacturing	This sector leads the way with IoT. There is a 30% projected increase in connected machine-to-machine devices over the next five years, driving the need for real-time information to optimize productivity for quality products for consumers.
Retail	Automated order fulfillment for grocery replenishing for curb-side pick-ups and/or home deliveries; prescribe other goods and products for in-store shopping experience to build customer loyalty and consumer satisfaction.
Transportation	Approximately 24 million cars have navigation systems and Internet access to locate nearby attractions for customers on the road; sensors have been implemented to parallel park cars and detect drivers who become drowsy or swerve while driving.

Source: Author.

Specifically to healthcare, IoT complements the analytics ecosystem, which includes medical devices, consumer wearable devices, and innovative sensors integrated in a variety of tools and objects. IoT can generate massive amounts of data that are subsequently analyzed by health IT systems. IoT devices are becoming mainstream and an integral part to population health management strategies and predictive analytics.

As referenced in Table 6.1, healthcare is an industry that is very applicable to IoT. Use cases in healthcare for IoT are on the rise. Wearable technology has become more than a fashion statement. It is very popular among millennials and a necessity particularly for senior citizens and the aging population. Wearables such as smartwatches and Fitbits are more than just telling time, seeing text messages, or playing your favorite tunes. They are collecting our health data and becoming a life-changing and lifesaving device. These wearable devices are able to capture vital data on heart rate, activities (steps, calories), sleep, location, and emergency contact. These types of data can provide insightful, proactive actions to improve the quality of care and services in healthcare.

The Internet of Things has changed the world of medicine. What was considered impossible to treat has become possible with IoT coupled with analytics. When connected to the Internet, ordinary medical devices can gather invaluable data with more frequency to give extra insight into symptoms and enable remote care such as telehealth (more later in this chapter). With IoT, more data and better analysis give patients more control over their lives and caregivers can provide proactive treatment. Some real-life use cases include cancer treatment, diabetes, and asthma ailments. Technologies such as Bluetooth and sensors are enabling IoT with data to monitor patients and alert their physicians of key vitals. Clinical research organizations are likely to use IoT as they seek to collect more data and information from patients both internal and external to the clinical environment.

Use cases leveraging IoT applications are limitless: everything from analyzing social media by collecting tweets, blogs, and posts to determine what consumers are recommending as a service/product to security and surveillance of login sessions and data access for data security breaches – and all else in between. Going beyond collection of data for exploration, and even analysis – IoT data can uncover patterns in events as they occur. Analyzing IoT data can drive prescribed actions to prevent unnecessary outages and costs. By sending alerts and notifications, updating situational war-room dashboards, and even providing instructive action to other objects, the need for real-time actions has never been greater.

On the downside, as IoT grows, the growing use of detectors and sensors must excite the hackers and cyber-criminals. They can leverage these devices to hack into the systems. Many traditional fraud detection techniques do not apply because detection is no longer seeking one rare event or anomaly but requires understanding an accumulation of events in context. One challenge of cybersecurity for IoT involves constant data analysis and streaming data events is managed and analyzed differently. We expect advanced analytics to shed new light on detection and prevention with event streaming processing. Another challenge is the plumbing of the data generated by IoT. An even bigger challenge for IoT will be to prove its value. There are limited implementations of IoT in full production at the enterprise level.

AI – ARTIFICIAL (AND AUGMENTED) INTELLIGENCE

Artificial intelligence (AI) is *the* buzzword of the decade. The promise of AI ranges from talking robots to using machine learning and deep learning for complex analytical-driven decisions. An entire chapter or book can be written about artificial intelligence and its intentions to deliver anything and everything. Hollywood even made AI popular in the form of science fiction with memorable and recognizable movies such *The Terminator* (1984) and *I, Robot* (2004). What was science fiction has become nonfiction to a certain extent. The good news is that we do not anticipate robots or machines to be bad, evil characters.

AI has existed for many years, even before those infamous movies were made. It was first referenced in 1956 by John McCarthy, who was an American computer scientist and one of the founding fathers of AI. Mr. McCarthy defined AI as "every aspect of learning or any other feature of intelligence can in principle be so precisely described that a machine can be made to simulate it." The potential of AI has the attention of many organizations, including hardware and software vendors.

The potential for AI is tremendous, particularly for healthcare artificial intelligence. Many analysts, thought leaders, and investment firms are excited about AI. Tractica, a marketing intelligence firm that focuses on emerging technologies, researched and published a report on healthcare artificial intelligence. Tractica revealed that this market is expected to exceed US$34 billion[9] by 2025. Healthcare AI is primarily driven by the growing need to automate tasks and harness deep insights into clinical and financial matters.

In healthcare, we personally believe that the healthcare industry can greatly benefit from the use of artificial intelligence to do extremely good deeds. AI is a game changer with its applications for insight-driven decisions. Technology companies, academia, and venture capitalists have invested millions and even billions over the years to deliver AI. Technology advancements have enabled the ability to process unlimited amounts of unstructured data such as scans, images, and exams and transform them into intelligent information. AI programs combined with healthcare analytics are helping professionals in healthcare to better interpret and translate patient data to deliver tailored and personalized care.

We all can agree that healthcare is expensive, particularly in the United States. You and I as consumers and patients in the healthcare system endure and feel the pain of the costs each time we visit a doctor or hospital. Remember the personal story from Chapter 1? The costs of ER visits and to doctors totaled over US$45,000. Luckily, insurance covered some of the costs but we still had to pay a large portion out of our own pocket. In addition, prescription medications are extremely costly. In some cases where costs are extremely high, patients are looking outside the United States or even at underground or black markets for their medications. The healthcare industry as a whole continuously looks for ways to reduce costs and AI is the leading driver of many healthcare initiatives. The intent is to incorporate AI technologies to decrease costs for both the providers and patients.

Vendors in the analytical and data management marketplace are adding AI applications to their solution portfolio. The global market will look to develop AI applications to fuse the ever-growing and

[9] https://www.tractica.com/research/artificial-intelligence-for-healthcare-applications/.

massive volumes of data and apply them to machine learning techniques, deep learning algorithms such as linear regression, time series, and neural networks. These applications are designed to tackle specific, real-world healthcare use cases that will make diagnosis, monitoring, and treatment of patients more reliable, efficient, and available around the world.

AI Use Cases in Healthcare

Healthcare has many functions in which AI can be implemented, such as key clinical and operational areas. These areas include imaging analytics, drug discovery and clinical trials, clinical decision support, natural language processing, biomarker discovery, and patient management. Here are some use cases where AI has been implemented in healthcare organizations.

In the same report from Tractica, top-10 use cases for healthcare are:

1. Medical image analysis
2. Healthcare virtual desktop access
3. Computational drug discovery and drug effectiveness
4. Medical treatment recommendation
5. Patient data processing
6. Medical diagnosis assistance
7. Converting paperwork into digital data
8. Automated report generation
9. Hospital patient management system
10. Biomarker discovery

At a recent AI summit in London in 2019, two care providers presented their AI adoption, which caught the attention of many attendees. Cleveland Clinic and Carers UK provided very noteworthy insights into their organizations' use of AI and its future.

Cleveland Clinic (CC) is a not-for-profit healthcare organization that handles 5.4 million patient visits each year. It is expected to grow year over year. In the presentation, CC described how they embark on IA as a solution to one of the healthcare industry's biggest challenges: worker burnout. According to CC, 54% of healthcare professionals suffer from burnout while other industries experience on average about 23%. Physicians in particular are under more stress today than ever due to the amount of time on the job and number of patients to see. Technology can be a friend and a foe in healthcare. On one hand, technology can help doctors to access more information at their fingertips. On the other hand, it also adds pressure for the physicians to produce the data (clinical documentation) and ingest the latest medical journals, professional articles, patient-provided data, clinical trials, etc. Using AI is a way to become more efficient delivering patient-focused analysis and predictive care.

CC is applying data management, analytics, and AI to connect nearly 1 billion points of data to analyze predictive readmission, length of stay, and personalized survival modes. This global organization discovered that a significant number of their patients were readmitted after being released from the hospital. The ability to analyze clinical, demographic, chronic diseases data is very insightful. CC was able to identify patterns and develop predictive data models for personal treatment and length of stay for specific illnesses. The outcome has significantly reduced readmissions and length of stay. In addition, CC has insights into the profiles of the current patients, and can predict the type of generalist and specialist care needed for staffing needs to manage the clinic's operations.

Carers UK is another organization using AI for healthcare. Carers UK is a national, nonprofit membership charity whose purpose is to provide expert advice, information, and support for care providers. The presenters from Carers UK provided a perspective on an evolving trend and pressure on caregivers for seniors and children. The scope of the AI application is to build a monitoring system designed to help senior citizens live more independently. The solution consists of a mobile app for the caregiver that remotely monitors activity in the senior's living space. Sensors are placed around the home and set up to deliver activity status such as the TV, cabinet doors, kitchen, ovens, kettle, toaster, etc. Reports can display daily and weekly patterns of activity. As the system captures data and learns patterns, caregivers can set up profiles for when their loved ones are sleeping, their wake-up period, when they have activity, and when specific appliances are being used. In addition, customer notifications can be set up, such as no activity or too many activities. For example, a notification was sent to the caregiver that her mother had not gotten up and she had an appointment for a physical within the hour. Another example was that an alert was notified that the back door was left open longer than normal. The caregiver gave her mother a call and learned that she was gardening outside. The results reveal that the stress of caregiving is reduced via this AI application and caregivers do not have to be physically present to monitor and be available for their loved ones. With this monitoring system, Carers UK admitted that the challenge was gaining permission from seniors to place monitors and having Big Brother watching and following them around the clock.

It is great to see that two healthcare organizations are leveraging AI to practical problems and challenges. AI can be overwhelming but, with a defined problem, it can deliver solutions to many aspects in healthcare. Here are some other use cases:

Image Analysis

AI technology is taking the complexity and uncertainty out of interpreting patient scans with image analysis algorithms. With AI, machine learning algorithms have the ability to pinpoint and highlight problem areas on images, assisting in the screening process. This image analysis serves as an additional degree of certainty in the diagnosis of a patient's condition. This technology has seen greatest adoption in fields such as dermatology, neurology, and ophthalmology, but its specialty reach has expanded with time.

Patient Triage

AI is popular for patient triage and is aiding with the issue of doctor burnout by providing a safe and reliable method from manual to automated outreach to patients. To alleviate unnecessary patient visits for trivial or nonexistent conditions, AI is being deployed to collect patient data via text messaging or application by asking the patient a series of questions about their symptoms. After collecting sufficient information, analyses are being performed to recommend a visit to the doctor, or to send along the information for further review and consultation visit. The patient triage application is taking the guesswork out of self-diagnosis and saving both the patient and healthcare provider money and time. Working smarter and providing better care for patients is the goal of AI in healthcare.

Patient Outcomes

Effective decision support is another application in which AI is improving patient outcomes. Even the most experienced doctors or nurses encounter challenges suggesting next steps for a complicated patient with a complex case file. For this reason, clinical decision support systems are needed and necessary for healthcare providers. With AI, the ability to reduce clinical variation and repetitive testing is a value-added benefit for patient outcomes. Ensuring patient safety is superior with decision support applications that can quickly make sense of all the data within a physician's electronic medical records system.

Language Translation for Medical Treatment

AI is leveraging machine translation (AI complete) interpreting non-English-speaking patients. From personal and direct experience, the aging population has a real need for this AI application. When you are in pain or sick and cannot share your symptoms with your care provider either in speech or written text, it can be very stressful and frustrating for all participants. Patients who may not be proficient in English can have a very hard time telling or describing their symptoms to their physicians or nurse. At the same time, care providers are not able to diagnose the patient's conditions correctly without understanding the patient's ailment. AI machine translation is being used to translate, for example, Vietnamese into English, so that what is being spoken can be understood. A patient can speak into their phone and have it translated for the doctor or nurse to evaluate the patient's condition. This capability is much needed for non-English-speaking patients and senior citizens who may have a family member or a companion to accompany them to the doctor's office or hospital.

Mental Health and Depression

This is an area topping the news media and in the political arena. The landscape is ideal for AI to address mental health and depression. For the first time, technology and the IoT can capture real-time, objective metrics for state of mind and mood like tone of speech, breathing pattern, smartphone communication, and physical activity. In today's society, we are learning and accepting that people would rather share their deepest and most private feelings with an avatar over another human being; hence the emergence of chatbots, which leverage advances in natural language processing to create avatars and develop virtual therapists. Chatbots are constantly evolving to become more human-like and also to offer different language options. AI can now detect nonverbal cues such as facial expressions, gestures, and postures to analyze multisensory information and help evaluate the user. AI can be developed and programmed to augment the shortage of health professionals to alleviate the burden of depression and other mental health conditions.

AI technologies will contribute significantly to the growth of the IoT function, as will systems designed to enhance security around mobile devices and networks. Healthcare organizations anticipate that artificial intelligence, the IoT, and other advanced analytics solutions will produce prescribed actions, reduced costs, and quicker response times to regulatory changes.

AI may be the future but it is also bringing back the past by restoring "care" in healthcare, so that clinicians have more time with patients, avoid burnout and depression, and empower patients with proactive regimens for their ailments. AI will require substantial involvement of the medical community to care for their patients and not allow increased productivity to squeeze clinicians even further.

Challenges with AI

AI for healthcare is promising and expanding in many ways. The need to balance the risks and rewards of AI in healthcare will require concerted efforts from technology vendors and developers, regulators, end users, and consumers like you and me. There are many potential challenges and they can be overcome with the right balance. Here are some challenges facing AI for healthcare:

Data – Cleansed and Integrated
AI relies on and needs a tremendous amount of integrated, cleansed data for the various applications. Data is a commodity and can be invaluable in healthcare. The motto "garbage in, garbage out"

becomes an unfortunate reality when data quality is not addressed. Organizations base business decisions on insights gained from data, and healthcare is no exception. If anything, quality healthcare data is of the essence. If inaccurate data is analyzed without subsequent data quality checks, only inaccurate intelligence will prevail. Poor quality data can affect businesses in varying degrees, ranging from simple misrepresentation of information to multimillion-dollar errors.

In fact, numerous analysts and researchers have concluded that data quality is the culprit behind many failed projects in healthcare. With healthcare being an important topic in many communities, improving data quality has become a top management priority.

With healthcare data, you now have to store and manage a variety of data types in large volumes. Due to the tremendous amount of health data variety and sources, quality is often compromised. It is a common problem that many healthcare organizations are reluctant to admit and address. The single most challenging aspect for companies is to recognize and determine the severity of their data quality issues and face the problem head-on. Spending the money, time, and resources to collect massive volumes of data without ensuring the quality of the data is futile and only leads to disappointment.

Trust and Accuracy

Data privacy and security presents a new set of challenges for AI in healthcare. Health data and medical records cannot be handled recklessly. AI algorithms need access to massive datasets for training and validation in order to provide the right actions for physicians and clinicians.

Healthcare organizations shuffling terabytes of data between disparate systems is a common practice. The shuffling of data increases the risk of a data breach. When a data breach occurs, the financial burden and reputation of the healthcare organization is on the line and trust is broken between the patient and the healthcare provider.

Most healthcare organizations do keep their data assets closely guarded in highly secure, HIPAA-compliant systems. As AI needs to access different data types from data storage, there are more ways for hackers to deliver ransomware.

Another side of trust is the accuracy of the AI application. As machine learning is becoming more popular and common, physicians and those who interact with patients may become complacent in trusting all computer-generated assessments to be perfect. Trusting AI programs becomes even more risky over time as the training dataset becomes outdated and conflicts with the unavoidable reality in the changing healthcare practice and disease characteristics.

As machine learning becomes more commonplace, clinicians and those who interact with machine learning are at risk of becoming complacent and treating all computer-generated assessments as infallible. Trusting a program becomes even more dangerous over time as the training data set gets older and clashes with the inevitable reality in medicine of changing practice, medications available, and changes in disease characteristics over time.

Ethics

The trickiest issue about AI healthcare is the philosophical and ethical debate among practitioners and regulators. What happens when an AI application makes the wrong decision? Who is responsible and where is the blame? How can practitioners verify? How do AI systems avoid bias and protect patient data? These are the questions that have been raised within the healthcare community involving AI.

In the traditional practice, doctors rely on the health data by reviewing your history and current symptoms. Such practice asks the patient questions about the current ailment and a course of action is recommended by the doctor. If the doctor misdiagnosed, then at least you know the source and the trails that the doctors took. With AI, it may be a black-box phenomenon where a patient may not know how the decision was made and what information led to that diagnosis.

In addition, AI developers may be biased with their data using only certain demographics or regions for analysis. When biased data is used, patient care is at risk as AI systems can be taught to push practitioners toward a misaligned clinical action. Worse yet, AI applications could be programmed to promote decisions that profit a specific drug developer or healthcare manufacturer.

Ensuring that AI develops ethically and safely will be the responsibility of all stakeholders: patients, physicians, payers, providers, and programmers – and everyone in between.

It is an exciting, challenging, but optimistic time to be in healthcare, and the continuing maturity of AI will only add to the mixed emotions of these ongoing, controversial debates. There may not be any clear answers to these fundamental challenges at the moment, but humans still have the opportunity to take control, make the hard choices, and shape the future of patients in healthcare.

3D PRINTING

3D printing was invented in 1983 by Chuck Hall. Considered the father of 3D printing, he manufactured the world's first 3D printer and used it to print a tiny eyewash cup. Even though it was just an ordinary, small black cup, it paved the way for changes in the healthcare industry in the most innovative ways.

3D printing technology is resurfacing in the medical world. Using 3D printing technology, medical devices can be made to match the exact specifications of a patient. The medical devices can be customized and designed to be more compatible with a patient's anatomy. With today's technology, medical devices modeled from patient's images have shown greater acceptance by the body, increased comfort for the patient, and improved performance outcomes after leaving the hospital. The flexibility provided by 3D printing gives healthcare practitioners the ability to provide patients the most advanced care and minimize the risk of complication.

Here are a few current and future medical adoptions of 3D printing and how it affects the patients and alters the healthcare industry:

Prosthetic Limbs
You and I can go online, access a website (such as National Institutes of Health, https://3dprint.nih.gov/collections/prosthetics), print the correct pieces, and construct an affordable prosthetic limb. It sounds ridiculous, but it's all true and cost-efficient. While a traditional fitted and manufactured prosthetic hand can cost thousands of dollars, a similar 3D device can offer similar and if

not a better level of performance for US$50![10] When a 3D-printed prosthetic can be manufactured at a fraction of the cost compared to the traditional method, amputees can print and have a number of different parts for a variety of uses – driving, exercising, or getting around – and can experiment with different models to see what works the best for them. In addition, 3D printing of prosthetics will dramatically reduce the time spent on fitting and measuring, enhancing the convenience and efficiency of the patient. Patients with limited access to quality healthcare such as rural areas and warzones can take advantage of 3D printing technology. While access to and costs of this technology will continue to improve, so will the prosthetic limbs themselves as variety, printing processes, designs, and materials evolve.

Alternative Prosthetics

Although 3D printing shows great promise for prosthetic limbs, they are just a few of the numerous body parts this new technology could replicate. With its ability to print nearly any three-dimensional object, 3D printing in medicine is the tipping innovation the healthcare industry has been yearning for. In addition, 3D-printed body parts can easily be engineered to fit different shapes and sizes to accommodate the human body. Its flexibility, adaptability, and compatibility with various printing materials makes it ideal for everything including prosthetic skin, molds for hearing aids, and dental and orthopedic implants. 3D printing has also shown potential for bone replication, with one such technology using digital scans to create custom implants that bond with the patient's own facial structure. Other future solutions work as a sort of high-flexibility bone-grafting agent, providing a highly adaptable "scaffold" on which bones can integrate and grow.[11]

Organs

Not only has 3D printing technology been used to produce custom body parts as mentioned above, but medical researchers have also

---

[10] https://dealingwithdifferent.com/3d-printing-prosthetics/.
[11] https://www.theverge.com/2016/9/28/13094642/hyperelastic-bone-graft-substance-unveiled.

begun to explore implanting living 3D-printed tissue. While this technology is still in the research and development stage, there is discussion of 3D-planted internal organs such as kidneys. If this is successful, then it would effectively end the high-demand waiting lists and painful selection processes of the organ donor industry.

3D printing technology has also been found valuable in surgical planning. For surgeries that are new or complex in nature, careful measures must be taken to ensure comprehension of the situation. Proactive printing of a patient's anatomy as a visual aid has been found very practical and useful in the preparation for complicated surgeries. The ability to see and hold a physical model of the patient's anatomy gives surgeons the ability to conceptualize the ideal course of action prior to operating. To date, the technology has been used for many complicated heart surgeries, and even the Cleveland Clinic's most recent total face transplant. With the expanding healthcare applications, 3D printing is increasing the attention to detail in patient care, and technology is making it possible to change the healthcare industry and millions of lives.

VIRTUAL REALITY – TEACHING, EDUCATION, LAB

Virtual reality (VR) is popping up in areas such as entertainment, gaming, and education. You are fastened in a high-flying rollercoaster car approaching the top of a sharp hill. As you approach at a stop before the descent, your anticipation makes your heart race, your palms sweat, and you think "Why am I here?" As the front of your car descends down the steep hill and plunges to the valley below, your heart and stomach may just fall out of your body. The scene and the feelings are surreal. In this instance, when the ride is over and you remove your goggles instead of stepping off the rollercoaster, it turns out that the ride you have just experienced was completely virtual and you remember that you are at a gaming convention and not at the amusement park.

VR is the use of computer technology to create a simulated environment. Different from traditional user interfaces, virtual reality engages the user inside an experience made to be interactive and personal. In a virtual reality simulation, users are able to interact with the

3D world in front of them as if they are a part of the scenario. VR invigorates the senses to transport the user to an artificial world and provide an experience that imitates real life. A headset with glasses is commonly worn to experience virtual reality.

Taking technology to the next step is mixed reality (MR). MR is the use of computer technology to combine real and virtual worlds, creating a new hybrid environment. In this hybrid environment, physical and digital objects coexist and interact in real time. MR technology attaches virtual objects to the real world, allowing users to interact with them. MR is often delivered with the use of glasses and a controller.

The practical concepts of virtual and mixed reality have amazed audiences for many years with easier access thanks to technology. VR/MR technologies are now commercially available for several applications and play a great role in many fields, particularly in healthcare. Naturally, their most important application has caught the attention of medical professionals who are eager to sharpen and expand their skills. For those in the healthcare field, virtual/mixed reality can provide training in procedures, teaching techniques, and equipment use in an effort to simulate patient interactions in a more immersive and caring way.

We all learn in different ways. According to the cone of learning from Edgar Dale, after two weeks the human brain remembers 10% of what it reads, 20% of what it hears, and 90% of what it does or simulates. By this logic, MR and VR have the opportunity to revolutionize completely the way medical professionals are educated and trained today. Education and training via simulation from MR/VR could be a productive step toward more adept and confident healthcare providers and professionals.

VR and MR can be a part of the training programs. They provide future and current physicians, surgeons, and emergency medical staff the "hands-on" experience needed to be competent in a medical procedure. The simulations made possible by the technology are a brilliant alternative to the traditional books and videos used to educate. Educational books and videos have been a useful way to disseminate information, but in light of advanced technology they seem a bit antiquated. With this emerging and immersive style of learning, VR/MR appeals to all types of learners in healthcare through audio, visual, and kinesthetic.

VR and MR are not meant to be a replacement for physical hands-on practice but rather to augment it. Virtual and mixed reality medical education is therefore useful for students who are not quite ready for the action in a hospital environment. Giving residents practice with the computer simulation is a low-risk alternative and, in extreme cases, can prevent patient harm.

Although VR/MR have been in development for years, the concepts of virtual and mixed reality are transformative now due to a shift in consumer-grade technology and costs. With technology vastly improving and prices falling due to competition, healthcare organizations will find it easier to engage and offer reality systems. To date, a number of pilot programs involving virtual and/or mixed reality training for medical students have been implemented worldwide. In 2016, the Cleveland Clinic began one such program for its medical students. In 2018, a well-known virtual reality company announced its partnerships with eight top US medical residency programs to provide hands-on training opportunities for new surgeons. Though not exclusive to medicine, this statistic demonstrates that the VR/MR usefulness in classrooms is nationwide.

CHAPTER **7**

Final Thoughts

"Learning is, by nature, curiosity."

— Plato

The future of healthcare is at a crossroads and being shaped dramatically by a variety of significant trends. While the cost of healthcare continues to rise, the industry is facing a movement toward preventive and value-based care. At the same time, technology like wearable devices, IoT, and home services is empowering patients to be more engaged and more proactive with their own health. At the same time, the industry is struggling with the dilemma of data sharing and maintaining patient privacy and trust. These developments are affecting the role of caregivers and their relationships with their patients. One underlying constant driving toward the digital transformation in healthcare is the power of data and analytics.

Data is growing exponentially and is pervasive in every aspect of the healthcare ecosystem. Analytics is becoming more common to aid with delivering intelligence affecting our daily health, patience experience, and cost control. Technologies such as AI, 3D printing, and augmented reality (AR)/mixed reality (MR) are advancing medical research, preventive and predictive diagnosis, and ongoing care. In addition, more people are needed to support the needs of healthcare and processes are being evaluated to sustain the growth in healthcare.

In the previous chapters, we discussed a lot about technology, which is a key factor moving the healthcare industry forward. In-database processing delivers the promise of analyzing the data where it resides in the database and enterprise data warehouse. It is the process of moving the complex analytical calculations into the database engine, utilizing the resources of the database management system. Data preparation and analytics can be applied directly to the data throughout the data analytical lifecycle. Benefits include eliminating data duplication and movement, thus streamlining the decision process to gain efficiencies, reducing processing time from hours into minutes, and ultimately getting faster results through scalable, high-performance platforms. In-memory analytics is another innovative approach to tackle big data using an in-memory analytics engine to deliver super-fast responses to complicated analytical problems. In-memory analytics are ideal for data exploration and model development processes. Data is lifted into memory for analysis and is flushed when completed. Specific in-memory algorithms and applications are designed to be massively threaded to process high volumes of models on large data sets. Both of these technologies are complementary in nature and not every function can be enabled in-database or in-memory.

Hadoop is a technology to manage your traditional data sources as well as new types of data in the semistructured landscape. Hadoop is an open source technology to store and process massive volumes of data quickly in a distributed environment. Many misconceptions around Hadoop have created false expectations of the technology and its implementation. However, Hadoop offers a platform to support new data sources for data management and analytic processing.

Python, R, and Spark are popular and trendy analytical tools to analyze the abundance of health data. These tools are being embraced by data scientists and data engineers to obtain intelligence. Healthcare organizations are attracted to these tools for their lower cost investment and open source communities. By integrating in-database, in-memory Hadoop, and open source, it delivers a collaborative and harmonious data architecture for healthcare organizations to manage structured and unstructured data. From departmental to enterprise-wide usage, healthcare organizations are leveraging new technologies to manage the health data better, to innovate with analytics, and to create/maintain competitive advantage with intelligence.

If there is one thing that we highly suggest it is to review the use cases. Not only do they provide information that many of you can relate to but they also provide some best practices. These use cases are the ultimate proof that integrating data, people, process, and technology adds strategic value to organizations and provides intelligence in decision-making. Whether you are an executive, line manager, business analyst, developer/programmer, data scientist, or IT professional, these use cases can enlighten the way you do things and help you explore options.

We are barely scratching the surface when it comes to analyzing health data. The future of data management and analytics is pretty exciting. We are personally excited for the maturation of artificial intelligence and virtual/mixed reality. These two technology advancements are complex in nature but they also provide the most value. In addition, AI/AR/MR encompass machine learning, reasoning, natural language processing, speech and vision, human–computer interaction, dialog and narrative generation, and more. Many of these capabilities require specialized infrastructure that leverages high-performance computing, and specialized and particular resources with specific technical expertise. People, process, and technology must be developed in concert with hardware, software, and applications that are deployed to work together in support of your initiative.

FINAL THOUGHTS

A key question facing healthcare providers today is how to transform healthcare delivery while anticipating and meeting an emerging set of new expectations from patients. This will require significant change to the current model of care. The healthcare system in the United States has historically been focused on getting patients better once they have become sick. There are five major themes that are shaping the future of healthcare. They are:

1. Industry transformation
2. Journey to value-based care
3. Investment vs. returns on technology and innovation
4. Applying augmented intelligence to support clinical, operational, and financial outcomes
5. Engagement on the healthcare delivery model to understand experiences and viewpoints

An analytics strategy is needed in order to navigate the uncertainty these themes present successfully. Each theme touches data, people, process, and/or technology in one way or another. Data will be at the forefront. Data will be collected and integrated into data models. Data will come in all forms, from claims and billing data to electronic medical records to Internet of Things (IoT) to public use data. People will use process and technology to build analytical models tying data together that was once impossible, or at least ineffective and resource intensive. The ability to take streaming data and link it to claims data to electronic medical records (EMR) data to Centers for Disease Control (CDC) files to weather will allow for the potential of new intelligence to be delivered through deep learning algorithms. Data management, people, analytical capabilities, and a technology ecosystem will fuel insight-driven decision-making and algorithms and visualization techniques will allow for discovery and action that was once hidden.

INDUSTRY TRANSFORMATION

Disruptive partnerships and market entrants will continue to challenge traditional business models, blur industry lines, and create new competitors and partners. Consolidations, both horizontally and vertically, will continue as organizations seek scale to help protect margins through efficiency and innovation. Cost pressures will drive flexible and innovative care delivery and require unprecedented modes of digital interaction. A deep understanding of population health and value-based care will become an essential factor for financial and competitive success. Patient engagement will be the crossroads of competition as all participants in the healthcare ecosystem seek to control it. An analytics strategy will help prioritize objectives and projects the stress that cost pressures and payment pressures of industry transformation will generate.

JOURNEY TO VALUE-BASED CARE

Medicare continues to create value-based programs to link performance of quality measures to payments. Their aim is to promote better care for individuals, better health for populations, and lower costs. Current programs include:

- End-Stage Renal Disease Quality Incentive Program
- Hospital Value-Based Purchasing Program
- Hospital Readmission Reduction Program
- Value Modifier Program
- Hospital Acquired Conditions Reduction Program
- Skilled Nursing Facility Value-Based Program
- Home Health Value-Based Program

As Medicare continues to build programs, commercial and Medicaid programs are joining the fray. Taking longitudinal care of patients will be the responsibility of healthcare providers. The level of risk hospital providers will be responsible for will continue to increase. Out are the old fee-for-service models and in are the new innovative value-based care shared savings and quality-metric-based models. Your analytics strategy will need to generate models from primary care risk models to models identifying patients who are at risk for increased healthcare spend to future inpatient admission risk models for specific conditions that are considered "impactable" to identifying the services needed to keep patients in network to provide them with the best possible care to understanding why patients choose another network for some of the most critical procedures to leveraging genomic data. You can see the important role an analytics strategy will play.

INVESTMENT VS. RETURNS ON TECHNOLOGY AND INNOVATION

You have probably heard Benjamin Franklin's quote, "In this world nothing can be said to be certain, except death and taxes." Had Benjamin Franklin been alive today, he would have probably modified his quote, "In this world nothing can be said to be certain, except death, taxes, and rising healthcare costs." According to the Centers for Medicare and Medicaid Services report, "National Health Expenditures Summary Including Share of GDP, CY 1960–2017," healthcare costs have risen since 1960. With the healthcare industry under a cost-increasing microscope, the amount of investment and returns generated from an analytics strategy needs to be thoughtful and strategic, making sure capturing, integrating, and interpreting data from all available sources can be leveraged to deliver value in the form of dollar savings and quality improvements.

APPLYING AUGMENTED INTELLIGENCE TO SUPPORT CLINICAL, OPERATIONAL, AND FINANCIAL OUTCOMES

Your analytics strategy will help you uncover a deeper understanding of the health of populations you manage. Predictive algorithms can surface clinical opportunities for intervention and prevention for the populations you manage. Providing the right services at the right location will challenge operational and financial models to maximize throughput while providing services for the lowest cost while maximizing revenue and operating margins while providing the best clinical outcome. Not everything will be best solved by AI, but at least informed by AI and combined with human intelligence to create an optimal augmented-intelligence decision.

ENGAGEMENT ON THE HEALTHCARE DELIVERY MODEL TO UNDERSTAND EXPERIENCES AND VIEWPOINTS TO CREATE TRUST BETWEEN PROVIDERS AND PATIENTS

Healthcare is unlike any other industry. Providers sit in a unique relationship in patient's lives. Today, providers have a personal relationship with patients that should continue to become even more personal. Your analytics strategy will help rethink service strategies, capabilities, delivering potentially life-changing diagnoses, and culture that drive connections between Baby Boomers, Generation X, Millennials, Generation Z, and future generations. You will have to consider how social media, online communities, wearable devices, mobile connections, health literacy, and patient-generated health data will interact among all healthcare participants.

CONCLUSION

You can begin to understand the importance of your analytics strategy and the comprehensive complexity that it needs to address. As you develop your analytics strategy, developing internal business partnerships will be the key to your program's success. Partnerships will range from clinical to financial to operational. You should develop use cases to share success stories. Those success stories can cover one or more of the four parts of the analytics strategy from data, people, process, and/or technology. The use cases can explore the success in using data that was once siloed or did not even exist and now resides in a unified data warehouse that enables clinical (EMR and streaming data), financial (billing and claims data), operational (surgical schedules, scheduled visits, etc.), plus any other external data sources you are collecting, like census data, NOAA weather data, air quality data, etc. The use cases can affirm the importance of people and the importance of changing roles, capabilities, and investment required to become an analytically mature organization. The use cases can promote the development of teams around the principles of design thinking, lean, and agile. The use cases can establish the tools and processes for understanding the work, doing the work right, and doing the right work. The use cases should evaluate new technologies alongside your business partners to ensure the enterprise has the right tools to support an agile analytics way of working by enabling the design and evolution of architecture based on requirements.

Success is sustained responsibilities between the data and analytics team and the rest of the enterprise. The data and analytics team needs to provide data expertise around making analytics easier to consume. There is no need to show the complexity or the math. It needs to educate the consumer of analytics in the methodologies and how to interpret the results in context. It also needs to provide continuous monitoring that can allow for dynamic model recalibration, monitoring of model performance KPIs, communication around changes, or interventions that can impact results and explore new features. The rest of the enterprise needs to communicate feedback on interventions or process changes that can enhance models, use data-related insights daily, and embrace developing the required skills necessary for interpretation and decision-making.

Your strategy will allow you to benefit in the following ways:

- Ability to apply advanced capabilities
- Ability to visualize data for insight
- Ability to change the discussion
- Ability to find hidden opportunities

The complexity of the healthcare problems we are being asked to solve cannot be delivered using traditional analytics. We are being asked to solve complex problems from demand modeling to capacity planning to population health management modeling to surgical suite planning, etc. The list continues to grow and the difficulty of the questions being asked continues to test the design complexities of model development. We are now picking from a list of techniques from Logistic Regression to Random Forest to K-Means and K-Nearest Neighbor Clustering methods to ARIMAX to Monte Carlo to Neural Network to Gradient Boost, by way of example. These techniques, coupled with the ability to visualize data differently, allows for insight that can unlock hidden opportunities that we were unable to identify before. It allows us to start changing the discussion. Is there opportunity where none may have been evident without using different analytical techniques or visualization tools? It is these opportunities to find insights that were hidden before the application of new visualization techniques that can give the healthcare industry the ability to lower costs while raising quality outcomes.

There is promise for AI in healthcare. It will give us better, more accurate predictive models. These models will be able to deliver meaningful clinical decision support functions, like problem list generation and differential diagnosis to operational throughput models to financial planning models. It will help with task automation like imaging analysis. But not everything is best solved with AI. Thoughtful augmented intelligence, the combination of human intelligence and artificial intelligence, will lead the way.

KEY TAKEAWAYS

Finally, we would like to share key takeaways, views, findings, and opinions from along the journey. These takeaways, views, findings, or opinions do not have any particular order of importance; nor should they. It is a learning process with continued curiosity. They are also not independent of each other. Each takeaway, view, finding, or opinion has some overlap with the others in some shape or form. We hope that at the end of this chapter you will agree that taking the first step of the journey will be well worth the effort required and gain some value from lessons learned.

Be agile in everything you do, from projects to strategy. As Nike would say, if you have an idea, just do it. George S. Patton said, "A good plan executed now is better than a perfect plan executed next week." Agile provides you the tools necessary to execute on a plan that will produce minimally viable projects instead of waiting until the perfect deliverable is produced. In fact, is there ever really a perfect deliverable? We believe not. Every project you will be delivering, from predictive analytical models to dashboards to a data warehouse, will require continuous monitoring and offer continuous improvement opportunities. Agile offers transparency in the work. All team members will have visibility as you track your project on a Kanban board. Sprint planning starts delivering feedback immediately and the team can start to show value instantly. The earlier you start delivering value, the easier it will be to manage expectations when project requirements change. Agile allows you to start to deliver working capabilities after every sprint, or at least progress that keeps the sponsor engaged. This invariably leads to higher satisfaction. Every project will not go as planned. There will always be roadblocks or changes in requirements, or at least the need for flexibility in changing requirements. Agile allows for the teams to control expectations and timelines and reduce the risk that the product deliverable will not meet the end user's needs. Agile methods maximize the opportunities for sponsor and end-user engagement by involving the sponsor and end user during the sprint planning cycle to product beta testing. It helps shape the "win-win" scenario for all involved.

Knowing your end user is a natural outcome as your analytic teams mature and complete projects. This will likely spur ideas from your team on potential improvements to end-user experience or tools to help end users do their daily work. Give your teams the freedom to "just do it." An idea not worked on is just an idea. How will you know if the idea has any value added to the end user? There is only one way to find out, and that is to get started. This not only pertains to your end user. What about your daily work? We know everyone out there has ideas. What normally holds you back is time. Do you have time to work on your ideas with all of the other work you are responsible for? While your entire job can't be "just-do-its," there should always be a balance between exploring new ideas and current workload. There is no magic number of hours per week we should allow for these types of initiatives, but leaders and team members should be able to discuss the potential value around ideas and find time to explore their viability. Remember, when you are sprint planning, you are in control of messaging and expectation management with your sponsors. You need to communicate the importance of bringing an idea into development to explore the potential benefits to the project. You do not want to stifle idea creation by not finding time to try new things. Not providing an avenue for team members to explore ideas they created will only diminish idea creation over the long haul. Attitude is everything and limiting the exploration of any team members will lead to a shutdown of ideas. They will have the mindset, "Why waste my time coming up with new ideas, when I can't work on them?" This is not to be confused with the lean principle we discussed earlier. Those just-do-its are quick-win, simple no-brainer solutions that have been identified and are in the backlog. These are known solutions just waiting to be resourced and can be grabbed during a sprint cycle when time frees up.

Check ego at the door. This requires lifelong learning – no one is too old to keep learning. Ego does not lead to collaboration. You have probably heard this phrase repeatedly. If you are the smartest person in the room, you are in the wrong room. When you are collaborating on your projects, who is in the room? Subject matter experts from many disciplines. Each expert brings smarts to the table. The collection of smarts allows the projects to move forward and produce successful outcomes. Checking your ego at the door allows you to objectively understand the strengths you bring to the team, the weakness you have, and your ability to convert that weakness by learning something new. It has been our experience that individual accolades stifle creativity and innovation through not actively listening. Don't jeopardize projects because you want to be singled out. Recognizing team wins creates a sense of accomplishment and participation from all individual team members. Success in this new era of advanced analytics and technology will require teams of subject matter experts. Don't allow egos to create an atmosphere of animosity. By checking egos at the door, you are already ahead without even realizing the benefits that will come throughout the project.

The only one holding you back is yourself. Healthcare is a complicated industry. Couple the rapidly changing technology landscape, advancements in artificial intelligence, and the rapidly changing healthcare landscape and you have a disaster waiting to happen if you are not committed to continuous learning. This doesn't come easy. There is a time commitment. That doesn't mean you need to learn for two to three hours daily. It means you need to make a commitment to learn every day. Maybe it is only 10 minutes, but make a goal. The best way to boost knowledge is through reading. Read every day. Maybe that goal is to read about something new every day related to the healthcare industry, or about a new technology or an artificial intelligence method. Maybe it is not healthcare-related, but business leadership–related, or learning from a different industry. Maybe that goal is to watch a video about AI or a new technology. There are other alternatives to reading, like audiobooks and podcasts. The point is, learning can be in any subject area. Take the time and effort to try and schedule that time to learn. If you do not make a habit of carving out the time to learn, that time will be filled with other activities, either work-related or personal activities. There is nothing more rewarding than learning something new. Continue to add to your knowledge base. Not only will you feel better, but your brain will thank you and you will be ready for any opportunity that comes.

Don't let technology drive the solution. Count on understanding the problem and requirements and designing a solution around solving the problem. AI is not a verb. You will be tempted to think the next bright shiny object, in this case, technology, will solve the problem. If it were that easy, everyone would have done it. Technology is part of the solution. As we have laid out in the book, driving to success requires a strategy around data, people, process, and technology. Understanding how technology will play a role in the deliverable of the solution involves gathering business requirements and functional requirements. It is making sure you can clearly define the objective(s). What business insights are you trying to deliver and how do you plan to show them? How often do they need new insights? What happens if the new insights are not delivered timely? What type of functionality do you need? Who will be using the outputs? Do you need different levels of details? It is important to interview the end users and document their answers to provide the teams with clear understanding and accountability of what needs to be delivered. It is at that time that the teams will be able to design the most appropriate solution with the right underlying technology to deliver a successful business value.

This may sound simple, almost a no-brainer. Projects often fail because we do not take the necessary time to understand the problem fully, or collect the necessary requirements and design a solution that works for the end user. Solutions are built by the analytics team without enough time spent with the end users. We have explored many different tools to help the teams make sure no stone is left unturned. The most important tool is curiosity. Most of you have heard of the five *whys*. Use it here by asking "Why?" five times; it really helps you understand every element in the requirements. This level of due diligence now will save time later. No one wants to stop a project because a requirement wasn't fully vetted. Spending the time at the beginning to collect details that will lead to full understanding of the problem, all the necessary requirements, and a minimally viable product will lead to an ultimate solution that is unambiguous to all teams.

Many times, we get caught up in the artificial intelligence hype cycle that AI will solve everything. Whether you go to conferences, talk about projects internally, or converse with your peers, AI seems to be at the forefront of every conversation. In fact, you see or hear comments like, "Just do some AI and see what happens." AI should not be used without business judgment. Instead of just "AIing" a project, can we take advantage of data and AI techniques to disrupt business, clinically, operationally, and financially through thoughtful augmented intelligence to enhance decision support.

Collaboration and engagement is needed at every layer of the organization between sponsors and analytical teams. Mutual victories. Communicate success stories. Project success relies on collaboration and engagement at every level. Think about why most of your projects fail or get put on hold. I suspect the reason outside of funding the project is a lack of collaboration and engagement. Business requirements are naturally dynamic and leveraging real-time feedback from end users through their engagement keeps alignment around project objectives to potential timeline adjustments to challenges that need to be addressed across horizontally and vertically team dynamics. Without the necessary collaboration and engagement, projects just stall and lose focus and direction. Collaboration and engagement will encourage innovation and inspire fresh thinking. When has a brainstorming session been unproductive? That is not to say every brainstorming session will be considered a success. Some sessions will generate volumes of ideas; some may not. People never really turn off their brains after a session and a seemingly unproductive previous session may wind up very productive in the next session. Brainstorming sessions will create a melting pot of ideas that the team owns. It is this ownership of ideas by the team that generates new ideas. The inescapable conclusion, collaboration, and engagement breeds project excitement through accountability, ownership, and learning. This ultimately continues to drive projects forward toward the first minimally viable product. Once you reach that milestone, the only barrier is believing you can let up on collaboration and engagement efforts.

No matter how the project originates, whether you have a sponsor, it supports organizational goals or objectives, or your analytics team sees value in exploring a project and then taking it to potential end users, all projects should have mutual victories. Why wouldn't they? This theme of the book is about a strategy that is applied to enable shared success from providing insights to the decision-making process to leveraging work across multiple projects to learnings from all projects, whether they were successfully put on hold indefinitely or just dissolved when value could not be realized. Building models is easy; answering the right questions to achieve mutual victories is hard.

Success is not just a local event and shared with only the teams involved. Find ways to communicate success stories to the organization. This will draw people in. Who doesn't want to be part of a success story that is shared? Whether it is through the internal intranet, monthly or quarterly analytics meetings, or corporate email communications, find a way to share the success stories. Not only does sharing create goodwill, but it creates excitement and interest. Interest will draw additional use cases and, as interest continues to grow, you create a self-sustaining backlog of projects. Isn't that what you want?

Analytics is like taking a class in reverse. You are asked to take the exam without knowing the content and then you take the class. This is best explained by an example. Let's assume you built a forecast. What is the purpose of a forecast? To provide an estimate of what the future will look like. Let's assume you produce a forecast for the next eight weeks. This is the exam. Now, for the next eight weeks, the "content" is unveiled. That is, over the next eight weeks the actual results will come in and you will see how your forecast performed. You see, it's like taking the test first. You do not get the luxury of knowing the actuals or understanding the content until after the forecast period is over. It will be like that for every model you build. Sure, you have training sets, but the actual exam is what is important. This can represent a challenge in gaining confidence in using and interpreting the results. It is just like playing a musical instrument. The more you practice, the better musician you become. Treat analytics the same way. The more you use analytics, the more confident you will be in consuming the results and applying them in your daily decision-making process.

There will be hard times and frustrations, don't let that consume you. Put setbacks behind you. Celebrate every win, no matter how small or insignificant you think it is. Take time to reflect – learn from your wins, but learn more from your mistakes. This is probably one of the hardest lessons to learn. When you have setbacks, it is how you respond and it starts with attitude. You will definitely be disappointed and perhaps even angry. That is normal behavior but you have to move on. Think of a football player or baseball player who just lost a game, a Super Bowl or World Series. What do you hear from them? You hear disappointment and anger. What do you also hear? They put it behind them. When we are talking about a game during the regular season, they need to put it behind them within 24 hours. If they do not? There is a good chance it will affect their performance on the field during the next regular season game. What if it is the Super Bowl or World Series? Sure, it may take longer, maybe weeks or until the next training camp starts, and they eventually put it behind them. The one consistency is they use the time on how long they will focus on feeling disappointed or angry. The same holds true here. There will be times during your career where there will be a setback. You will have a range of emotions. The same principle holds as for a sports athlete. You need time to express your feelings, and then you need to refocus your energy. There will be learnings to be had. You need to understand how you contributed and what you can do next time to circumvent the same outcome. Acceptance allows you to move on and ask, "What's next?"

Think about what you are embarking on. Four seemingly separate parallel journeys (data, people, process, and technology) are connected in driving toward one goal. That goal is to execute on your analytics strategy to create a competitive advantage. Think about any project that you will be starting up or the analytics strategy you are executing against. Your analytics strategy is not going to be completed overnight, nor will it be completed in a week or month. We are talking year(s) potentially to deliver on all parts of your analytics strategy. Projects will act much like your analytics strategy. These projects will not be completed overnight, and probably not be completed within the next week. Projects will have project plans with backlogs, tasks, and milestones with a targeted delivery of a minimally viable product that will lead to a product with full functioning capabilities at some point in the future. As we learned earlier in the book, there are plenty of different tools, like lean principles and agile techniques to help you navigate to the finish line. As tasks are starting to be completed, you move them through the Kanban board. Do you really take the time to celebrate? Should you really celebrate all of those little tasks that lead to significant stages of the project or strategy? The simple answer: yes. Why? A few reasons come to mind – attitude, importance of the current moment, and appreciation. The attitude of the team is a collection of the individual attitudes of its members as well as the leaders and sponsors. Positive attitude is contagious. When one person succeeds, everyone feels better. Creating an atmosphere of positive attitude will help overcome the most difficult challenge. Understanding the importance of the current moment can give the team confidence it is on the right path. Every task completed inches you closer to completion. Quitting is the only way a project fails, so make sure the current moment is celebrated and appreciated. Every step you take, no matter the size, is a step forward. You cannot change the past, so making sure you understand the current moment will make for a brighter future. Appreciation is important in two respects. First is around people and second around the work. Appreciation does not mean bringing in coffee and bagels or throwing a pizza luncheon for the team for every little task completed. Appreciation is showing every person on the team respect. There will always be a chance for a pizza luncheon after a milestone. Respect and acknowledgment of work well done creates positive influence, energy, and outlooks. Appreciation is a way to ignite a person's inner passion to do a job well. Appreciation is the celebration of excellence in one's work. The work is going to be hard. Acknowledging that fact is important and teams will appreciate that. There are going to be times when the team is challenged to find a solution, maybe even change course, or does not have an answer. Appreciation means the team has the power and confidence to say, "We don't know" or "We don't have the answer." One thing is clear, we are certain that will lead to answers. Appreciate the fact that not everyone has all of the answers. What the team is really saying is, "We don't have the answer – yet." The team will find a way. Never take for granted people and the understanding the work is hard.

In today's business climate, where analytical productivity is measured in throughput of projects, algorithms, or dashboards that are placed into production environments, we normally fail to account for reflection. There will be projects that succeed, others that fail, and some that are just put on hold never to be resurrected. There are so many lessons that can be learned if we take the time to do a postmortem. Part of every project should be a discussion and reflection. We should focus on questions like: What worked well? What didn't work so well? What should we continue to do? What would we do differently? Did we meet timelines? How were our time estimates for completed tasks? What recommendations would we make to other teams? Collecting great feedback is time misused unless you disseminate the information, whether it is written or verbal.

Be creative – don't be afraid to try something new. Explore everything. Have accountability. We tend to lack creativity for a couple of reasons. First, it may take more time than the end user may be willing to wait for their minimally viable product. Second, with creativity comes failure. Not every creative solution will work and failures can be seen as time and resources wasted. Third is the old adage of, "This is how we have always done it in the past." Fourth, leaders might not be comfortable with creative failure. Creative setbacks can lead to missing milestone timelines. Don't let any of these reasons stop creativity. There will be times when taking chances on creative ideas is wide of the mark and doesn't produce the desire result. Make sure you can clearly articulate the benefits you expected to receive and what experience was gained. Every project you work on does not come with a step-by-step instruction book. Granting creative licensure to the team will motivate them to build the best solution possible. It is invoking critical thinking skills that can be leveraged in future projects. Creativity keeps the team fresh and interested. Creativity will lead to more successful outcomes. Competitive advantages do not come from doing the same thing over and over again. Competitive advantages will be stimulated by creativity. Big breakthroughs come on the heels of creativity, not doing the same old routine. In the end, creativity will bring value to the end user. You just need to make them see that failures were lessons applied in disguise.

Accountability should lead to high performance, not punitive actions. When you think of accountability, it is normally around situations where something went wrong and people want to know who was responsible. Or when someone is going to hold you accountable, it leads to fear. Accountability should be a positive experience and starts from within. Accountability is making commitments and being helped to them. Commitments should be specific. Some examples are: I will do some task by some date. I will follow up with you by some date. I will provide you feedback by this date. As you can see, we are not using indecisive words like "try," "should," or "might." We are also making accountability at the individual level. There is no team accountability. When you think of your Kanban board, tasks are assigned to an individual. Therefore, accountability at the individual level follows. Accountability starts with those individuals not afraid to lead the effort. A great resource is *Winning with Accountability* by Henry J. Evans for understanding how you can create a culture of accountability in your organization.

Trust your strategy. Success is not perfection. You will exhaust an immense amount of time building an appropriate strategy, whether it is around projects or creating your analytics strategy roadmap. When you have gotten that far, then you are on your road to success. There is no such thing as a perfect strategy. There are always going to be roadblocks, challenges, and difficult times. You had the right skills to get you that far. Don't look around thinking someone else is challenging your strategy. Trust in yourself. Trust in your skills that got you this far. Not using your skills will lead to doubt. Doubt will lead to uncertainty. Uncertainty will lead to fear. Now, you have skepticism creeping into strategy execution. Your strategy will have weaknesses. Trust that your team will find ways around those weaknesses. Your strategy will require help. Asking for help instills trust in others.

Speaking up shows humility, not lack of intelligence. People will see this as you are not the smartest person in the room and can foster learning, problem-solving, and innovation, exactly the outcome you are looking for. Ultimately, trusting your strategy comes down to one simple point. You built the strategy because you thought it was best for your organization. What better reason do you need?

We have all heard some variation on "Don't let perfect get in the way of good." Striving for perfection on a project just leads to delays, frustration, and disengagement. Why? What is the definition of perfection? Everyone has a different interpretation. We discussed the concept of a minimally viable product (MVP). Are these MVPs perfection? Of course not. It is an agreed-upon product that everyone agrees can be used. Is that the measure of success? They are the products that will continue to be enhanced over time. Capabilities will be tested. Some of the capabilities will be accepted, and some will not. There will always be new ideas generated over time. Striving for perfection leads to paralysis, that is, a project never gets off the ground because there is a fear that we are missing something. There is always another "what-if" we are evaluating. Success comes from being able to use the first MVP as intended. Continued success comes from enhancements and releases based on ideas generated over time. Perfection is a myth that needs to be discouraged in project-based work. It is subjective and everyone's "perfect" outcome cannot exist simultaneously.

Don't be intimidated by titles. Always challenge ideas and thought leaders in your organization. Always put your ideas out there. Have you ever sat in a meeting with an idea, thought, or input and never spoke up because of who is in the room? Do not let titles intimidate you from sharing ideas to thoughts to comments to concerns to recommendations. We cannot begin to list all of the characteristics that make great leaders. But a few of the characteristics that apply here are focus, passion, respect, confidence, caring, shared visions, and engagement. You will probably see some or all of these characteristics as they define a leader's style. What other characteristics can you think of that define their style? Would any of these cause you consternation to the point that you would feel uncomfortable or even silly to share your thoughts? Why are you working for the company? Why is your leader? Don't you believe you share the same drive toward your company's mission and values?

Every case study we examined in this book, the many projects that are ongoing, and the many projects that live in your backlog or have not been identified will benefit from challenging ideas and thought leaders. How else do you guarantee the best product? The best ideas are the ones that spur conversation and debate. Many times, without even realizing it, these conversations and debates take the form of strengths, weaknesses, opportunities, and threats (SWOT) analyses. When you challenge ideas, you should always consider a SWOT analysis or similar methodology as a tool to help you document your challenges. Whatever the final outcome on challenging ideas, this analysis will help you communicate to the necessary sponsors how you came to your decision. What is one thing that thought leaders of your organization excel at? Informed opinions. These informed opinions live in your strategies or projects. As a good steward to your organization, it is essential to challenge your thought leaders. We cannot think of a successful thought leader whose purpose is to just have their employees execute as automatons. Thought leaders always offer an unusual or unique perspective that should generate questions or thoughts.

Your analytics strategy will create opportunities that once may not have been possible. Maybe you didn't have the right data, the computational power, or technology to execute previous projects? Maybe your projects were always on a wish list that never could be activated? Ideas should always be considered, whether they are projects or parts of projects. Make sure you surface every idea. Being able to make sure every idea is heard gives the project teams every opportunity to explore value adds. Isn't it better to debate, discuss, and challenge every idea? The only bad idea is the idea not communicated. The only bad idea is an idea not vetted. The only bad idea is one that cannot be considered. Be mindful of your project's size and scope. That doesn't mean you should not put your ideas out there; it means managing expectations, deliverables, and release schedules. The project direction could be a straight path or it could pivot, based on changing requirements.

Don't be afraid to ask what the value add is on every project. Intellectual return on investment has value also. Not every project is going to have a calculable return on investment (ROI). Check that, calculating ROI on some projects will be very difficult, could require years to see, or you may not have the necessary data to do the calculation. Regardless, you would be able to define clearly what the value add is on every project. If there is no value added, a more important questions needs to be considered: "Should we even move the project forward?" Some projects will have immediate ROI returns that you can calculate. One of the easiest ROIs to consider at the beginning of your journey is efficiency. Even with implementing new advanced analytics in your projects, many of the new technologies will offer efficiencies and gains in freeing up resources due to enhanced data gathering and computation techniques. Some of the ROI is based on adoption of the strategy. It is people coming to the platform and data and then leveraging data, people, process, and technology to create the value.

We discussed in Chapter 2 that people were the most important asset in an organization. It is the human element that adds intangible value to every organization. It can be hard to quantify intellectual ROI because the components are abilities like business knowledge, idea generation, innovation, and creativity. Intellectual ROI can also be things like algorithms and dashboards. Employee retention needs to be a key strategy every organization considers. When you find those "high performers" or "diamonds in the rough," the cost of replacing those employees is not only in trying to find suitable replacements, it is the intellectual property that leaves the organization. Investing in people leads to consistency in your analytics team output. The last thing you want is to lose key intellectual resources to competitors.

We hope you have enjoyed reading about transforming healthcare as much as we did sharing our thoughts and insights. The quest for healthy intelligence is accomplished through a comprehensive strategy around data, people, process, and technology and cannot be accomplished by technology alone. Putting together a comprehensive strategy requires plenty of hard work, collaboration, and support across your organization, both horizontally and vertically. Find key business partners that share your vision and want to be part of your journey. Develop a framework of key use cases that will help communicate success to the organization along the journey. The key use cases should highlight building the components of the strategy to finding engaged business partners to delivering successful project outcomes. The journey will be long, difficult, and challenging and, at the same time, rewarding. Building consensus and support around your strategy will require support from key business partners that share your vision. Find projects that will show value. There will be times when the path in front of you appears to be blocked. Don't let those times discourage you. The quest for healthy intelligence starts with the first step. That first step is deciding to build an analytics strategy for the future. Now that you have decided to move forward, continue to put one foot in front of the other. Each step you take doesn't need to be a big step. Find those business partners that want to share in the excitement that is generated around being proactive instead of reactive. Good luck, and have a healthy journey!

Index